REFORMING THE LAW OF THE SEA TREATY

Opportunities Missed, Precedents Set, and U. S. Sovereignty Threatened

Peter M. Leitner

University Press of America, Inc.
Lanham • New York • London

Copyright © 1996 by
University Press of America,® Inc.
4720 Boston Way
Lanham, Maryland 20706

3 Henrietta Street
London, WC2E 8LU England

Library of Congress Cataloging-in-Publication Data

Leitner, Peter M.
Reforming the law of the sea treaty : opportunities missed, precedents
set, and U. S. sovereignty threatened / Peter M. Leitner.
      p.   cm.
Includes index.
1. Maritime law--United States. 2. Maritime law. 3. United Nations
Convention on the Law of the Sea. (1982). I. Title.
JX4422.U5L45   1996   341.7'566'026 --dc20   96-21570   CIP

ISBN 0-7618-0393-9 (cloth: alk. ppr.)
ISBN 0-7618-0394-7 (pbk: alk. ppr.)

Contents

Tables

Charts

Figures

Preface

My involvement in the Law of the Sea Conference began innocently enough in 1973 as an undergraduate student when my academic advisor, Dr. Francis Manno, suggested that I look into the conflict between the United States and Chile, Ecuador, and Peru over their continuing seizure of U.S. tuna boats fishing off their coasts. This was to begin a 23-year on-again/off-again love-hate romance with the U.N. Conference on the Law of the Sea that influenced the preparation of three of my master's degree theses, landed me my first real job in the federal government, established me as a congressional observer to several of the Geneva and New York Conference sessions, and finally saw me lead a ten-country review of the prospects for establishing an ocean mining industry under prevailing political and economic constraints.

My attendance at negotiating sessions began in 1977 with the seventh and ended with the eleventh or final session in 1982, which, I believe, represented the zenith of U.S. diplomatic courage since the Cuban Missile Crisis. It was at the eleventh session that the Reagan administration faced down a variety of internal and external ideological opponents in a successful effort to unashamedly declare and protect vital U.S. economic, strategic, and political interests.

The Reagan administration's declaration that there are indeed vital American interests worth protecting and an identifiable bottom line beyond which the United States will refuse to compromise came as a shock to allies and adversaries alike. This unequivocal but practical negotiating style put an end to the continuous diplomatic free fall characteristic of the Carter administration where mixed signals, indecision, vacillation, broken promises, public castigation of allies, and failure to criticize foes were the order of the day. It also served notice to those pulling the strings within the Law of the Sea Conference that their years of tampering with negotiating texts, attempting to use the treaty as a vehicle for Third World demands for a new international economic order (NIEO), and the near universal assumption born from experience that the United States and its industrialized allies will always seek accommodation when faced with confrontation had ended.

I had become convinced of the dangers the treaty represented to vital U.S. interests years earlier. It was in 1976, when I was hired by the U.S. General Accounting Office as its Law of the Sea expert, in response to congressional requests for an alternative to the delegation reports provided by the State Department, that I was able to more fully understand the complexities and day-to-day mechanics of how the negotiations were proceeding. It was during the seventh session in Geneva, when I accidentally found myself in the middle of a four-hour G-77 strategy meeting, that I came to appreciate the extent of the vitriol many of the members of this voting bloc of 110 developing and communist nations held for the United States and its allies. I saw firsthand the danger of U.S. interests being engulfed by what former Secretary of State Dean Rusk described to me as a "swarming majority." Unfortunately, the Carter administration was busy attempting to bury differences, issuing "sanitized" delegation reports, and actively lobbying Congress for support of its negotiating efforts.

Little was seen or heard about the treaty outside of professional journals for over a decade until the Clinton administration announced that it had been engaged in quiet negotiations to make the treaty more acceptable to the United States. These negotiations yielded a "1994 Agreement," which the president felt was good enough to justify reversing long-standing U.S. policy and signing the United States on to the treaty. Unfortunately, the treaty is not "good enough" to merit ratification as many of its provisos are still inimical to a variety of U.S. national interests. The 1994 presidential signature appears to represent a return to the Carter administration's failed foreign policy agenda, which should come as no surprise as many of Carter's key foreign policy advisors have returned to government in the present administration after a twelve-year hiatus.

Unfortunately, ratification of the Law of the Sea treaty will not only obligate the United States to an esoteric set of guidelines concerning navigation, fisheries, pollution, and scientific research; but it also carries with it a set of dramatic precedents regarding exploitation of natural resources in unclaimed international areas, establishes a powerful international bureaucracy with regulatory and enforcement powers, and calls upon the United States to finance at least 25 percent of the operating costs for an organization whose very existence is at odds with fundamental U.S. national interests and will likely one day be the source of direct confrontation. In addition, a long-standing concern that the treaty may be used as "political cover" for potential U.S. adversaries to acquire militarily sensitive technology has actually come to pass with the People's Republic of China (PRC), in 1995, acquiring state-of-the-art 6,000-meter-capable underwater surveillance and micro-bathymetry equipment for use on its "mine site." The weak justification offered by the PRC was sufficient to persuade the dysfunctional U.S. export control system to approve such strategic technological capability in spite of the obvious degree of overkill for the intended application.

In one sense, Clinton's signing is a form of payback to the U.N. system for the multinational "cover" it has provided on behalf of several failed U.S. foreign policy adventures during the past decade. It appears that the U.S. insistence upon multinationalizing U.S. policy initiatives in Haiti, Rwanda, Somalia, and Bosnia, which span both the Bush and Clinton administrations, played a public role in their failure but has also exacted another hidden price U.S. accession to the Law of the Sea treaty. This treaty was on the verge of coming into force without a single developed/industrialized country participating and would have been a great embarrassment to the U.N. system and doomed to irrelevancy had not last-minute negotiations provided sufficient alterations for President Clinton to proclaim the treaty "fixed."

In reality, while the treaty has been altered or amended, it has not been "fixed." The guiding principles underlying the treaty are still those of the NIEO, and the procedure of using the 1994 Agreement to refer to alterations or application of various aspects of the treaty itself, without actually modifying the Treaty, is a dubious proposition at best and a tactic that invites deep suspicion of the reality, durability, and indeed the purpose of these "changes." The present administration has made considerable use of the term "political optics" to describe non-changes or political sleight of hand aimed at convincing the American people and Congress that a particularly insidious policy initiative is really in their interest to accept or at least not actively oppose. Such appears to be the case with the Law of the Sea treaty.

The opinions expressed in this book are my own and do not necessarily represent the views of the Department of Defense.

Acknowledgments

This book would not have been possible without the guidance of Professor Francis Manno, who first guided me into studying the Law of the Sea treaty in 1973. Other key mentors were Professor John Stanley Bennett, who chaired my 1976 thesis on the economics and technology of ocean mining, and Professor James L. Regens, who chaired my 1977 thesis on territorial sea claims. Appreciation is also due the International Division of the U.S. General Accounting Office, which hired me to be its law of the sea expert in 1976 and afforded me the opportunity to attend Conference sessions and observe developments first-hand. At GAO I had the honor of working with Mr. Val Bielecki on a multi-country review of ocean mining prospects. I would also like to recognize the excellent work of the Congressional Research Service, from which I drew most of the chronology found in Appendix 1, and the Tufts University Multilaterals Project database, which is located on its readily accessible internet web-site, *http://www.tufts.edu/fletcher/multilaterals.html*, which provides access to a useful array of documents relating to the activities of the International Seabed Authority and a variety of other treaties. Finally, my greatest debt is owed to my wife, Cynthia, and my children, Lucy, Richy, Wendy, and Sarah, who offer constant inspiration and support.

Chapter One

Minerals and National Power

Survival is the primary concern of all nations, but the increase of national power, wealth, and culture is a related and nearly equal motivating force. The means for gaining these ends have nearly always been governed by expediency. While ethical and philosophical considerations enter national policy in varying degrees, few people would not condone their government's transgression of "international law" when their material interests were at stake. Self-interest as the primary motivation of nations may be decried or acclaimed; its reality should be recognized. It is also a fact that an industrial power will go to war whenever economic pressures become too oppressive. When it is believed that war will win the control of sources of raw materials and permit territorial expansion, an industrial power will go to war regardless of any international treaties or agreements. Mineral production has been instrumental in determining the course of history many times in the past and promises to be of increasing importance in the future.

After the First World War, much political friction was created in Europe by the redistribution of territories under the peace treaty, which deprived some nations of much-needed raw materials. Austria was almost stripped of its mineral deposits, and Germany lost important mineral districts in both the east and west. The control of iron ores was an important factor in the German seizure of Lorraine in the war of 1870, and the subsequent occupation of Lorraine, Alsace, and the Saar by the French has had as its principal goal the acquisition of mineral resources.

New industries, new technology, and the rise of competition among industrialized nations gave a new importance to the role of raw materials. The struggle for the control of iron ore and coking coal on the European continent is a familiar story. Even more important was the pressure to gain control over distant territories whose value assumed new relevance. Barraclough summarizes this trend as follows:

> The voracious appetite of the new industrialism, unable of its very nature to draw sufficient sustenance from local resources, rapidly swallowed up the whole world. It was no longer a question of exchanging European manufactures— predominantly textiles—for traditional oriental and tropical products or even of providing outlets for the expanding iron and steel industries by building railways, bridges, and the like. Industry now went out into the world in search of the basic materials without which, in its new forms, it could not exist. (Barraclough 1967)

> Germany's deficiency of raw materials prior to the second World War is perhaps the most striking case that could be cited. Here was a nation of tremendous industrial development built up primarily around the coal of the Ruhr and the iron of the Lorraine since 1870. Prior to the first World War it had been active in exploiting minerals in its colonies and elsewhere. Through the high development of its smelting enterprises, a heavy flow of minerals converged in Germany from all parts of the world. Suddenly it was stripped bare of its lead and zinc in Silesia, and of all the potential developments in its colonies. Even the remaining coal supply of the Ruhr was for a time endangered by the French occupation of the Ruhr. Germany was left only coal and potash. Outside sources of supply were almost without exception controlled commercially and politically by former enemies. The situation was one of unstable equilibrium which required wise and delicate handling if future trouble was to be avoided. The natural desire of the Germans to secure needed raw materials was intensified by subsequent restrictions and disadvantages placed by the other powers on the flow of raw materials into Germany. On the other hand, these powers feared that German industrial development would follow unrestricted supplies, which is, in effect, what actually developed. (Clark 1918 76-77)[1]

Thus the question of mineral resources plays an important role in causing war, and in the event of war a nation's capacity to produce the necessary mineral products may be a matter of life or death. Stocks of metals and minerals may be built up from outside sources, and even during a war they must be supplied by an outside nation, but to be powerful from a military standpoint a modern nation should be able to produce most of the required minerals from domestic sources. With these facts in view one may understand more clearly the reasons for Germany's activities prior to 1939 in the development of, and preparation to produce from, mineral deposits that in normal times would have been considered of little value. (Wright 1936, 34)

In addition to emphasizing the importance of the availability of a stable flow of resources to develop and industrialize nations, another purpose of this book is to highlight what may well turn out to be the most dramatic and far-reaching development since the first Industrial Revolution, that being the extension of that original force into the seven-tenths of the earth's surface commonly termed the "marine environment." The technological sophistication that marks our historical period seems very likely, to result in the reversing of recent trends toward global interdependence and integration occasioned by raw material scarcities. Global interdependence could shatter because the oceans hold enormous resources, resources that dwarf land-based supplies, and because the technology required for their exploitation is the exclusive possession of a handful of developed nations, primarily the United States. Ocean mining will disrupt international commodity markets through the sudden expansion of the global resource base and through the development of this resource base by nations that are historically net importers of the principal minerals found in manganese nodules.

Conventional wisdom argued that the United States was the principal nation to watch regarding marine mineral exploitation because it possessed the technology to access, mine, and process manganese nodules and it had a strategic need for the metals embedded in the nodules. Until the July 1994 signing of the U.N. Convention on the Law of the Sea (UNCLOS) by the Clinton administration, this perception was correct. However the anti-private investment climate created by the UNCLOS will likely be the death knell of direct U.S. ocean mining activities. Instead U.S. participation will be relegated to the role of technology supplier or subcontractor to either the United Nations or a developing country ocean mining venture.

If ratified by the United States Senate the revised UNCLOS may permanently preclude direct U.S. access to the mineral resources of the deep seabed. Shutting the United States out from direct access to this vast source of mineral wealth will unnecessarily perpetuate a pattern of import dependence that carries with it serious national security, balance of payments, and foreign assistance implications.

The United States' mineral position is, at present, becoming rather fragile; hence new sources of supplies must be located to fuel its growing industrial base. Augment this development with the long-range U.S. policy of mineral self-sufficiency in the face of producer cartels and you arrive at a situation where the United States, in order to reduce its exposure to the vicissitudes of unstable third world regimes, will now seek to extend its resource base directly, through the exploitation of unclaimed territories, the seabeds. This represents, in fact, a return to eighteenth-century imperialistic policies regarding the acquisition of new territories for natural resources. It is also a return to policies that many historians have attributed to the origins of the first two world wars. The major distinction between these two periods is that future expansion will be into uninhabited areas.

Instead of expanding its imports of vital raw materials or drastically limiting its consumption of those materials, the United States is more likely to expand its resource base via the utilization of the new techniques. The next fifty years will witness at least two events of tremendous importance for the world order: first, the extension of the Industrial Revolution to the seabed in quest of natural resources that are becoming too expensive, economically or politically, to acquire on land; and second, the development of a competitive world economy more deeply divided along the lines of rich and poor nations than that which exists now, leading to an increasing polarization of the two spheres.

The central problem confronting the poor nations is that their very place within the world economy is dictated by developments within the developed nations. Their current paradoxical situation, in which they dominate certain developments within the developed countries (DCs) by controlling raw materials, resulted from an ever-burgeoning technological growth in the DCs themselves, which outran their ability to satisfy their basic needs.

But this same technological giant, relying on the same succession of developments that brought on this problem in the first place, will soon be able to satisfy its own needs by applying the technological prowess necessary to bypass traditional land-based sources in the search for mineral supplies and annex vast portions of the world's oceans. Hence, the recent ascendance of less developed countries (LDCs) as power brokers in world affairs will be on the wane as rapidly as it arose. The paradox is that the LDCs in order to pursue their own interest and procure as much advantage from their new position as possible, by raising raw material prices to consuming nations will also increase the incentives for DCs to accelerate development of this new technology that threatens the long-term interest of the LDCs. On the other hand, if the LDCs intentionally keep prices low so as to forestall this developing technology, they will be able neither to profit from their new-found power nor to prevent the eventual implementation of this technological threat.

To compounding their problematic future the end of the cold war brought an end to some East-West rivalries that included a competitive scramble for influence and alliances with third world countries. Competition swirled over the various forms of direct and indirect assistance including economic, humanitarian, military, and political in the form of subsidies, grants, loans, and concessionary contract arrangements. In stark strategic terms, the LDCs in Africa, Asia, and Latin America lost much of their potential political or military value to the great powers of North America and Eurasia. As superpower military forces and mission requirements were cut back, no longer were basing or port access agreements with countries like the Philippines, Singapore, Kenya, Cuba, Djibouti, Yemen, Egypt, and Somalia necessary to support far-flung military requirements.

---

[1]"It is not unlikely that one of the most important resources of the entire Ukraine from the German standpoint will prove to be her deposits of manganese. . . Germany, as far as is known, has within her borders no sources capable of supplying anything like the quantity her steel foundries require. . . The leaders of the German Steel Trust have long looked forward to the day when an adequate supply of manganese might come under direct German control." (Clark 1918, 76-77)

Chapter Two

Law of the Sea Treaty

With its central organs in deadlock, the U.N. shifted resources to secondary activities staffed by a bloated bureaucracy more intent on advancing its own goals than the cause of world peace. Today, lines of authority are confused, blurred and duplicated. Basic missions and activities have ballooned into plodding exercises that produce mountains of paper and little, if any, real results. (Kassebaum and Hamilton 1995, C7)

Negotiation and U.S. Rejection

On July 9, 1982, President Reagan announced that the United States would not become a signatory to the U.N. Convention on the Law of the Sea (hereinafter referred to as UNCLOS, the treaty, or the convention) sponsored by the United Nations.

In its broadest terms, the treaty attempts to settle the question of who owns the seas and it affects almost every aspect of maritime life-- commercial, economic, military, and legal. For example, it covers the right of passage through, under, and over straits for international navigation. It permits every country a territorial zone of 12 miles and an economic zone of 200 miles. It addresses fishing rights, the continental shelves, and the exploration and exploitation of the oceans' resources beyond national jurisdictions.

The Convention and U.S. Interests

The Law of the Sea convention and the 1994 Agreement are extensive, complex documents touching on a wide range of policy issues and U.S. interests. Many consider non-seabed issues to be the most significant areas addressed by the convention.

Naval Power and Maritime Commerce Interests.

United States interests as a naval power provided the initial impetus for U.S. policy makers to promote Law of the Sea negotiations. The increasing number of claims made by other states over offshore high seas areas--such as territorial sea, fishing zones, and economic zones--was expected to limit freedom of navigation to an unacceptable extent and increase the likelihood of international disputes over access to the world's oceans. The convention sets a 12-nautical-mile territorial sea limit and a 200-nautical-mile exclusive economic zone (EEZ). The convention also protects high seas freedoms throughout the zone and innocent passage through the territorial sea, so long as such activities are not "prejudicial to the peace, good order, or security of the coastal state." Submarine and other underwater craft are required, however, to navigate on the surface and show their flags.

The convention adopts the concept of transit passage for movement through straits that lie within the territorial seas of the states. Over 135 straits that may have been closed by the expansion of the territorial sea limit to 12 miles would be open to transit under this provision. All ships also have a right of innocent passage through archipelagic waters.

Opponents of U.S. adherence to the overall convention argue that the United States already benefits from the convention's navigational provisions, on the basis of customary international law. The United States has already declared a 12-mile territorial sea limit and a 200-mile EEZ and is exercising its rights through a Freedom of Navigation Program, using diplomatic protests, operational challenges, and bilateral agreements to promote adherence to the naval and maritime obligations established in the convention. Indeed, such a program is a routine part of peacetime naval operations and will continue, with or without the UNCLOS. Since the end of UNCLOS negotiations, for example, the U.S. Navy has challenged claims by Libya in the Gulf of Sidra (1985) and the continuous (1993-95) challenges to Chinese territorial claims in and around the Spratley Islands and the South China Sea. In addition, it is difficult to find anyone who believes that Turkey will accept the Greek stranglehold of its Aegean/Mediterranean coast awarded by the UNCLOS.

Coastal State Interests.

The 1945 Truman Proclamation, claiming U.S. jurisdiction over U.S. continental shelf resources, has been viewed as the initial salvo in the explosion of claims made by coastal states around the world to extend territorial seas and fisheries and economic zones in the years since.

The convention allows each coastal state to claim a 200-mile EEZ in which it has "sovereign rights" over exploring, exploiting, conserving, and managing the natural resources--whether living or non-living--of the waters superadjacent to the seabed and its subsoil. In the EEZ, the coastal state also has jurisdiction to regulate the establishment and use of structures for economic purposes, marine scientific research, and protection of the marine environment within the EEZ.

Protection of the Marine Environment.

Under the convention, states are to take measures to deal with *all* sources of pollution of the marine environment: a) from land-based sources, from or through the atmosphere, or by dumping; b) from vessels; c) from installations and devices used in exploration or exploitation of the natural resources of the seabed and subsoil; and d) from other installations or devices operating in the marine environment. (Article 194)

For land-based sources, which account for 80percent of marine pollution, the convention requires states to adopt laws and regulations to prevent, reduce, and control such pollution, taking into account internationally agreed rules, standards, and recommended practices and procedures. Rather than rely solely on flag states for enforcement of vessel source pollution rules, the convention charges coastal states and port states, as well as flag states, to act against vessels suspected of violation of anti-pollution regulations within territorial or EEZ waters.

Marine Scientific Research.

The convention grants the coastal state jurisdiction over marine scientific research conducted within its EEZ and on its continental shelf and requires coastal state consent for the conduct of such research. Some claim that the prospects for U.S. marine scientists to gain increased access to other nations' offshore areas--the location of the most useful marine scientific research--would be limited.

Dispute Settlement.

A number of legal experts believe that U.S. interests in a stable Law of the Sea are strengthened by the comprehensive compulsory dispute settlement provisions in the convention. The goal of the convention is to promote compliance with its provisions and ensure that disputes are settled by peaceful means. It provides for the settlement of disputes that may arise from the interpretation or application of the convention; it also includes a supplementary system for the settlement of disputes arising under Part XI of the convention relating to deep seabed mining. The underlying principle in the convention is that parties to a dispute can select by agreement any dispute settlement procedure they desire.

U.S. Reviews and Rejects UNCLOS

President Reagan's 1982 statement was preceded by a series of events that cast serious doubt that the United States intended to sign the treaty. In March 1981 the president announced that his administration would undertake a comprehensive review of the draft treaty to assure that it met U.S. interests. On January 29, 1982, he reported that the results of the review concluded that major elements of deep seabed mining provisions were not acceptable and would have to be changed during the final (March 8 - April 30, 1982) negotiating session in New York. At the conclusion of that session the United States voted "no" on the adoption of the final treaty text because negotiating objectives had not been achieved.

The long-awaited conclusion of the United Nations Conference on the Law of the Sea (hereinafter referred to as the conference) resulted in the adoption of the formal treaty on April 30, 1982. The treaty, which was opened for signature in December 1982, contains over 300 articles and creates a new body of international law, establishes a series of sweeping political precedents that will compete with, and erode, the sovereign powers of national governments, and, at the same time, codifies major aspects of traditional high seas freedoms.

The conference, which had been meeting periodically since 1973, drafted broadly accepted language for much of the treaty, but major sections of the deep seabed mining provisions were unacceptable to the United States and most industrialized allies. The concern that the Reagan administration voiced over the treaty draft on coming into office led the administration to replace a significant segment of the U.S. delegation and suspend U.S. negotiating efforts while it conducted its review of U.S. participation in the conference to determine the degree to which the treaty met U.S. interests especially in the areas of navigation, overflight, fisheries, environment, and deep seabed mining.

This review culminated in the presidential statement of January 29, 1982, that most provisions of the draft were acceptable and consistent with U.S. interests but that major elements of the deep seabed mining portion were not. The president identified six goals necessary to the deep seabed mining provisions before the treaty could be supported by the United States. As Reagan stated:

> . . . we will seek changes necessary to correct those unacceptable elements and to achieve the goal of a treaty that:
>
> --Will not deter development of any deep seabed mineral resources to meet national and world demand;
>
> --Will assure national access to these resources by current and future qualified entities to enhance U.S. security of supply, to avoid monopolization of the resources by the operating arm of the International Authority, and to promote the economic development of the resources;
>
> --Will provide a decision making role in the deep seabed regime that fairly reflects and effectively protects the political and economic interests and financial contributions of participating states;
>
> --Will not allow for amendments to come into force without approval of the participating states, including in our case the advice and consent of the Senate;
>
> --Will not set other undesirable precedents for international organizations; and
>
> --Will be likely to receive the advice and consent of the Senate. In this regard, the convention should not contain provisions for the mandatory transfer of private technology and participation by and funding for national liberation movements . . .

The administration also maintained that the treaty reflected a protectionist bias, discriminated against free enterprise, and was contrary to broader U.S. interests. Chief among these were production ceilings and limits on the number of mine sites that could be operated by any one country. Also, concern about the constitutionality of the treaty was raised by the possibility that future amendments to the treaty would be binding even if the United States voted against them or the Senate did not give its consent.

The U.S private sector was concerned that certain provisions affected the long-term stability and economics of deep seabed mining. It argued there would be no absolute assurance that once the first miners completed necessary research and development they could build a commercially viable system and operate it under initially established terms and conditions over the long term (twenty years or more). Other provisions that the private-sector saw as affecting the financial aspects of ventures included mandatory technology transfer, and a requirement that private sector miners provide information (to the international "enterprise" the treaty creates to do deep seabed mining) on a minesite of value equal to their own site(s).

The U.S. delegation had a difficult task in returning to the eleventh session of the conference (March 8 - April 30, 1982), billed as the final negotiating session, to renegotiate elements of the treaty in order to achieve the president's stated objectives. When the conference opened, the U.S. delegation presented a list of general principles for consideration. These were promptly rejected, however, by the Group of 77 (a coalition that included over 110 third world countries organized into a fairly cohesive voting bloc), which demanded a listing of specific word change amendments to the text, arguing that the time for the negotiation of basic principles had long since passed. The U.S. delegation prepared what became known as the "Green Book," a compilation of over 100 proposed amendments. This, too, was rejected as a basis for negotiation--the Group of 77 insisting that the proposed amendments would affect the basic character of the treaty and were thus unacceptable.

Negotiations between the United States and the Group of 77 continued through intermediaries for the balance of the conference. The primary set of intermediaries known as the Group of 11 (Australia, Austria, Canada, Denmark, Finland, Iceland, Ireland, New Zealand, Norway, Sweden, and Switzerland) offered numerous compromise texts, but they were largely ineffective in an atmosphere of increasing polarization.

On April 30, 1982, the last day of the conference, the leadership attempted to have the treaty adopted by consensus but the United States exercised its right to have the treaty, as a whole, put up for a two-thirds vote. The final outcome was 130 in favor and 4 against, with 17 abstentions. The four states voting against adoption of the treaty were the United States, Israel, Turkey, and Venezuela. The seventeen abstentions were cast by the United Kingdom, the Federal Republic of Germany, Belgium, the Netherlands, Luxembourg, Italy, Spain Thailand, and the Soviet bloc with the exception of Romania.[2]

Two countries with major potential for ocean mining, France and Japan, voted in favor of the treaty.

When the conference concluded, the United States began another review of the outcome of the negotiations, the results of which President Reagan announced on July 9, 1982:

> ... Our review recognizes ... that the deep seabed mining part of the convention does not meet United States objectives. For this reason, I am announcing today that the United States will not sign the convention as adopted by the Conference, and our participation in the remaining Conference process will be at the technical level and concerned with those provisions that serve United States interests.

How Did the Treaty Get This Way?

Four seminal events marked the errant course that led to the eventual rejection of the treaty by the United States. These are:

1. The acceptance without definition, of the principle that the mineral resources of the seabed, in areas beyond national jurisdiction, are "the Common Heritage of Mankind." While the principle is a noble statement and easily acceptable, it has come to be defined in such a way that justifies the creation of a supranational regulatory agency that will control most activities occurring within the "Area."

2. The 1975 proposal to the U.N. General Assembly, by then-Secretary of State Henry Kissinger, to support a "Parallel System" of ocean mining whereby commercial miners and their sponsoring states would support direct competitive U.N. mining operations in the deep seabed. This bombshell of a proposal was a complete surprise to U.S. industry, other government departments, and even to most of the U.S. Law of the Sea delegation. While aimed at cooling off New International Economic Order rhetoric in other U.N. fora by throwing them a bone, this action raised the Group of 77's level of expectation of further concessions and was a contributing factor in emboldening them.

3. The U.S. decision to return to treaty negotiations even after a small group of developing country delegates fundamentally altered the agreed-on ocean mining negotiating text after the sixth session of the conference was adjourned. The U.S. decision to return was, in effect, acceptance of the legitimacy of an illegitimate anti-free enterprise text and created an insurmountable obstacle to achieving an acceptable treaty.

4. The U.S. decision to provide conference participants full access to a U.S.-financed model of an ocean mining venture. While the purpose was to narrow the debate on levels of taxation, fees, and production limits to be placed on potential ocean miners, its effect was to provide ammunition to third world negotiators to use against U.S. free market proposals.

The Common Heritage of Mankind Principle

In a 1967 statement at the United Nations, Ambassador Pardo of Malta proposed that seabed resources be regarded as the "common heritage of mankind" and that this Area not be subject to national appropriation. Two years later the General Assembly passed the Moratorium on Seabed Exploration and Exploitation (Resolution 2574-D (XXIV)), which called on all states to refrain from seabed resource exploitation until the establishment of an international seabed regime that would administer the Area in the interest of all mankind. The General Assembly Declaration of General Principles on the Seabed (Resolution 2749 (XXV)), adopted in 1970, endorsed the common heritage principle but included no definition of the Area itself. The United States and many other nations opposed the Moratorium Resolution.

The common heritage concept, however, has wide support among both developing and developed nations, including the United States. However, interpretations of this principle differ markedly. The developed nations feel that free and open exploitation of the seabeds, so long as territorial sovereignty is not claimed, is in the interest of all nations and allowable under both the common heritage principle and the traditional doctrine of freedom of the high seas. The developing nations, however, lean toward a more collectivist interpretation of the term "common heritage of mankind" to mean that individual states are barred from exploiting mankind's possession unless it is conducted under the auspices of a generally accepted international regime. Despite these differing interpretations, the principle itself has been the chief impetus behind efforts to establish an International Seabed Authority to administer the "common heritage" in the interest of all mankind.

The Parallel System of Mining

In an attempt to accelerate the pace of the treaty negotiations, Secretary of State Kissinger made an unprecedented offer to the U.N. General Assembly. The deal he proposed sought:

> . . . to insure that all nations, developed and developing, have adequate access to seabed mining sites:

—The United States proposes that the treaty should guarantee nondiscriminatory access for states and their nationals to deep seabed resources under specified and reasonable conditions. The requirement of guaranteed access will not be met if the treaty contains arbitrary or restrictive limitations on the number of mine sites which any nation might exploit. And such restrictions are unnecessary because deep seabed mining cannot be monopolized; there are many more productive seabed mining sites than conceivably can be mined for centuries to come.

The United States accepts that an "Enterprise" should be established as part of the International Seabed Resource Authority and given the right to exploit the deep seabeds under the same conditions as apply to all mining.

—The United States could accept as part of an overall settlement a system in which prime mining sites are reserved for exclusive exploitation by the Enterprise or by the developing countries directly—if this approach meets with broad support. Under this system, each individual contractor would propose two mine sites for exploitation. The Authority would then select one of these sites, which would be mined by the Authority directly or made available to developing countries at its discretion. The other site would be mined by the contractor on his own.

—The United States proposes that the International Authority should supervise a system of revenue sharing from mining activities for the use of the international community, primarily for the needs of the poorest countries. These revenues will not only advance the growth of developing countries; they will provide tangible evidence that a fair share in global economic activity can he achieved by a policy of cooperation. Revenue sharing could be based either on royalties or on a system of profit sharing from contract mining. Such a system would give reality to the designation of the deep seabeds as the common heritage of all mankind.

—Finally, the United States is prepared to make a major effort to enhance the skills and access of developing countries to advanced deep seabed mining technology in order to assist their capabilities in this field. For example, incentives should be established for private companies to participate in agreements to share technology and train personnel from developing countries.

. . . In response to the legitimate concerns of land-based producers of minerals found in the deep seabeds, we offer the following steps as an additional major contribution to the negotiations:

—The United States is prepared to accept a temporary limitation, for a period fixed in the treaty, on production of the seabed minerals tied to the projected growth in the world nickel market, currently estimated to be about 6 percent a year. This would in effect limit production of other minerals contained in deep seabed nodules, including copper. After this period, the seabed production should be governed by overall market conditions.

—The United States proposes that the International Seabed Resource Authority have the right to participate in any international agreements on seabed-produced commodities in accordance with the amount of production for which it is directly responsible. The United States is prepared to examine with flexibility the details of arrangements concerning the relationships between the Authority and any eventual commodity agreements.

—The United States proposes that some of the revenues of the Authority be used for adjustment assistance and that the World Bank, regional development banks, and other international institutions assist countries to improve their competitiveness or diversify into other kinds of production if they are seriously injured by production from the deep seabeds. An urgent task of the International Authority, when it is established, will be to devise an adjustment assistance program in collaboration with other international institutions for countries which suffer economic dislocations as a result of deep seabed mining.

These proposals on the issue of deep seabed resources are offered in the spirit of cooperation and compromise that characterized our economic proposals at the seventh special session and that guides our policies toward the developing nations. The United States is examining a range of commodity problems and ways in which they might be fairly resolved. . .

The United States believes that the world community has before it a grave responsibility. Our country cannot delay in its efforts to develop an assured supply of critical resources through our deep seabed mining projects. We strongly prefer an international agreement to provide a stable legal environment before such development begins, one that insures that all resources are managed for the good of the global community and that all can participate. But if agreement is not reached this year, it will be increasingly difficult to resist pressure to proceed unilaterally.

An agreement on the deep seabed can turn the world's interdependence from a slogan into a reality. A sense of community which nations have striven to achieve on land for centuries could be realized in a regime for the oceans. (Kissinger 1976, 540-41)

This Kissinger sop to the Group of 77, in an attempt to placate ever-increasing New International Economic Order demands, opened up a Pandora's box of convoluted logic, historic precedents, and escalating demands that set the stage for even bolder expectations by the Group of 77. Expectations and perceptions of U.S. weakness set the stage for the Engo treachery at the sixth session of the negotiations.

Engo's Treachery

The sixth session of the conference was held from May 23 - July 15, 1977. As was the standard practice since UNCLOS III first convened in 1972, the work of the conference was organized around three committees. Committee I dealt with seabed mining issues. Committee II focused on fisheries, territorial sea claims, and activities on the continental shelf. Committee III dealt with dispute settlement, research, and environmental matters.

While the sixth session made slow but steady progress on most issues, Committee I under the chairmanship of Paul Bamala Engo of Cameroon was responsible for fanning a smoldering set of confrontational North/South issues into a conflagration whose effects are still felt today, some eighteen years later.

The following excerpts from the U.S. delegation report describe the events, as well as the mood, of that period most effectively:

Under the fair and judicious leadership of Minister Jens Evensen of Norway a responsible and effective discussion of seabed issues took place. This discussion and the texts formulated by Minister Evensen offered real prospects that the impasse on seabed mining issues could be resolved on terms acceptable to both the developed and developing nations.

Regrettably, however, the new 'composite' text concerning the system of exploitation and governance of the deep seabed Area (Part XI) is now fundamentally unacceptable. It deviates markedly from the proposed compromise text which had been prepared on the basis of full, fair and open discussion under Minister Evensen's leadership.

The Evensen text, although not without problems, was generally viewed as a useful basis for further negotiation. The newer text—produced in private, never discussed with a representative group of concerned nations, and released only after this session of the Conference terminated--cannot be viewed as a responsible substantive contribution to further negotiation. Indeed, the manner of its production--treating weeks of serious debate and responsible negotiation as essentially irrelevant--raises an equally serious procedural problem: whether the Law of the Sea Conference can be organized to treat deep seabed issues with the seriousness they, and the Conference which depends on their satisfactory resolution, demand.

Among the serious points of substantive difficulty in the latest deep Seabeds text, and the system it would define are the following:

• It would not give the reasonable assurance of access that is necessary if we and others could be expected to help finance the Enterprise and to accept a 'parallel system' as a basis of compromise.

• It could be read to make technology transfer by contractors a condition of access to the deep seabed--subject, at least in part, to negotiation in the pursuit of a contract.

• It could be read to give the Seabed Authority the power effectively to mandate joint ventures with the authority as a condition for access.

• It fails to set clear and reasonable limits on the financial burdens to be borne by contractors; indeed it simply combines a wide range of alternative financial burdens, as if such a combination could be a compromise--when, in fact, it is likely to prove a compound burden sufficient to stifle seabed development.

• It would set an artificial limit on seabed production of minerals from nodules--which is not only objectionable in principle; it is also far more stringent than would be necessary to protect specific developing country producers from possible adverse effects, and is incompatible with the basic economic interests of a developing world generally.

• It would give the Seabed Authority extremely broad new, open-ended power to regulate all other mineral production from the seabed "as appropriate."

• It would appear, arguably, to give the Authority unacceptable new power to regulate scientific research in the Area.

• It would fail adequately to protect minority interests in its system of governance and would, accordingly, threaten to allow the abuse of power by an anomalous "majority."

• It would allow the distribution of benefits from seabed exploitation to peoples and countries not party to the convention.

• It would seriously prejudice the likely long-term: character of the international regime, by requiring that--if agreement to the contrary is not reached within 25 years--the regime shall automatically be converted into a "unitary" system, ruling out direct access by contractors, except to the extent that the Authority might seek their participation in joint ventures with it.

With this unfortunate, last-minute deviation from what had seemed to be an emerging direction of promise in the deep seabed negotiations, I am led now to recommend to the President of the United States that our government must review not only the balance among our substantive interests but also whether an agreement acceptable to all governments can best be achieved through the kind of negotiations which have thus far taken place. (U.S. Department of State 1977, 5-6)

It was astounding that after months of public brooding over the Engo double-cross, the Carter administration decided to return to the conference and continue negotiations based on the Engo draft. The United States lost enormous ground at that point when it "blinked first" in the game of chicken between the interests of industrialized states and the redistributive demands of the Group of 77 promoting the New International Economic Order.

The Odyssey of the MIT Model

Within the context of UNCLOS III negotiations over the creation of a future seabeds regime, the old maxim "knowledge is power" has taken on a special meaning. While it is true that the accumulation, manipulation, and selective dissemination of specialized bits of information have in the past formed a powerful negotiating tool, the possibility that the premature or unnecessary release of information may result in a serious erosion of one's own negotiating position deserves some study.

One of the most notable characteristics of Committee One (Deep Seabed Regime) negotiations throughout the life of UNCLOS III prior to the seventh session convening in 1978 in Geneva was the paucity of technical information concerning future ocean mining operations. Prior to Geneva'78, the main source of technical information had been the United Nations Secretariat, which attempted to quantify the potential impact that ocean mining would have on traditional mineral markets. Lacking more accurate information, the secretariat made reasoned estimates of nodule mineral content and abundance based on an extremely weak database. As a result, the secretariat studies, although quite interesting to read, were painfully inadequate from a technical standpoint.

Up until that point, only the United States and a handful of other industrialized potential ocean mining countries had some degree of understanding of the likely economic dynamics of an ocean mining operation. As most of the hard data associated with projecting internal rates of return for business activities are considered proprietary, even sponsoring governments did not have complete information.

In spite of this widely perceived lack of hard data, the conference sought to regulate an as yet nonexistent industry about which nothing for certain was known. In an attempt to overcome the obvious handicap created by an informational vacuum, the Sea Grant program of the National Oceanic and Atmospheric Administration (NOAA) commissioned the Massachusetts Institute of Technology (MIT) to create a detailed computer model of a future U.S. ocean mining corporation. This project sought to be able, by building in a high degree of flexibility, to predict the economics of a commercial venture under a variable set of assumptions and was to be used for U.S. government planning and negotiating purposes.

The study created a computer model that estimates the costs for a single, first-generation ocean mining project located in the eastern central Pacific, where the nodules are found in sufficient quantity to make them commercially attractive. Both the technological and financial prospects for mining manganese nodules were considered, evaluating the major components of a five-phase mining operation cycle: prospecting, exploration, mining, transportation, and processing. The operating costs—energy, labor, materials, and fixed and miscellaneous costs—were also estimated. These features were assumed for a mining operation handling 3 million tons of nodules a year over a twenty-five-year recovery period. The hypothetical project would go into commercial production in its sixth year, with its annual production and revenues projected through the thirtieth year.

The research results were released in a report dated March 1978 entitled "A Cost Model of Deep Ocean Mining and Associated Regulatory Issues." (Massachusetts Institute of Technology 1978) This report was widely distributed to governmental and private entities and a number were supplied to the U.N. Secretariat for distribution among all the national delegations to UNCLOS III.

The wide distribution of the MIT model (a problem that the U.S. delegation refused to recognize) raised the state of negotiations at UNCLOS to a level that the United States and its industrialized allies were ill-prepared to manage. While a slow, evolutionary process of sophistication within Committee One was underway prior to Geneva, it was possible to influence the conference gradually toward the U.S. position both by waiting for a gradual weakening of the Group of 77 as a dominating political bloc and by selectively releasing information to the conference.

The release of the MIT model had a threefold effect on the conference:

1. The model instantly galvanized conference participants along a generally accepted set of assumptions. This was most clearly expressed in the statement of Tommy Koh of Singapore, the chairman of the subgroup of financial experts:

> In the group of financial experts we were immediately confronted with the need to agree on a set of assumptions. Without an agreed framework of assumptions it would not have been possible for us to carry on with our discussions. We agreed that the best study to date was that undertaken by the Massachusetts Institute of Technology, entitled "A Cost Model of Deep Ocean Mining and Associated Regulatory Issues," hereinafter referred to as the MIT Study.

The act of agreeing on a common set of principles raised the tenor of negotiations to a level far more advanced than previously anticipated. This quantum leap in the level of discussions obviously caught the U.S. negotiators unprepared as they were forced to admit, after repeated questions from other delegates, that the administration had not acted on such advanced questions as the domestic tax treatment to which contributions to an international authority would be subject. This admission proved an embarrassment to the U.S. delegation and should have served as a warning of other potential embarrassments that the delegation would face later.

2. The model had the psychological effect of imparting to LDC conference participants an air of expertise regarding an advanced technological subject, thereby making them "as sophisticated"

technically as their DC counterparts. This mind-set of presumed technical equality created an atmosphere conducive to a proliferation of unrealistic proposals. It is now quite easy, and in some respects more legitimate, to seize on a particular number in the study and "run with it" without necessarily understanding how the number was determined or what its interrelationship with other assumptions might be.

3. The presentation of the model and the subsequent release and promotion of conflicting data on the part of the U.S. delegation have resulted in a cascade of technical misinformation.

It is counterproductive for the United States to release a complete information package one day, which it touts as "the best available data," and to apologize for inaccurate bits and pieces the next day. This is particularly serious because those assumptions within the model which the United States had been trying to withdraw from discussion provide the economic/commercial underpinnings of the entire industry as postulated in the model.

This introduction, praise, and withdrawal of supposed "best available data" in the midst of ongoing negotiations lent an image of guesswork to the position of the U.S. delegation. To the more suspicious delegations, the process created an image of tinkering with the figures in an attempt to put U.S. proposals in the most favorable light. Under such negotiating conditions, it is difficult for the United States to criticize other delegations for submitting proposals that may be considered outrageous or unsubstantiated. In effect, the conflicting nature of the U.S. presentation bestowed an equivalent legitimacy on both LDCs and to DCs regarding the validity of their proposals.

With these facts in mind it was rather startling that the U.S. delegation compounded its errors by sponsoring a special seminar at Cambridge under the auspices of MIT for the express purpose of imparting to from eighteen to twenty LDC delegations a degree of sophistication in the use of the model. The delegates were given open access to the model itself. In addition, the MIT team and the U.S. delegation established an on-line capability while the conference was underway when it reconvened in New York that August.

Most striking in all of this unprecedented generosity to U.S. negotiating adversaries was the timing. The United States provided the means to undermine its technical proposals right on the heels of the Engo treachery at the sixth session only one year earlier. That treachery immediately followed Kissinger's offer of a parallel system of mining replete with loan guarantees for third world and U.N. activities. Such lemming-like behavior on the part of U.S. negotiators was unfortunately not an aberration; it was repeated several times in negotiations in several other fields with equally disastrous results.

It is interesting to note that the motivation behind the release of the model to the conference was to prevent, through education, the expression of unrealistic proposals, which would confuse the negotiating process. It appears that this well-intentioned action brought about exactly what it sought to eliminate.

Who Has Ratified UNCLOS?

The legitimacy of any regime depends on a variety of factors, including its perceived importance, relevance, reasonableness, and practicality. These factors are in large part influenced by the power and importance of states that recognize, or are parties to, the regime. In the case of UNCLOS, we are faced with the unprecedented fact of a treaty entering into force having been ratified by over sixty states (six of which are landlocked), without the participation of any Western industrialized nations.

Such an eventuality would be of greater concern to treaty signatories than to the rest of the world as it would be doomed to irrelevancy. Fearing the prospect of irrelevancy for the U.N.'s premier New International Economic Order achievement, then-Secretary General Javier Perez de Cuellar, himself a former UNCLOS delegate, reopened talks in 1993 aimed at making the treaty more palatable to the industrialized countries.

Most industrialized countries followed the U.S. lead in refusing to accede to the treaty. Some shared the various concerns expressed by the United States. Others, however, were fearful that without U.S. participation and contribution of 25 percent of all financial assessments they would be required to bankroll the treaty themselves. Perhaps this is the ultimate source of U.S. leverage in governing the support of other nations as nonparticipants in UNCLOS.

As seen below, the list of UNCLOS ratifiers is long but unimpressive and collectively represents less than 5 percent of the U.N. schedule of assessments. An ISA/Enterprise complex relying on these subscribers would be financially unviable and little threat to a nonparticipating United States.

Table 2.1
Ratification of the 1982 UNCLOS

As of July 1, 1994, the following sixty-two nations had deposited their instruments of ratification or accession (figures in parentheses indicate U.N. scale of assessment) (United Nations 1992):

Coastal Island Nations	Dates of Ratification
Angola (.01)	December 5, 1990
Antigua and Barbuda (.01)	February 2, 1989
Bahamas (.02)	July 29, 1983
Bahrain (.03)	May 30, 1985
Barbados (.01)	October 12, 1993
Belize (.01)	August 13, 1983
Bosnia-Herzegovina	January 12, 1994
Brazil (1.59)	December 22, 1988
Cameroon (.01)	November 19, 1985
Cape Verde (.01)	August 10, 1987
Comoros (.01)	June 21, 1994
Costa Rica (.01)	September 21, 1992
Cuba (.09)	August 15, 1984
Cyprus (.01)	December 12, 1988
Djibouti (.01)	October 8, 1991
Dominica (.01)	October 24, 1991
Egypt (.07)	August 26, 1983
Fiji (.01)	December 10, 1982
Gambia (.01)	May 22, 1984
Ghana (.01)	June 7, 1983
Grenada (.01)	April 25, 1991
Guinea (.01)	September 6, 1985
Guinea-Bissau (.01)	August 25, 1986
Guyana (.01)	November 16, 1993
Honduras (.01)	October 5, 1993
Iceland (.03)	June 21, 1985
Indonesia (.16)	February 3, 1986
Iraq (.13)	July 30, 1985
Ivory Coast (.02)	March 26, 1984
Jamaica (.01)	March 21, 1983
Kenya (.01)	March 2, 1989
Kuwait (.25)	May 2, 1986
Malta (.01)	May 20, 1993
Marshall Islands (.01)	August 9, 1991

Mexico (.88)	March 18, 1983
Micronesia, Federated States of (.01)	April 29, 1991
Namibia (.01)	April 18, 1983
Nigeria (.20)	August 14, 1986
Oman (.03)	August 17, 1989
Philippines (.07)	May 8, 1984
Saint Lucia (.01)	March 27, 1985
St. Kitts and Nevis (.01)	January 7, 1993
St. Vincent and the Grenadines (.01)	October 1, 1993
Sao Tome and Principe (.01)	November 3, 1987
Senegal (.01)	October 25, 1984
Seychelles (.01)	September 16, 1991
Somalia (.01)	July 24, 1989
Sudan (.01)	January 23, 1985
Tanzania, United Republic of (.01)	September 30, 1985
Togo (.01)	April 6, 1985
Trinidad and Tobago (.05)	April 25, 1986
Tunisia (.03)	April 24, 1985
Uruguay (.04)	December 10, 1992
Yemen (.01)	July 21, 1987
Yugoslavia (.42)	May 5, 1986
Zaire (.01)	February 17, 1989
Landlocked Nations	**Dates of Ratification**
Botswana (.01)	May 2, 1990
Mali (.01)	July 16, 1985
Paraguay (.02)	September 26, 1986
Uganda (.01)	November 9, 1990
Zambia (.01)	March 7, 1983
Zimbabwe (.01)	February 24, 1993

---

[2]Of the seventeen countries abstaining, all but Belgium, Italy, Luxembourg, Spain, the Federal Republic of Germany, and the United Kingdom signed the Treaty in December 1982.

Chapter Three

Fatal Flaws in the Seabed Mining Regime

> The biggest single problem with the U.N. is that it involves in every decision too many nations that don't have a stake in the outcome . . . That's a prerequisite for irresponsible decision-making. (Kirkpatrick in McManus 1991)

The central feature of the seabed mining regime is the creation of the International Seabed Authority. Because its powers and functions and decision-making procedures will control the implementation of the regime, the International Seabed Authority provides the focal point for this analysis.

No evaluation of the seabed mining regime can be definitive at this time because key elements of the regime have been left to be worked out in the rules and regulations of the Authority. The rules and regulations will be drafted by the Preparatory Commission after the treaty negotiations are completed. If discussions in the Preparatory Commission reflect those during treaty negotiations, the industrialized countries will seek objectivity and specificity in the rules and regulations while the developing countries will seek broad discretion for the Authority. In any case, the rules and regulations cannot cure treaty deficiencies but can compound problems or effectively invalidate "protections and understandings" previously agreed to.

In fact, no nation has greater experience or a higher level of understanding of how excessive regulatory implementation or oversight can undermine, or even change, the character of judicial or legislative intent than does the United States. The growing furor over federal wetlands rules is an excellent example of overzealous regulators stifling investment and economic activity in Areas, and to a degree, far outside of the original legislative intent.

The clearest and most extensive analysis criticism of the treaty's seabed mining provisions is paraphrased below, except where otherwise noted. It is derived from a U.S. government White Paper that was presented to the delegates to the eleventh session in a last-ditch attempt to negotiate a more acceptable treaty.[3] Most of the objections and concerns raised in the 1982 analysis are still valid today.

The International Seabed Authority

The convention establishes an International Seabed Authority, composed of all states parties, with control over access to the minerals of the deep seabed and with broad regulatory, operational, and revenue-raising powers. The primary objectives of the regime do not promote the development of seabed mineral resources but instead closely parallel the objectives of the New International Economic Order, such as control over availability of the minerals, guaranteed prices, forced technology transfer, income transfers, and protection for inefficient land-based producers.

•All organs of the Authority will be dominated by the developing countries, with the United States and industrialized countries that share its views forming only a small minority. The decision-making system within each of these organs is based on the principle of one-nation-one-vote, with the result that the interests of the United States and other industrialized countries can in most cases be easily overridden.

•The Assembly is the supreme organ empowered to establish general policy by a two-thirds majority. Other organs of the Authority and of seabed miners *must* act in conformity with the general policies established by the Assembly.

•The thirty-six-member Council is the executive organ of the Authority. The Council establishes the specific policies of the Authority and administers the seabed mining regime. United States representation on the Council, although likely, is by no means guaranteed. Russia, on the other hand, is guaranteed direct representation on the Council through its domination of Eastern Europe because specific treaty provisions guarantee a minimum of three seats for Eastern Europe. The majority of the Council will consist of developing countries. Only six states (including the United States) can be anticipated to share the general interests of the United States.

• The convention establishes a one-nation-one-vote, three-tiered voting system in the Council for substantive questions, although it is unclear as to who decides whether an issue is considered "substantive" or not. Fundamental changes in the mining regime, such as amendments to the treaty or rules and regulations, require consensus on the Council, enabling the United States (and any other Council member) to block such changes. The United States and like-minded industrialized states would not be able to block any other substantive decisions of the Council, since these questions require only three-quarters or two-thirds majorities. The United States would be unlikely to obtain affirmative action by the Council.

•The commissions of the Council would control approval of contracts to mine the seabeds, help administer the seabed mining regime, and monitor the economic effects of the seabed mining. Although their decision-making procedures are not yet established, their composition ensures that industrialized countries would be only a small minority. The Enterprise, the mining arm of the Authority, and the Seabeds Disputes Chamber, the judicial arm of the Authority, would also be dominated by the developing countries.

Scope of the Authority

Under the Authority, the resources of the seabed are vested in all mankind, on whose behalf the Authority shall act (Article 137). The Authority's control over oceans resources is expressly limited to the seabed and ocean floor and subsoil thereof beyond the limits of national jurisdiction (Articles 1 and 157). The Authority has no jurisdiction over the waters superadjacent to the Area (ocean surface, water column) or the airspace above those waters (Article 135).

Objectives of the Authority

In their noteworthy deficiency, in the objectives outlined in the convention fail to proclaim mineral resource development of the deep seabeds as the principal goal or even an important goal of the Authority and of the seabed mining regime. The text, in the midst of a long list of policy goals, simply states that "activities in the Area . . . shall, as specifically provided in this part, be carried out . . . with a view to ensuring . . . the development of the common heritage for the benefit of mankind as a whole" (Article 150). Such a weak "pro-production statement" encourages the Authority to foster neither the development of ocean resources nor the free flow of investment in response to market forces. Indeed, when read in the context of other policies, it may actually hinder development.

Most of the other policy goals of Article 150 are bases for market intervention, forced transfer of resources from industrialized countries to developing countries, and other impediments to investment, rather than a framework to allow goods, capital, and technology to flow freely in response to market forces. These stated goals are (emphasis added):

--the orderly and safe development and rational management of the resources of the Area;

--the expansion of opportunities for all state parties, especially developing states, to participate in seabed mining;

--the participation by the Authority in revenues generated by seabed mining and the transfer of seabed mining technology to the Enterprise and developing states;

--the increase in the availability of the minerals produced from the resources of the Area *as needed* in conjunction with minerals produced from other resources;

--the promotion of just and stable prices remunerative to producers and fair to consumers for minerals produced both from the resources of the Area and from other sources, and promoting long-term equilibrium in supply and demand;

--*the protection of developing countries from the adverse effects* on their economies or on their export earnings of a reduction in the price of an affected mineral, or in the volume of that mineral exported, to the extent that such reductions are *caused by activities in the Area.*

These policy objectives incorporate many goals of the New International Economic Order put forward by the developing countries in other international fora and strongly resisted by the United States. The only stated policy goal in Article 150 that reflects any effort to allow goods, capital, and technology to flow freely in response to market forces is the so-called market-access clause, which states that "conditions of access to markets for the imports of minerals produced from the resources of the Area and for the imports of commodities produced from such minerals shall not be more favorable than the most favorable applied to imports from other sources." Otherwise, the treaty text seems to exhort the Authority to manage the development of seabed resources, control the availability of seabed minerals, maintain guaranteed prices for minerals, force the transfer of technology and revenues to itself and to developing states, and insulate land-based producers from competition from seabed mining.

Organs of the Authority

The operating arms of the Authority established in the convention include the following:

1. The __Assembly__, consisting of all states parties, is declared the "supreme organ of the Authority" to which all other organs are accountable. It has the power to establish the general policies of the Authority (Article 160, paragraph 1), with which the actions of other organs must conform. Because each state party has one vote and substantive decisions are taken by a two-thirds majority (Article 159, paragraph 6), the developing nations can control the decisions of the Assembly. The United States and other major industrialized nations would form a small minority without enough votes to achieve a majority on any issue and would have to win over a substantial number of developing countries in order to block any Assembly actions. Therefore, the general policies of the Authority, which will significantly affect Authority operations and the overall investment climate, cannot be made or blocked by the industrialized countries.

2. The __Council__ is the executive organ of the Authority. It has the power to set the specific policies of the Authority and administer the seabed mining regime. The text gives no guidance as to what is meant by "specific policies," nor does it distinguish them from "general policies." Such ambiguities on the division of power between the Assembly and Council could result in unnecessary tensions between the two organs and confusion in the determination of Authority policies.

The thirty-six states that are members of the Council are elected by the Assembly (Article 161, paragraph 1) to five separate chambers of the Council, which reflect the various groupings of states with "major interests" in the seabed mining regime:

(a) The seabed mining chamber consists of four members from among the eight states parties that have the largest investments in preparation for and in the conduct of seabed mining, either directly or through their nationals, including at least one state from the Eastern (Socialist) European region.

Figure 3.1
International Seabed Authority

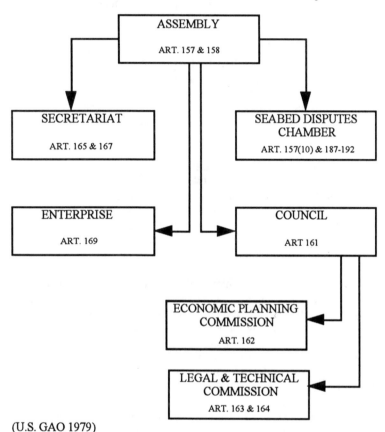

(U.S. GAO 1979)

(b) The consumer/importer chamber consists of four members from among those states parties which, during the last five years for which data are available, have either consumed more than two per cent of total world consumption or have had net imports of more than 2 percent of the total imports of nickel, copper, cobalt, and manganese, and *in any case* one State from the Eastern (Socialist) European region.

(c) The exporter chamber for land-based producers consists of four members from among those countries which mine domestically and are major net exporters of nickel, copper, cobalt, and manganese, including at least two developing countries whose exports of such minerals have a substantial bearing on their economies.

(d) The special interest chamber for developing nations consists of six members that represent the interests of states with large populations; states that are landlocked or geographically disadvantaged; states which are major importers of copper, nickel, cobalt, and manganese; states that are potential producers of such minerals; and least developed states.

(e) The general chamber consists of eighteen members elected according to the principle of ensuring an equitable geographical distribution on the Council as a whole, provided that each geographical region would have at least one member in this chamber. The geographical regions are Africa, Asia, Eastern Europe (Socialist), Latin America, Western Europe, and others.

The determination of which states are eligible for each category plays a central role in the composition of the Council, because the treaty requires that "each group of states parties to be represented on the Council is represented by those members, if any, which are nominated by the group" (Article 161, paragraph 2.c.). The eligibility criteria for category (a), the seabed miner chamber, are quite vague and will have to be spelled out in detail in the rules, regulations, and procedures of the Authority. Although it will be fairly obvious which nations are major seabed miners, it will be difficult to establish criteria that can measure the relative level of the seabed mining activity of each state. There are already *thirteen* nations that may be deemed eligible on the basis of seabed mining investment for the three unreserved seats in category (a): the United States, Canada, the United Kingdom, Germany, France, Japan, the Netherlands, Belgium, Italy, Russia, South Korea, India, and the People's Republic of China. The number of states with a direct interest in seabed mining, however, could expand over the years, especially if processing facilities are located in developing countries.

The eligibility criteria for category (b), the consumer category, attempt to be more specific by requiring that members account for at least 2 percent of world consumption or imports of copper, nickel, cobalt, and manganese. A number of very difficult technical problems associated with metal statistics (in particular the definition, availability, and measurement of metal statistics; the choice of metal statistics; and the aggregation of metal statistics when dealing with more than one metal) will have to be resolved satisfactorily in the rules and regulations of the Authority. The choice of aggregation method in particular has profound effects on eligibility. If the metals are weighted by value, eight States would be eligible for category (b) (the United States, Russia, Japan, Germany, the United Kingdom, France, China, and Italy). If all metals are weighted equally in the calculation, the number of eligible states increases to as high as eleven (the same eight as above plus Belgium/Luxembourg, Canada, and possibly Sweden). The text also requires "in any case" that an Eastern European Socialist state be a member of category (b), whether or not it meets the statistical eligibility requirements.

The eligibility criteria for category (c), the land-based-producer chamber, are so general that virtually any major exporter of any one commodity could be deemed qualified. The criteria would have to be spelled out in more detail in the rules and regulations before the caucus could be convened.

Virtually every developing state party would be eligible for category (d), the developing country chamber.

All states parties are eligible for category (e), the general chamber. Members of chamber (e) will be chosen to restore, to the degree possible, whatever geographical imbalance remains after the selection of the first four chambers. In U.N. practice, the ideal standard for "equitable geographical distribution" in a thirty-six-member organ would likely be ten to eleven states from Africa, nine states from Asia, six states from Latin America, three states from Eastern (Socialist) Europe and six to seven states from Western Europe and other areas. Because the Eastern European and Western Europe and Others (W.E.O.) groups would be well represented in the first four categories, only one W.E.O. country and one East European country are likely to be elected to category (c); the rest will be African, Asian, and Latin American states.

The United States cannot be certain that it will be elected to the Council, even in category (a) and category (b). Since the treaty does not specify how each caucus would nominate its representatives, the selection procedures are presumably left to the caucuses themselves. If the seabed miner and consumer caucuses opt for a one-nation-one-vote procedure, U.S. selection for the Council, although likely, is by no means guaranteed. The United States must expect keen competition for the six unreserved category (a) and (b) seats as each state affected by the treaty will consider a Council seat necessary to protect its own interests. *Even if the United States obtains an initial seat on the*

Council, the text calls for rotation of Council membership, which could be interpreted to preclude permanent seats for any one country. The Former Soviet Union, on the other hand, is guaranteed direct representation on the Council through its domination of Eastern Europe due to specific treaty provisions that assign seats in chambers (a), (b), and (e) to Eastern Europe.

The composition of the Council ensures that the developing nations will have the numerical majority, while the United States and other major industrialized countries will be only a minority on the Council. The Council will most likely consist of only six states (including the United States) that can be relied on generally to share U.S. views, three Eastern European Socialist states, one small Western European state, and twenty-four to twenty-six developing states (depending on the membership of the land-based producer chamber). Even U.S. allies cannot be expected to vote with the United States on each issue of importance to the United States. For example, the Europeans and Japan have strongly opposed the United States in the conference on such issues as anti-monopoly and anti-subsidy provisions.

The treaty establishes a one-nation-one-vote, three-tiered voting system in the Council for substantive questions (Article 161, paragraph 7).

The text specifies the majority to be applied to each particular power and function of the Council. In the case of fundamental changes in the treaty regime (for example, amendments to the seabed text or changes in the rules and regulations), the Council must agree by consensus. Operational and institutional decisions are made by either a three-quarters majority or two-thirds majority, depending on the importance of the issue. Procedural questions are decided by a simple majority. If the issue arises as to which majority should be required to invoke a particular power, the question is treated as requiring the higher majority (Article 161, paragraph 7.g.). Any decisions for which no voting requirement is specified must be taken by consensus (Article 161, paragraph 7.d.).

If the United States is elected to the Council, it could block any Council decision requiring a consensus. All other members of the Council, be they Chad or Russia, would have the same power. The composition of the Council, however, effectively precludes the United States and like-minded industrial states from blocking Authority actions that require either a three-quarters vote (ten states to block) or a two-thirds vote (thirteen states to block). Since the United States can count on at most six votes in the seabed miner and consumer chambers, it would have to draw on land-based producers, the Eastern Socialist bloc, some developing countries, or a combination thereof to block a three-quarters majority. Even a coalition of Western industrialized states, East European Socialist states, and China would be unable to block a two-thirds majority. Obviously, the United States and like-minded states would be unable to effect positive action in the Council.

3. The **Legal and Technical Commission and the Economic Planning Commission** are both organs of the Council that will, respectively, help administer the seabed mining regime and monitor the economic effects of seabed mining (Articles 163, 164, and 165). Each commission consists of fifteen technically qualified members elected by a three-quarters majority of the Council (Article 163; paragraphs 2 and 3; Article 161, paragraph 7.c.). Because the selection of commissioners should pay due regard to "the need for equitable geographical distribution and representation of special interests" (Article 163, paragraph 4), the developing countries will have a majority while Western industrialized countries will have no more than five representatives on each commission. The decision-making mechanisms for the commissions are not specified but are to be determined in the rules, regulations, and procedures of the Authority (Article 163, paragraph 11). It is clear, however, that the United States and its allies would be unable to effect positive action and would have difficulty blocking Commission initiatives in either Commission.

4. The **Enterprise** is the organ through which the Authority will mine the seabed directly, as well as transport, process, and market recovered minerals (Article 170, paragraph 1). The Governing Board directs the business operations of the Enterprise (Annex IV, Article 6). Its fifteen members are elected by the Assembly (two-thirds majority), on the recommendation of the Council (three-quarters majority) with due regard for equitable geographical distribution (Annex IV, Article 5, paragraph 1), (Article 160, paragraph 2.c.: Article 159, paragraph 6; Article 162, paragraph 2.c.; Article 161, paragraph 7.c.). Because the United States and its allies cannot significantly affect the election of the Governing Board, the Enterprise will be dominated by representatives of the developing countries.

5. The **Seabeds Disputes Chamber** is not an organ of the Authority but a part of the Law of the Sea Tribunal. Under Article 187, it has jurisdiction over disputes between states parties, parties to contract, and the Authority. The eleven-member Chamber is selected by a majority of the International Tribunal for the Law of the Sea, with the proviso that the representation of the principal legal systems of the

world and equitable geographical distribution is to be assured (Annex VI, Article 36). The Tribunal itself is elected at a special meeting by a two-thirds majority of the states parties present and voting (Annex VI, Article 4). In light of these election procedures, the developing countries will have a numerical majority of both the Tribunal and the Chamber.

Revision of the Regime

The fundamental components of the Law of the Sea seabed mining regime could be revised in four ways: (1) amendments to the seabed mining regime proposed by the Council and Assembly; (2) changes in the rules and regulations of the Authority; (3) amendments to the seabed mining regime proposed by the Review Conference; and (4) expansion of the Authority's powers and functions.

If the United States is on the Council permanently, the text enables the United States to resist changes in the fundamental components of the seabed mining regime over the first twenty years after production commences under the treaty, because amendments to the treaty and changes in its rules and regulations require Council consensus. However, all other members of the Council have the same power, thus leading to an excessively rigid regime. The fundamental components of the regime could be revised by the Review Conference over U.S. objections after the twenty-year period. These amendments would enter into force for the United States, unless the United States denounced the *entire* treaty. Finally, there are no institutional safeguards to counter usurpation of new powers and functions by the Authority. Thus, the United States could be forced by an aggressive Authority or review conference to denounce the entire treaty (including the non-seabeds portions), which could create additional legal and political problems for the United States.

Amendments

The basic amendment procedures of the treaty provide that any states party may propose amendments to the seabed mining regime (Article 314, paragraph 1). The proposed amendment would be subject to approval by the Assembly by a two-thirds majority following its approval by the Council by consensus (Article 314, paragraph 1; Article 159, paragraph 6; Article 161, paragraph 7.d.). Such adopted amendments shall enter into force for all states parties following the deposit of instruments of ratification or accession by three-fourths of the states parties (Article 316, paragraph 6). The treaty may also be amended by entirely separate Review Conference procedures discussed below.

If the United States were elected to the Council, it would be able to block any amendments contrary to its interests by blocking a consensus on the Council. At the same time, because of the consensus rule, the United States would face a virtually impossible task in obtaining amendments beneficial to its interests adopted by the Council and Assembly.

Rules and Regulations

The text provides two different procedures for adopting rules, regulations, and procedures of the Authority. Those relating to prospecting, exploration, and exploitation of the seabeds and the financial management and internal administration of the Authority would be drafted by the Preparatory Commission and would apply provisionally pending their adoption by the Authority (Article 308, paragraph 4; Article 162, paragraph 2.n.ii.). The Council would adopt by consensus and apply these rules, regulations, and procedures provisionally, pending approval of the Assembly (Article 162, paragraph 2.n.ii; Article 161, paragraph 7.d.). The Assembly is empowered to consider and finally approve by a two-thirds vote, the rules, regulations, and procedures provisionally adopted by the Council (Article 160, paragraph 2.f.ii; Article 159, paragraph 6). Any changes in the rules, regulations, and procedures would have to be agreed in the Council by consensus and in the Assembly by a two-thirds vote.

This approval procedure enables the United States to know the initial rules, regulations, and procedures of the Authority prior to their ratification. If the United States were elected to the Council, it would be protected from any changes in these rules, regulations, and procedures that would be contrary to its interests because it couldn't block consensus on the Council. (The doubts only arise because the text is slightly ambiguous about whether the Assembly can change the rules, regulations, and procedures adopted by the Council.) Unfortunately, the consensus requirement would also result in a rigid set of rules, regulations, and procedures since any other Council member could block changes. As a result, the Authority would be unable to adapt its rules and regulations to changing conditions that are likely to arise in a new industry such as seabed mining.

The second procedure applies to rules, regulations, and procedures on the equitable sharing of financial and other economic benefits derived from activities in the Area and the payments and contributions resulting from revenue sharing from the continental margin beyond 200 miles, "taking into particular consideration the interests and needs of the developing states and peoples who have not attained full independence or other self-governing status" (Article 160, paragraph

2.f.ii). These rules, regulations, and procedures would not necessarily be drafted by the Preparatory Commission, nor would they be adopted and provisionally applied by the Council. Instead, the Council would "recommend" by consensus such rules, regulations, and procedures, and the Assembly would either approve them by two-thirds majority or, in case of disapproval, return them to the Council for reconsideration (Article 160, paragraph 2.f.i; Article 159, paragraph 6; Article 162, paragraph 2.n.i; Article 161, paragraph 7.d.).

The United States could use the consensus requirement provision to control criteria for the distribution of funds to states, and in particular, to block the financing of liberation movements such as the Palestine Liberation Organization. If the United States exercised a veto, however, it could be charged with contravening a basic principle of the seabeds regime, in which liberation organizations are deemed legitimate recipients of Authority revenues (Article 140). Such charges could undermine U.S. efforts to ensure that the Authority abide by the letter and spirit of the convention in other areas.

Review Conference

The Review Conference, composed of all states parties and convened fifteen years after the commencement of commercial production under the treaty, is empowered to review and draft amendments to the seabed mining regime (Article 155). If the Conference cannot reach agreement after five years of negotiation, it is empowered to adopt amendments by a two-thirds majority of the states parties. Such amendments would enter into force for all states parties one year after the deposit of instruments of ratification, accession, or acceptance by two-thirds of the states parties (Article 155, paragraph 4).

Since most states parties are likely to be developing nations, the Review Conference could amend the treaty over the objections of the United States and the other major industrialized nations. The United States would face the choice of accepting amendments contrary to its interests or denouncing the entire treaty (Article 317). The United States would likely be challenged if it asserted a right to mine the seabeds unilaterally, because it had already operated under the regime for twenty years or more. The customary right to mine the seabed under international law existing prior to the treaty would be uncertain.

Expansion of Authority Power

The Authority may attempt to extend its powers and functions beyond those expressly granted in the treaty. The United States could have difficulty blocking the usurpation of power, because no voting rule is provided for such contingencies. Although the United States could bring such a dispute before the Seabeds Disputes Chamber (Article 187; paragraph b; Article 188), the composition of the Chamber (which would be dominated by the developing countries) and the need for the Council and Assembly to implement the Chamber's findings could allow the Authority to continue to usurp powers and functions.

Access to Seabed Minerals

The convention does *not* provide assured access, on a non-discriminatory basis, for the United States and U.S. corporations. The treaty does not provide that any entity that has or can obtain the necessary capital, technology, and know-how would receive exclusive rights to explore and exploit specific areas of the seabed in a stable and reasonable regulatory environment, which permits profits sufficient to attract venture capital.

Only two features of the text have a positive effect on the access question, and their positive effects are partially offset by other considerations: (1) The treaty grants exclusive rights to a seabed miner to mine a particular area of the seabed. But such rights are vulnerable to suspension or termination because the composition, powers, and decision-making systems enable the Authority, dominated by the developing countries, to rescind such rights over the objections of the United States and other potential seabed mining countries. The exclusive rights may also be eliminated through amendments adopted at the Review Conference. (2) The treaty provides that the rules, regulations, and procedures of the Authority may not be changed unless such changes are agreed to by all members of the Council, and that such new rules, regulations, and procedures would not apply to any operator holding a previously approved plan of work. These provisions add a degree of certainty to the system of access but also could lead to a very rigid regime, which would be unable to respond to changing needs and circumstances.

Assured access to the deep seabed minerals is denied the United States primarily through: (1) the powers, composition, and decision-making mechanisms of the organs of the Authority; (2) the mechanism for contract approval; (3) the limitation on mineral production and mechanism for production authorization; (4) the obligations and limitations under an approved plan of work, particularly in regard to the reservation of mine sites, the technology transfer obligations, the financial terms of contracts, and the other operational requirements.

The primary impediments to U.S. access are the institutional structure and the decision-making systems of the Authority. The organs of the Authority, taken as a group, have a formidable array of powers to bring to bear on any U.S. entity that wants to mine the seabeds. They control entry into seabed mining, allocate production shares, supervise and control mining operations, suspend mining operations, and adjudicate contract disputes. Although the United States and its allies have the greatest stakes in seabed mining as both miners and consumers, the developing nations would dominate all organs of the Authority.

The convention establishes a highly discriminatory set of qualification standards, which would be considerably more stringent for private firms sponsored by industrialized states than for industrialized states, developing states, entities sponsored by developing states, joint ventures, and the Enterprise. Private firms sponsored by the United States would face more decision points where their qualifications could be questioned by the Authority (sponsorship, technical capability, financial capability, etc.) whereas the other entities seem to be presumed qualified. The United States, since it currently dominates seabed mining development, would be the only nation whose entities would likely be denied a contract because of the quota and anti-density provisions. The composition of the organs empowered to approve contracts prejudices the process against industrialized countries and in favor of the Enterprise and developing countries. Finally, the treaty does not have a workable and fair appeals mechanism to provide a U.S. miner with a realistic chance of successfully appealing rejection of an application.

The text threatens U.S. access because the production control formula limits the amount of minerals allowed to be produced from the seabeds and thereby the number of entrants into seabed mining. If two or more applicants compete for an authorization to commence commercial production, the Council has broad discretion to choose even the least efficient among them. The production limitation and the allocation process deter seabed investment by creating the risk that an operator might never be permitted to mine his site.

The obligations and limitations imposed on seabed miners by the convention impede access by substantially increasing the costs, constraints and complexity of mining. The costs of mining the seabeds for U.S. miners are increased substantially by requirements to prospect sites for the Enterprise, share revenues with the Authority, and transfer technology to the Enterprise and developing countries. Although the revenue-sharing obligations are flexible and generally responsive to profitability, they also require heavy front-end financial payments to the Authority. The text also mandates that U.S. mining firms sell their proprietary mining technology to the Enterprise and certain developing countries on "fair and reasonable terms and conditions." While the mandatory sale provision is objectionable on ideological grounds,, the obligation would also lower the commercial value of the technology, increase the operating costs of the miner, threaten the exclusivity of the technology, and discourage technological innovation.

The convention fails to provide nondiscriminatory access for U.S. mining corporations. First, the treaty explicitly urges discrimination in favor of developing countries. Second, the contract approval and production authorization mechanisms favor the Enterprise, developing countries, joint ventures, and to a certain extent industrialized states operating through state-owned ventures, as Russia does. Third, reserved site and technology transfer obligations represent a significant impediment to U.S. corporations and a major advantage for the Enterprise and developing countries. Joint ventures are exempt from technology transfer. The revenue-sharing provisions also discriminate in favor of the Enterprise, developing countries, and joint ventures. Finally, the institutional structure is strongly biased in favor of developing countries, joint ventures, and the Enterprise.

As a result, the current seabed mining regime, if it ever entered into force, could cause the interests of the United States and the U.S. corporations that are pioneering seabed mining to diverge. A rational corporation, when faced with the significant bias in the system against entities sponsored by the United States and its allies, would search for ways to circumvent the system. The existing text contains significant incentives for mining corporations either to (1) negotiate joint ventures or production-sharing arrangements with the Enterprise or (2) seek sponsorship from a developing nation. Thus, the seabed mining regime may in practice evolve into a joint venture system. Corporations may be able to operate under such a system. but it certainly does not assure access for the United States. In addition, pioneer seabed mining companies that get into commercial production (and thus under the production ceiling) would be operating within an internationally sanctioned cartel. This cartel would restrain any new entrants, to the advantage of the pioneer miners. Finally, the obvious burdens of the text could increase corporate hopes of receiving financial offsets from the U.S. government that would in effect guarantee profitability. Again, this would be a case of corporate access but not U.S. access.

The System of Governance and Access

The International Seabed Authority would administer the system of access in accordance with the provisions of the treaty and its rules, regulations, and procedures (Article 153, paragraph 1). The rules, regulations, and procedures are to be developed initially by the Preparatory Commission and would enter in force with the treaty (Article 308, paragraph 4). The Authority is empowered to control and organize exploration and exploitation activities in the seabed (Article 157, paragraph 1). Authority organs have a significant bearing on access:

--The Assembly has the power to establish the general policies of the Authority (Article 160, paragraph 1). All seabed miners are required to act in conformity with these general policies. Other powers and functions of the Assembly which have an impact on access questions include final approval of the rules, regulations, and procedures of the Authority (Article 160, paragraph 2.f.) and of the Authority's budget (Article 160, paragraph 2.g.).

--The Council has the power to set the specific policies of the Authority (Article 162, paragraph 1). The Council is entrusted with control over the system of access in the treaty through its powers in Article 162 to (1) exercise control over activities in the Area, that is, deep seabed mining (paragraph 2.k.); (2) approve plans of work for mining the seabeds (paragraph 2.j.); (3) select which applicants will receive shares of the allotted seabed production if the amount of production requested exceeds the amount available (paragraph 2.p.); (4) direct and supervise the inspection of activities in the Area (paragraph 2.y.); (5) close off parts of the seabeds or suspend mining operations in order to prevent serious harm to the marine environment (paragraphs 2.w. and 2.v.); (6) issue directives to the Enterprise, (paragraph 2.i.); (7) initiate proceedings in the Seabeds Disputes Chamber and recommend appropriate measures on a finding of the Chamber (paragraphs 2.t. and 2.w.); (8) review the collection of all payments to the Authority (paragraph 2.o.); (9) submit the annual budget of the Authority to the Assembly (paragraph 2.q.); and (10) provisionally adopt the rules, regulations, and procedures of the Authority. (Rules produced by the Preparatory Commission would already be provisionally applied without Council action.)

--The Legal and Technical Commission is a subsidiary organ of the Council which will administer many aspects of the system of access on behalf of the Council. Under Article 165, the

Commission (1) reviews and makes recommendations on plans of work submitted by seabed mining applicants (paragraph 2.b.); (2) supervises mining activities (paragraph 2.c.); (3) recommends rules, regulations, and procedures of the Authority (paragraph 2.f. and 2.g.); (4) monitors the impact of mining on the environment and recommends appropriate actions to the Council (paragraphs 2.d., 2.h., 2.k., and 2.l.); (5) calculates the production ceiling (paragraph 2.m.); and (6) recommends the initiation of proceedings in the Seabeds Disputes Chamber and appropriate measures to be taken on findings by the Chamber (paragraphs 2.i. and 2.j.).

--The Seabeds Disputes Chamber has jurisdiction in Article 187 over disputes with respect to activities in the Area which have an impact on access such as (1) disputes between States concerning the interpretation or application of the treaty's seabed mining provisions (paragraph a); (2) disputes between parties to a contract concerning (a) the interpretation or application of a plan of work, or (b) acts or omissions of a party to a contract (paragraph c); and (3) disputes between the Authority and a prospective contractor concerning a refused plan of work or a legal issue in the negotiation of the plan of work (paragraph d). The contractor has the option, however, of taking contract disputes which do not involve treaty interpretations to commercial arbitration rather than the Chamber.

Thus, organs of the Authority have a formidable array of powers to bring to bear on any entity that wants to mine the seabeds. Such powers are closely akin to those of a national government administering development of resources subject to its sovereignty. The Authority has powers never before granted to any international organization.

Each of these organs will be dominated by the developing countries, while the Western industrialized countries will form a very small minority and Eastern European countries another small minority. The only constraints on the Authority in the exercise of these formidable powers are limitations expressly contained in the treaty. These "constraints" will be evaluated below as they apply to various aspects of the access question.

Different Systems of Access Under the Treaty

Access is granted only through the so-called "parallel system." This system establishes different procedures of access for states and entities sponsored by states on the "nonreserved" side of the parallel system and for the Enterprise and developing countries and their entities on the "reserved" side (Article 153; Annex iii, Articles 8 and 9). The central feature of the parallel system is that a prospected mine site is set aside for the reserved side of the parallel system for each mine site approved on the nonreserved side (Annex III, Article 8). Developing countries and their entities have access to a reserved site if the Enterprise agrees to relinquish a site to them; otherwise, developing countries would have access on the nonreserved side. In fact, the text goes beyond establishing just two systems of access and instead establishes five systems of access for each type of entity:

(1) States, which must ratify or accede to the treaty before their right to mine the seabeds or sponsor applicants is recognized (Article 153, paragraph 2.b.).

(2) Entities sponsored by states, which would include either state corporations (particularly in the case of the Eastern-Europeans) or "natural or juridical persons which possess the nationality of or are effectively controlled by states," such as private corporations (Article 153, paragraph 2.b.).

(3) Developed states or entities sponsored by developing states that operate on the reserved side of the parallel system (Article 153, paragraph 2.b.).

(4) The Enterprise, the operating arm of the Authority, which will engage directly in all phases of seabed mining including exploration and exploitation, transportation, processing, and marketing (Article 153, paragraph 2.b.; Article 158, paragraph 2; Article 170, paragraph 1).

(5) Joint ventures negotiated between the Enterprise and either states or entities sponsored by states, which may also mine the seabeds (Article 153, paragraphs 2.b. and 3).

United States access to seabed minerals would normally be through the system of access for entities sponsored by states. The conditions of U.S. access are not only very different from those for other types of entities, but also considerably more burdensome. These major disadvantages will be discussed in more detail in the context of the various stages of a contract. In summary, the major advantages of other entities follow:

--The convention obligates states parties to provide the Enterprise with seed money in the form of interest-free loans and loan guarantees to finance the equivalent of one fully integrated project at an approximate cost of $1.5 billion (Annex IV, Article 11, paragraph 3). In addition, the Authority is empowered to transfer funds to the Enterprise throughout the life of the treaty (Article 173). As a result, the opportunity costs of investing in seabed mining are much higher for states and corporations than for the Enterprise. The opportunity costs for state and private investors arise from their equity participation in seabed projects; the opportunity cost is the return on capital from alternative investments forgone in order to invest in seabed mining. Since the Enterprise is financed through interest-free loans and guarantees from States, the opportunity costs of its initial investment are borne not by the Enterprise but by the states. In later projects, the Authority may bear the opportunity costs, to the extent that it transfers funds to the Enterprise.

--The Enterprise, developing states, and entities sponsored by developing states operating on the reserved side can all force the mandatory sale of seabed mining technology for ten years after the Enterprise commences commercial production (Annex III, Article 5). The implementation of this obligation, however, may extend beyond this period. As a result, these other entities have guaranteed access to the best available technology, most likely at less-than-market prices.

--The Enterprise is exempt from payments to the Authority under the financial terms of contracts for ten years after it commences commercial production (Annex IV, Article 10, paragraph 3).

--Developing countries, entities sponsored by developing countries, and joint ventures that operate on the reserved side are given access to mine sites prospected by private corporations under the "banking" system (Annex III, Articles 3 and 4) and may be granted financial incentives under the "banking" system (Annex III, Articles 3 and 4) and under the financial terms of contracts (Annex III, Article 13, paragraph 1.d.).

--The terms and conditions for joint ventures with the Enterprise are quite vague in the text compared with the terms and conditions specified for private U.S. corporations (Annex III, Article 11). In essence, the Governing Board of the Enterprise sets the terms and conditions for joint ventures (Annex IV, Article 6, paragraph e). The technology transfer obligations of the treaty are waived (Annex III, Article 5, paragraph 6) and financial payments to the Authority are lowered for joint ventures. However, joint ventures to exploit reserved sites may be subject to special rules and regulations of the Authority (Annex III, Article 9, paragraph 3).

Prospecting

The text places obligations on any entity (state, commercial, Enterprise, or joint venture) that wants to prospect the seabeds. Any proposed prospector must provide the Authority with a written undertaking that he shall (1) comply with the convention and relevant rules and regulations concerning protection of the marine environment and cooperation in training programs and (2) accept verification by the Authority of compliance (Annex III, Article 2, paragraph 1.b.). The proposed prospector shall also notify the Authority of the broad area or areas in which prospecting is to take place (Annex III, Article 2, paragraph 1.b.).

The prospector faces the following difficulties at this stage:

--The text discriminates against industrialized states and the entities they sponsor in favor of the other types of entities by requiring compliance with rules and regulations concerning "cooperation in training programs." Such cooperation includes providing opportunities for LDC and Enterprise personnel to participate in activities in the Area (Articles 143 and 144, Annex III, Article 15). Although this obligation theoretically applies to all proposed prospectors, its actual invocation is likely to affect only industrialized states and the corporations they sponsor (and thus add to their costs). This obligation could be particularly onerous because crew space is at a premium on board ship.

--There is some risk that the Authority may abuse its powers of verification. Under the treaty, the Authority controls activities in the Area by a three-quarters vote in the Council (Article 161, paragraph 7 e, Article 162, paragraph 2.h.). Unless the procedures of verification are tightly prescribed in the rules and regulations (and such rules cannot be expected to foresee every contingency), the Authority could interfere in the activities of the prospector, especially under the guise of environmental considerations.

--The Authority may question whether an undertaking is satisfactory and thus delay the commencement of prospecting.

Approval of a Plan of Work

Any entity mining the seabeds under the treaty must have its "plan of work" approved by the Authority. The treaty specifies some of the content of a plan of work, including rights of the operator and obligations and limitations on the operator. The rules, regulations, and procedures of the Authority will outline these requirements in greater detail. Except in the case of the Enterprise, an approved plan of work will take the form of a contract between the operator and the Authority.

The procedures for approving a plan of work contain two major elements: (1) the qualification standards for applicants; and (2) the institutional procedures for reviewing and deciding on a plan of work. The qualification standards in particular draw important distinctions between the various entities entitled to mine the seabeds, while the institutional mechanisms, because of their composition and decision-making systems, are likely to operate with certain biases.

(1) U.S. access. U.S. corporations that apply for contracts must establish that (a) they have the nationality of or are under the control and sponsorship of a state party; and (b) they follow the procedures and meet the qualification standards established in the treaty and its rules, regulations, and procedures (Annex III, Article 4, paragraph 1).

Normally, a sponsorship requirement would be fairly straightforward. Unfortunately, the treaty complicates the process by *requiring* multiple sponsorship in the case of a partnership or consortium of entities from several states and dual sponsorship when a corporation is a national of one state but "effectively controlled" by another (Annex III, Article 4, paragraph 2). The convention forces the multinational consortia that are likely to pioneer seabed mining to make complex arrangements with a number of different governments. The mechanics of the system have yet to be defined. Since "effective control" is not defined, the Authority could also use this provision arbitrarily as an excuse to delay the process of contract approval by insisting on rummaging through the web of corporate ownership.

The qualification standards for a corporation include whether the applicant has the financial and technical capability to mine the seabeds and has performed satisfactorily under previous contracts (Annex III, Article 4, paragraph 4). Specific criteria for these qualification standards have not been established in the text but presumably would be set out in more detail in the rules and regulations (Annex III, Article 17, paragraph 1.b. XIV). Nonetheless, broad criteria such as financial capability, technical capability, and previous performance could be open to broad interpretations and thus result in considerable discretion for the Authority. Such discretion is *not* subject to judicial review by the Seabeds Disputes Chamber (Article 190).

In order to qualify for a plan of work, the U.S. operator would have to provide the Authority with a number of written agreements (Annex III, Article 4, paragraph 6). The applicant must undertake:

--to accept as enforceable and to comply with the applicable obligations created by the treaty and its rules and regulations, decisions of the organs of the Authority, and the terms of his contract with the Authority;

--to accept control by the Authority of his mining operations;

--to assure the Authority that his obligations under the contract will be performed in good faith; and

-- to comply with the provisions on technology transfer.

These undertaking have significant legal consequences. First, the corporations agree to subject themselves to the formidable powers and control of the organs of the Authority (Article 157; Article 160, paragraph 2; Article 162, paragraph 2). Second, the corporations submit to the procedures established in the treaty and rules and regulations, including the adjudication process. The adjudication process may lead to monetary penalties, suspension, or termination of a contract (Annex III, Article 18, paragraph 1 and 2). Third, a sponsoring state is responsible to ensure, within its legal system, that its contractor carries out activities in conformity with the treaty; otherwise, the state itself is liable (Article 139, paragraph 1; Annex III, Article 4, paragraph 3). Fourth, provisions on technology transfer commit the contractor to include in his plan of work a series of additional undertakings that compel the sale of his technology on demand by the Enterprise or developing countries (Annex III, Article 5, paragraph 3). (This issue is discussed in detail in the section on obligations under a plan of work.) Finally, the undertaking that a contractor act "in good faith" significantly increases the Authority's discretion to challenge a contractor's performance, either in litigation or in evaluating subsequent applications. A contractor's performance is measured not only in terms of the letter of his contract but also in terms of some vague concept of the intent of the contract.

An industrialized state, which applies for a contract to mine the seabeds directly, faces fewer hurdles in order to qualify. First, it would not face the sponsorship requirement because by definition it meets the nationality and effective control standards (Annex III, Article 4, paragraph 2). In addition, the qualification standards relating to financial and technical capability might not be applied, since the treaty may presume that states will be technically and financially qualified. "The procedures for assessing the qualifications of states parties which are applicants shall take into account their character as states" (Annex III, Article 4, paragraph 5). The industrialized State, however, would be required to include in its contract the same undertakings as a private corporation (Annex III, Article 4, paragraph 6). These undertakings would also have the same onerous legal consequences, except that the state would be directly liable for its activities (Article 139, paragraph 1).

A developing state that applies for a contract to mine the seabeds could face considerably fewer hurdles than an industrialized state, especially if it operates on the reserved side of this system. The sponsorship requirements are straightforward (Annex III, Article 4, paragraph 2), and the treaty already presumes a developing state will be financially and technically qualified (Annex III, Article 4, paragraph 5). Most important, the treaty explicitly permits the Authority to discriminate in favor of developing states without defining "developing state." Although the developing state must agree to the same general undertakings as an industrialized state (Annex III, Article 4, paragraph 6), these undertakings would have a different meaning for developing states that operate on the reserved side. For instance, "compliance to the technology transfer provision" does not mean that the developing state is compelled to sell its mining technology on demand (as is the case for industrialized states and the entities they sponsor). Instead, the technology transfer provisions give developing states access to mining technology by empowering them to compel its sale for reserved sites (Annex III, Article 5, paragraph 3.e.). In addition, a developing state could be eligible for special financial incentives (Annex III, Article 13, paragraph 1.d.), prospected sites (Annex III, Article 4), and other benefits that make complying with the provisions of the treaty quite attractive. Entities sponsored by developing states would be treated the same as developing states, except that sponsorship requirements may create some complications if these entities are multinational.

The Enterprise, since it operates under an approved plan of work rather than a contract, faces an different set of qualification standards. The Enterprise is exempt from sponsorship requirements (Annex III, Article 4, paragraph 1). Although the Enterprise must present evidence that it is financially and technically capable of mining the seabeds

(Annex III, Article 12, paragraph 2), such capabilities can be presumed because the financing of its first integrated project is provided by states parties (Annex IV, Article 11, paragraph 3). Financing for subsequent projects could come through financial transfers from the Authority (Article 170, paragraph 4, Article 173, paragraph 2.a.; Annex IV, Article 11, paragraph l.a.), and the Enterprise has access to technology since it can compel the sale of the best technology available (Annex III, Article 5).

The text is vague about the qualification standards and procedures for a joint venture between the Enterprise and another entity. The text, although somewhat convoluted on the point, seems to indicate that contracts for joint ventures must be sponsored by a state party (Annex III, Article 11, paragraph l; Annex III, Article 3, paragraph 5; Article 153, paragraph 2.b.). If this is the case, a joint venture faces the complexities of the sponsorship provisions. The joint venture, because of its access to technology and financing through the Enterprise, would presumably be deemed financially and technically capable to mine the seabeds. If the joint venture were part of an Annex III, Article 3(5) contract, the joint venture would have to include the same undertakings as other contractors in its plan of work (Annex III, Article 4, paragraph 6). Much like the Enterprise and developing countries, however, the requirement to comply with technology transfer provisions is meaningless, since obligations to transfer technology are waived in the case of joint ventures (Annex III, Article 5, paragraph 6).

The text thus provides a highly discriminatory set of qualification standards, which are considerably more stringent for private commercial entities sponsored by the United States and like-minded states than for seabed mining entities. Corporations sponsored by the United States face many more decision points where their qualifications can be questioned by the Authority (sponsorship, technical capability, and financial capability) whereas the other types of entities seem to be presumed qualified. U.S. corporations also accept more burdens than other entities when they agree to operate under the terms of the treaty. As a result, entities may be ranked according to stringency of qualification standards:

> (A) Private entities sponsored by industrialized states (most stringent qualifications);
> (B) Industrialized states, including state mining companies;
> (C) Joint ventures between the Enterprise and other entities;
> (D) Developing countries and entities sponsored by developing countries operating on reserved sites; and
> (E) The Enterprise (least stringent qualifications).

(2) Institutional steps in approving a plan of work. These steps, seen in conjunction with the composition of the Authority organs and their decision-making systems, severely prejudice the access of corporations sponsored by the United States. The procedures differ significantly for contractors on one hand and the Enterprise on the other.

The institutional procedures faced by contractors (states, entities sponsored by states, and perhaps joint ventures) follow:

(a) Proposed plans of work submitted to the Authority would first be reviewed by the Legal and Technical Commission to ascertain whether the applicant has complied with the procedures established for applications, has given the Authority, and possesses the requisite financial and technical qualifications (Annex III, Article 6, paragraph 2; Article 165, paragraph 2.b.). Because contractors sponsored by industrialized states are not presumed qualified (unlike other contractors), they will have to undergo close scrutiny by the Legal and Technical Commission. The decision-making system of the Commission is not specified in the text but instead is left to be worked out in the rules and regulations (Article 163, paragraph 11).

(b) The Commission would evaluate the plans of work to determine their compliance with the terms of the treaty and its rules and regulations (Annex III, Article 6, paragraph 3). Plans of work would not be approved: if part or all of the proposed mining area is included in a previously approved plan of work or a previously submitted proposed plan of work not finally acted on; if part or all of the mining area has been set aside for environmental reasons; or if approval of the plan of work would result in a single state mining more than 2 percent of the total seabed area or 30 percent of a circular area of 400,000 square kilometers (these are the anti-monopoly and density provisions).

(c) On completion of these investigations, the Legal and Technical Commission would decide whether to recommend approval or disapproval of the plan of work to the Council (Article 165, paragraph 2.b.). If the Commission recommends approval of a plan of work, the plan of work shall be approved by consensus, minus the state submitting or sponsoring the plan of work (Article 162, paragraph 2.j.i.). If the Commission recommends disapproval or makes no recommendation, the plan of work can only be approved by a three-quarters majority of the Council (Article 162, paragraph 2.j.ii.). There are no time limits on the deliberations of the Commission.

The institutional procedures faced by the Enterprise follow:

(a) The Governing Board of the Enterprise proposes to the Council projects for carrying out not only mining activities but also activities related to transportation, processing, and marketing (Annex IV, Article 12, paragraph 1; Annex IV, Article 1, paragraph 1). The Enterprise would include a plan of work for mining the seabeds as part of this project (Annex IV, Article 12, paragraph 1).

(b) The Legal and Technical Commission would evaluate the plan of work to determine its compliance with the terms of the treaty and the rules and regulations (Annex IV, Article 6, paragraph 3). The Enterprise's plan of work would not be approved (if part or all of the proposed mining area overlapped previously approved or submitted plans of work or) if the area had been closed to seabed mining for environmental reasons. The density and anti-monopoly provisions do not apply to the Enterprise (Annex III, Article 6, paragraph 3.c.).

(c) On completion of the investigation the Legal and Technical Commission would recommend approval or disapproval of the plan of work (Article 165, paragraph 2.b.). The voting mechanism in the Council for Enterprise plans of work would be the same as for other plans of work (Article 162, paragraph 2.j.).

This contract approval mechanism does not ensure U.S. access to the minerals of the seabeds:

--Only qualifications of applicants sponsored by industrialized states would undergo close scrutiny by the Legal and Technical Commission. The Enterprise, on the other hand, would be effectively exempt from the requisite financial and technical qualifications.

--The anti-density and quota/anti-monopoly provisions are primarily efforts of certain industrialized countries (Russia, France) to restrict the United States, which was expected to dominate pioneer mining.

--The decision-making system for the Legal and Technical Commission is not specified in the convention, so the United States cannot predict how its applications will be acted on but must await the promulgation of Authority rules and regulations.

--The composition of the Commission casts doubt on its objectivity and fairness in evaluating applications. The majority of its members will be from developing states. No matter what decision-making system is finally adopted, the minority of representatives from industrialized states will not be able to ensure that the Commission will act objectively and find all bona fide miners "qualified." Because of the complexities of the qualification standards applied to entities sponsored by industrialized states, the Commission could use its discretion to obfuscate, delay, and perhaps even justify turning down a qualified U.S. miner. Since the Commission is dominated by the developing countries, they would tend to look more favorably on Enterprise and developing country applications.

--The decision of the Legal and Technical Commission will bind the Council if the Commission finds a U.S. miner "unqualified" or makes no recommendation. The United States would face the impossible task of mustering twenty-seven votes in a thirty-six-member Council dominated by developing countries in order to approve the plan of work. If the Commission approves a plan of work, however, it is virtually impossible to overturn the decision. Should the Enterprise or a developing country be deemed "qualified," it will almost automatically be approved by the Council.

--The text does not have a fair mechanism to appeal an adverse decision in the contract approval process. Such appeals could only be heard by the Seabeds Disputes Chamber (Article 187, paragraph d), which would be dominated by the developing countries. Even if the Chamber ruled an entity unfairly treated, its decision could only be implemented by a three-quarters vote of the Council (Article 162, paragraph 2.v.; Article 11, paragraph 7.c.). The contract approval process is not subject to commercial arbitration.

Production Limitations

The treaty establishes a limitation on seabed mineral production during an interim period, running for the first twenty years of commercial production, until the end of the Review Conference, or until international commodity arrangements affecting these minerals enter into force for the Authority (Article 151, paragraph 2.a.). The production limitation or ceiling is calculated using a complex formula based on the growth in world nickel consumption. Article 151 outlines the steps in determining allowable annual seabed production:

--The basic production limitation formula is the sum of (1) the tonnage growth of nickel consumption in the five years prior to the first commercial production from the seabed and (2) 60 percent of the tonnage growth in nickel consumption from the first year of commercial production to the year for which the allocation is being made. The production limitation is recalculated during each year of the interim period, based on the most recent data. Since the application for a production limitation may be submitted up to, but not more than, five years prior to the beginning of a company's commercial production, the production limitation must be calculated from estimates about future nickel consumption rates. These estimates are made by use of a trend line, which projects future tonnage consumption on the basis of the most recent fifteen years of past consumption data (Article 151, paragraphs 2.b.i., 2.b.ii., and 2.b.iii.).

--The basic production limitation is modified by provision for a "floor," which was developed to allow at least a minimum level of seabed production even if nickel consumption has been stagnant. If the compound growth of nickel consumption on the trend line was less than 3 percent annually, a new trend-line would be calculated as if there had been 3 percent compound annual growth; this trend line would pass through the original trend line value of nickel consumption for the first year of the fifteen-year database. The basic production limitation formula would then be applied to the new trend line in order to calculate the allotted annual seabed tonnage (Article 151, paragraph 2.b.iv.).

--The application of the "floor" would be subject to the restriction that nickel production from the seabeds may not exceed the total growth of nickel consumption at any time during the interim period. The total growth of consumption is calculated from the original trend line used in the first step of the calculation (Article 151, paragraph 2.b.iv.).

Estimates of the seabed tonnage that would be allotted annually are difficult to make because they require assumptions about short-term growth (which would be used for the fifteen-year database), about long-term average growth rates, and about the year of first commercial production from the seabeds. Under these scenarios, the production limitation would allow for four or five full-scale mining operations in the first year of commercial production. By the end of the interim period, the formula would allow between twelve mine sites (under a

2.0 percent growth rate) and twenty-five mine sites (under a 4.5 percent growth rate). The most likely case (3.5 percent growth) would allow approximately sixteen sites to be in operation at the end of the interim period. The treaty also expressly sets aside 38,000 tons of annual production for use by the Enterprise (Article 151, paragraph 2.c.).

The production limitation distorts the flow of capital into oceans investment and could significantly hinder the development of deep seabed minerals:

--The production limitation formula restricts the number of entrants into seabed mining. Since the Enterprise is guaranteed production for one mine site, only three to four sites will be available for full-scale commercial production in the first year and at most fifteen during the entire interim period. Five mining consortia from Western industrialized countries have already seriously engaged in prospecting and technology development and will probably require at least two mine sites apiece during the interim period. The Enterprise, the existing consortia, and Eastern European nations could already account for most of the available seabed mining production, so potential new investors are likely to shy away from seabed mining. If the production limitation in practice excludes miners that would otherwise engage in seabed mining, the United States could face underinvestment, supply shortages, and higher prices in the constituent metals, especially if land-based operators do not expand capacity sufficiently.

--Ironically, the production limitation could also distort investment patterns if the seabed miners decide to invest in seabed mining before such investment is economical. Companies would do this in order to avoid being frozen out of seabed mining altogether. Over-investment would lead to misallocation of capital and possibly severe fluctuations in the supplies and prices of constituent metals.

--The production limitation is the source of much of the Authority's discretion over access, as the Council is empowered to choose among competing applicants for a production allocation by a three-quarters majority (see section on production authorization). The United States and like-minded states cannot muster enough votes on the Council to guarantee production authorizations, and the developing country majority of the Council would look favorably on Enterprise and developing country applications; therefore, the Council may grant production to the least-qualified or least-efficient applicant. If a bona fide miner's commencement of commercial production is thus significantly delayed, he could face financial loss and perhaps bankruptcy. In this scenario, seabed miners would be tempted to apply for contracts under developing country sponsorship, to establish joint ventures with the Enterprise, or to locate processing facilities in developing countries, all of which would result in a corresponding reduction in U.S. access.

--The production limitation creates a number of practical problems of implementation and management. Since a contractor is allocated a slice of the growth segment well before he commences commercial production based on long-term trends, the production limitation cannot respond to short-range fluctuations in demand and is dependent on the accuracy, often absent, of contractors, forecasts of when and how much each project will produce. Projections made five years before production begins could lead to distortions in supply and prices if they seriously underestimate actual consumption. Finally, the production limitation allows no margin of error for the failures likely to occur in the early years of seabed mining. Because the allocation would not be available to other miners until such a failure is disclosed and there is a long leadtime for entering into full-scale commercial production, the actual production from the seabeds is likely to be less than the production allocated.

--The production limitation is based on nickel consumption, and has no relation to the demand for other nodule metals such as manganese, cobalt, and copper. Seabed mining could not respond to a surge in demand for any one of these constituent metals, if increased production would exceed the production limitation.

Production Authorization

An approved plan of work does not guarantee that an operator will be allowed to mine. A miner must also receive a production authorization from the Authority before he may commence commercial production. The treaty outlines the following procedures for granting production authorizations:

(1) The Legal and Technical Commission calculates the production ceiling available annually in accordance with the formula in the treaty text (Article 165, paragraph 2.n., Article 151).

(2) Each operator with an approved plan of work must apply for a production authorization not more than five years before he plans to

commence commercial production. In his application, the operator shall specify the annual quantity of nickel he plans to recover (Article 151, paragraph 2).

(3) The Authority, through the Legal and Technical Commission, shall issue a production authorization for the level of production applied for unless the sum of that level and the level already authorized exceeds the nickel production ceiling during any year of planned production (Annex III, Article 7, paragraph 1).

(4) An operator with a production authorization may in any year produce less than or up to 8 percent more than the level specified in his production authorization, provided that the overall amount of production shall not exceed that specified in the authorization. If the operator further expands production, he must first negotiate with the Authority a supplementary production authorization. The Authority may not authorize annual production in excess of 46,500 tons of nickel (Article 151, paragraph 2.e.).

(5) If an operator's planned production exceeds the production ceiling, he will not receive a production authorization (Article 151, paragraph 2). Applicants who are not selected in any period shall have a "priority" in subsequent periods until they receive an authorization (Annex III, Article 7, paragraph 4).

(6) The convention empowers the Council, by a three-quarters majority, to make a selection from competing applicants for a production allocation (Article 152, paragraph 2.p.). The treaty instructs the Authority to make the selection "on the basis of objective and nondiscriminatory standards set forth in the rules and regulations" (Annex III, Article 7, paragraph 2). In making the selection, the Authority shall "give priority" to operators that (a) give better assurance of performance (taking into account the financial and technical qualifications of the proposed operator and performance, if any, under previously approved plans of work); (b) provide earlier prospective financial benefits to the Authority (taking into account when production is scheduled to begin); and (c) have already invested most resources and effort in prospecting or exploration (Annex III, Article 7, paragraph 3). The text also grants a priority to the Enterprise or developing countries operating on the "reserved" side of the parallel system, when fewer sites are being exploited on the reserved side (Annex III, Article 7, paragraph 6). Finally, when considering priorities for production authorization, the Authority must take into account the need "to enhance the

opportunities of all states parties" to mine the seabeds (Annex III, Article 7, paragraph 5). This could be used by the Authority as a discretionary antimonopoly provision to deny a U.S. miner a production authorization.

If the production ceiling is reached or exceeded, the selection process can be used to delay or stop contractors sponsored by the United States from initiating commercial production:

--The Council has almost total discretion in making the selection since every conceivable type of operator has a "priority" of one kind or another. The text makes no attempt to rank priorities, so all applicants for production authorizations are theoretically equal.

--The U.S. and like-minded States cannot ensure that their applicants would receive production authorizations, because they would have to muster a three-quarters majority on the Council.

--The Council, because of its composition, would tend to favor production authorizations requested by the Enterprise or developing countries and, because the standards are so vague, could justify selecting less qualified applicants. In order to block such a selection, the United States would have to forge a coalition between all Western industrialized countries and the former-Soviet bloc or some developing countries.

--An operator could be delayed indefinitely from mining the seabeds. When production becomes available, there could be a competing applicant with an equal "priority" that would receive the production authorization. Delay could result in bankruptcy, especially for corporations sponsored by industrialized states that need to generate a return on their capital investments.

Commodity Arrangements

The terms and conditions set by commodity arrangements could also distort investment and markets. The text requires that "all interested parties including both producers and consumers participate" in such arrangements (Article 151, paragraph 1) before the Authority can participate, so the United States could challenge any Authority effort to join an arrangement that the United States did join.

Institutionally, however, it could be difficult precluding Authority participation in these arrangements as the United States and other major seabed mining states could not block the three-quarters majority on the

Council, the vote that enables the Authority to make arrangements with other international organizations (Article 162, paragraph 2.; Article 161, paragraph 7.c.). The United States could not be certain whether the Seabeds Disputes Chamber would uphold a U.S. challenge to such action.

Compensation Schemes

The text requires that the Authority establish a scheme to compensate land-based producers for losses in exports and export earnings, to the extent that such injury is caused by competition from the seabeds (Article 151, paragraph 4). The Economic Planning Commission draws up the compensation scheme (Article 164, paragraph 2(d)). The Council, by a three-quarters majority, recommends the scheme to the Assembly, which can adopt the scheme by a two-thirds majority. It would be virtually impossible to measure the direct effects of seabed mining on export earnings. Since the text establishes no time limitations, conditions, or criteria on the compensation program, compensation could result in subsidization of land-based producers.

Security of Tenure

A precondition for an investor to risk venture capital in seabed mining is security of tenure over a specific area of the seabeds. Exclusive rights to mine that area are required because intensive mapping and prospecting are required, and mining and processing technology tend to be site-specific. In addition, investors must be able to assess the financial prospects of the venture over the planned life of the project. A seabed miner is unlikely to be able to attract risk capital, unless he can demonstrate that he can service the debt over the entire commercial life of the debt.

Rights Under an Approved Plan of Work

All entities with approved plans of work receive only one important right--security of tenure against other parties in the treaty. The approved plan of work confers on the operator exclusive rights for the exploration and exploitation of the specified categories of resources in the Area covered by the plan of work in accordance with the rules and regulations of the Authority (Article 153, paragraph 6; Annex III, Article 3, paragraph 4). The actual duration of the plan of work is not specified in the treaty but will be addressed in the rules and regulations and should be related to the economic life of the mining project, taking into consideration such factors as the depletion of the ore, the useful life of the mining equipment and processing facilities, and commercial viability (Annex III, Article 17, paragraph 2.b.).

The text also provides that the total duration of a plan of work should be short enough to give the Authority an opportunity at the time of extension or renewal to amend the terms and conditions of the plan of work in accordance with rules and regulations that it can issue subsequent to entering into the plan of work (Annex III, Article 17, 2.a.iii). This provision ensures that the seabed miner will know the rules of the game at the time his plan of work is approved; new rules and regulations can be applied only on renewal of the plan of work. This provision strengthens the operator's security of tenure, but its value to the investor would be lost if the Authority established short durations for plans of work.

The text does not provide an absolute right of secure tenure over a mine site:

(a) A contractor's rights under a contract may be suspended or terminated "if, in spite of warnings by the Authority, the contractor has conducted his activities in such a way as to result in serious, persistent and willful violations of the fundamental terms of the contract, Part XI and the rules and regulations of the Authority" (Annex III, Article 18, paragraph 1.a.). No particular organ of the Authority has been empowered to determine whether there have been "serious, persistent, and willful violations." The text does not even specify that the question of suspension be addressed in the rules and regulations. Therefore, the power to suspend contractors devolves on the Assembly through its power to determine which organ of the Authority "shall deal with any question or matter not specifically entrusted to a particular organ, consistent with the distribution of powers among the organs of the Authority" (Article 160, paragraph 2.n.). At worst, the Assembly could decide itself whether to suspend contracts, which it could do by a two-thirds majority (Article 160, paragraph 6). At best, the Assembly could assign the issue to the Council, which is empowered to control mining activities by a three-quarters majority (Article 162, paragraph 2.k.; Article 161, paragraph 7.c.). In either case, a miner's "exclusive rights" could be suspended over the objections of industrialized states, thus jeopardizing security of tenure for corporations sponsored by industrialized states. Developing country operators would feel more secure given the composition of the Authority's organs. The Enterprise would not be subject to such threats on its security of tenure because only contractors are subject to monetary penalties, suspension, or termination of a plan of work.

The text contains one protection. The Authority may not execute the suspension until the contractor has been accorded a reasonable opportunity to exhaust the judicial remedies available to him, including commercial arbitration and the Seabeds Disputes Chamber. Since commercial arbitration concerns only disputes on the interpretation or application of a contract (Article 188, paragraph 2.a.), however, commercial arbitration is unlikely to cover the suspension question. The Seabeds Disputes Chamber would have jurisdiction over suspension questions through its power to resolve questions of interpretation of the treaty and to interpret plans of work (Article 187). The composition of the Chamber, however, undermines its "objectivity" as an appeals court for miners sponsored by industrialized states. The Chamber's composition would tend to favor developing countries and the Enterprise. Finally, the Chamber is prohibited from overturning the Authority's exercise of its discretionary powers (Article 190).

(b) A contractor's rights may also be suspended or terminated if he has failed to comply with "a final binding decision of the dispute settlement body applicable to him" (Annex III, Article 18, paragraph 2.b.). This could also represent a considerable threat to the operator. As pointed out above, the Authority is given considerable discretion in determining compliance, the Assembly is empowered to determine which organ handles the suspension question, and the composition of the Seabeds Disputes Chamber raises doubts as to the fairness of the appeals mechanisms. The Enterprise is *not* subject to monetary penalties, suspension, or termination, if it fails to comply with a "final binding decision of a dispute settlement body," since it does not have a contract.

(c) Twenty years after the commencement of seabed mining, a Review Conference is empowered to adopt amendments to the treaty by a two-thirds majority of states parties (Article 155, paragraph 4). Such amendments enter into force when ratified by two-thirds of the states parties. Since the Review Conference is empowered to adopt amendments to any provision in the treaty, including the right of security of tenure, the operators face considerable risk of losing mining rights to specific areas of the seabed. This risk is borne by any pioneer operator with a plan of work extending more than twenty years and by all late entrants; no operator can count on security of tenure beyond the Review Conference. The validity of the contract is also called into question, if the United States is forced to withdraw from the treaty.

Thus, although the treaty theoretically grants exclusive rights to contractors to mine a particular area of the seabed, such rights are vulnerable to suspension, because of the composition and powers of Authority institutions, or to elimination because of amendments by the Review Conference. Because only contractors are subject to monetary penalties, or termination of contracts, the Enterprise has a considerably more secure tenure over its sites. Security of tenure is the *only* right granted to contractors sponsored by industrialized states under a plan of work. Other entities receive additional rights; for instance, the Enterprise, developing states, and entities sponsored by developing states are granted access to prospected mine sites and seabed mining technology under the treaty. These rights will be discussed in detail in the next section.

Obligations and Limitations Under a Plan of Work

The treaty places a number of obligations and limitations on all seabed miners under an approved plan of work. These obligations and limitations fall into the following general categories: (1) reservation of mine sites; (2) technology transfer; (3) financial terms of contracts; and (4) operational requirements. Each category of obligations affects each type of entity mining the seabeds in fundamentally different ways. One half of the mine sites are reserved for the Enterprise or developing countries. Each operator applying for a contract is required to prospect two mine sites and, on approval of a contract, is required to turn over the prospecting data for one site to the Authority. The financial outlay required to prospect the extra mine site represents a significant front-end financial load ($16 to $20 million) for the contractor and a significant advantage for the Enterprise.

The treaty requires the sale of technology from seabed miners operating on nonreserved sites to the Enterprise and developing countries operating on reserved sites. The transfer of technology would not take place as a normal commercial transaction. These obligations significantly increase the risks and costs of seabed mining and jeopardize the exclusivity of the technology. As a result, these provisions could inhibit investment, stifle technological innovation, and discourage the development of new and more efficient techniques of seabed mining.

The treaty sets revenue-sharing obligations for seabed miners in considerable detail. The revenue-sharing arrangements are relatively flexible, resulting in a lower proportional share in revenues for the Authority in lean years. It is impossible to know at this time whether the payments to the Authority represent a fair economic rent for the exclusive rights to exploit a particular area of the seabed. If the required financial payments are higher than the value of the exclusive rights, then the financial terms of contracts could significantly discourage investment. The treaty theoretically allows for the revenue-sharing rates to be adjusted downward (Annex III, Article 13, paragraph 14). Unfortunately, the mechanism for the adjustment would be through adopting new rules and regulations, which could be blocked by a single member of the Council. In effect, the financial terms of contracts are rigid and cannot be lowered to reflect the real economic rent of an exclusive right.

Contracts must also include a number of operational requirements: (1) transfer of data; (2) training programs; (3) performance requirements; (4) mining standards and practices; and (5) transfer of rights and obligations. Since most of the operational requirements have been left to be fleshed out in the rules and regulations of the Authority, it is difficult to gauge the effect of these operational requirements on access. If the negotiation of rules and regulations reflects the treaty negotiations, the industrialized countries will insist on objectivity, whereas the developing countries will insist on substantial discretion for the Authority. Since the final result will probably fall somewhere in between, these operational requirements are likely to present some costs and risks for operators.

Reservation of Mine Sites

The treaty stipulates that any industrialized state or any entity sponsored by an industrialized state applying for a contract must have prospected two mine sites of equal value and submitted the data on both sites to the Authority (Annex III). On approval of a plan of work, the Authority grants the applicant an exclusive right to mine one of the prospected sites and reserves the other for the Enterprise, developing countries, entities sponsored by developing nations, or joint ventures (Annex III). This "banking" system doubles the prospecting costs for industrialized states and entities sponsored by industrialized states. The costs of prospecting one mine site have been estimated at $16.0 to $20.0 million.

The reserved, prospected mine sites and attendant data are turned over to the Enterprise, developing countries, entities sponsored by developing countries, or joint ventures operating on the reserved side at no charge. The Enterprise has the first opportunity to explore and exploit the reserved mine site, either itself or through a joint venture (Annex III, Article 9). If the Enterprise enters into a joint venture, it must offer developing states the opportunity to participate in such joint ventures (Annex III, Article 9, paragraph 2). Developing countries and entities sponsored by developing countries may explore and exploit a reserved site if the Enterprise decides it will not mine the site (Annex III).

Any corporations sponsored by the United States is thus placed at a significant disadvantage:

--The additional financial outlay required to prospect an extra mine site represents a significant front-end financial load and, because the cost is incurred well before a mine site generates income, could have significant impact on the firm's internal rate of return.

-- Entities that operate on the reserved side of the parallel system, particularly the Enterprise, are not required to make such financial outlays, but instead are the beneficiaries of a valuable prospected site.

--The chance of site overlaps between particular miners is increased due to the requirement to submit two prospected sites with each application.

The treaty requires all contracts to contain a series of undertakings that obligate contractors to sell the technology they use to mine the seabeds to other operators. These undertakings must be included in each contract until 10 years after the Enterprise commences commercial production "and may be invoked during that period" (Annex II, Article 5, paragraph 7). The technology involved is broadly defined as "the specialized equipment and technical know-how, including manuals, designs, operating instructions, training, and technical advice and assistance necessary to assemble, maintain, and operate a viable system and the legal right to use these items for that purpose on a non-exclusive basis" (Annex III, Article 5). The application of these provisions varies substantially among the types of entities allowed to mine the seabeds.

When submitting a proposed plan of work, all applicants are required to make available to the Authority a general description of the equipment and methods to be used in mining the seabeds, as well as other non-proprietary information about the characteristics of such technology and information as to where such technology is available (Annex III, Article 5, paragraph 1). After the plan of work is approved, all operators are required to inform the Authority of revisions in this description and information whenever a substantial change or innovation is introduced (Annex III, Article 5, paragraph 2).

The convention requires industrialized states, entities sponsored by industrialized states, developing states interested in mining nonreserved mine sites, and entities sponsored by developing states to provide the following undertakings in their plans of work (Annex III, Article 5, paragraph 5):

--to make available to the Enterprise, if and when the Authority shall so request and on fair and reasonable commercial terms and conditions, the technology used in carrying out activities in the Area under a contract and which the mining entity is legally entitled to transfer. "This commitment may be invoked only if the Enterprise finds that it is unable to obtain the same or equally efficient and useful technology on the open market and on fair and reasonable commercial terms and conditions."

--to obtain a written assurance from third-party owners of any technology not covered above that the contractor uses in carrying out activities in the Area, which is not generally available on the open market, that the owner will, on a request from the Authority, make such technology available to the Enterprise to the same extent as made available to the contractor on fair and reasonable terms and conditions. If such assurance is not obtained, the technology in question shall not be used by the miner.

--to obtain, if and when requested to do so by the Enterprise and whenever it is possible to do so without substantial cost to the contractor, the right to transfer to the Enterprise any technology the contractor uses in carrying out activities in the Area under a contract that is not legally entitled to transfer and that which is not generally available on the open market. The corporate relationship between the owner and the contractor shall be relevant to the determination whether all feasible measures have been taken and to the applicant's qualifications for any subsequent proposed plan of work.

--to facilitate the acquisition by the Enterprise of the technology owned by third parties.

--to take the measures prescribed above for the benefit of a developing state or group of developing states that has applied for a plan of work for the reserved site "banked" by the contractor, provided that activities under the contract sought by the developing state or group of developing states would not involve transfer of technology to a third state or the nationals of a third state (the Brazil Clause). The contractor is freed from this provision when technology has already been requested or transferred by him to the Enterprise.

The treaty also establishes mechanisms to settle disputes and handle appeals on the technology transfer questions.

Disputes concerning any of these undertakings shall be subject to compulsory dispute settlement in accordance with the treaty (Annex III, Article 5, paragraph 4), which provides for binding commercial arbitration for disputes concerning interpretation or application of a contract and submission (by the commercial arbitral tribunal) to the Seabeds Disputes Chamber of any questions relating to interpretation of the treaty (Article 188, paragraph 2). The Authority may impose monetary penalties, suspend, or terminate any contractor found to have (a) conducted his activities in such a way as to result in "serious, persistent, and willful violations" of the fundamental terms of the contract, treaty, or the Authority's rules and regulations or (b) failed to comply with the final binding decision of a dispute settlement body (Annex III).

The narrower question of whether offers made by the contractor are within the range of "fair and reasonable commercial terms and conditions" may be submitted by "either party" to binding commercial arbitration in accordance with the UNCITRAL Arbitration Rules. In any case in which the finding is negative, the contractor shall be given forty-five days to revise his offer to bring it within that range before the Authority makes any determinations with respect to violation of the contract and the imposition of penalties (Annex III, Article 5, paragraph 4). These technology transfer obligations significantly increase the risks and costs of seabed mining and thus impair access for industrialized countries or entities sponsored by industrialized countries:

--The method for triggering the technology transfer obligation offers little protection for the contractors. In the case of transfers to the Enterprise, the Enterprise makes the determination that the same or equally efficient technology is not available on the market at fair and reasonable commercial terms and conditions. In the case of transfer to a developing country or countries applying for reserved sites, the developing country itself is empowered to make the same determination.

--The terms and conditions (especially the prices) for the transfers of technology to the Enterprise and developing countries are likely to be considerably less advantageous to the contractors and third party suppliers of technology than normal commercial transfers. First, the contractor holds a disadvantageous negotiating position since the text compels him to sell his technology. He does not have the option to refuse sale of his technology or to walk away from the negotiations, since his contract could then be suspended or he could be refused subsequent contracts. Therefore, he is likely to obtain less favorable terms and conditions than on the open market. Second, the developers of sophisticated and unique technology should be able to ask a monopoly price for such technology; otherwise, the incentive for developing the technology would be eroded. It is uncertain, however, whether a commercial arbitral tribunal would interpret "fair and reasonable commercial terms and conditions" as allowing for a monopoly price or whether the tribunal would rely on a cost-plus formula to make the determination. Finally, the phrase "fair and reasonable commercial terms and conditions" could be open to a wide range of interpretations because there are no standardized criteria. The phrase has no common meaning in international commercial practice, nor does it have meaning in most municipal legal systems. How it would be construed in commercial arbitration is quite uncertain. For example, what constitutes a reasonable profit on the sale? This would probably be viewed very differently by an arbitrator from a centrally planned country or developing country than it would be by an arbitrator from a Western industrialized country.

--The contractor and third-party suppliers face considerable risk that the competitive advantage of their proprietary technology for seabed mining would be eroded because such technology could be widely disseminated either through the Enterprise or through developing country purchasers.

If the Enterprise transfers technology to another party without the consent of the owner of the technology, the owner is unlikely to receive sufficient damages under the current text. Although the text prohibits the Enterprise from disclosing any industrial secret, any proprietary data, or any other confidential information of commercial value (Annex II, Article 14, paragraph 3), the treaty fails to establish a mechanism that effectively punishes the Enterprise or its staff for such actions. First, the Enterprise is not liable for any damages arising out of its operations, since the liability provisions apply only to contractors and the Authority (Annex III, Article 22). Secondly, in the case of an unwarranted transfer of proprietary technology committed by the Enterprise, the liability lies with the Authority, not the Enterprise (Annex III, Article 22). Third, the Authority is not empowered to suspend or terminate the Enterprise from work or impose monetary penalties, since such powers can be used only against contractors

(Annex III). Finally, although the owner of technology may seek redress through commercial arbitration or the Seabeds Disputes Chamber, the findings of these dispute settlement bodies would have to be upheld by the Authority. The Authority could only enforce such a finding through the Council's power to issue directives to the Enterprise. Industrialized countries and entities sponsored by industrialized countries could not be certain of a fair outcome, given the composition of the Seabeds Disputes Chamber and the Authority.

If the Brazil Clause is triggered, the owners of technology are also unlikely to be able to protect the proprietary nature and commercial value of their technology. Groups of developing countries are permitted to form joint ventures on reserve sites (Annex III, Article 5, paragraph 3.e). The entire group would then have access to a contractor's technology. In addition, even though the Brazil Clause expressly forbids developing countries from further transferring technology to third states or nationals of third states, the owner of technology would nonetheless have to depend on the organs of the Authority (which are dominated by the developing countries) to implement monetary penalties and/or suspensions in order to make the prohibition enforceable.

--The technology transfer provisions are likely to result in considerably higher costs for the seabed miner. First, all contractors will have to obtain written assurances from third-party suppliers of the technology, whether or not their technology is chosen by the Enterprise or developing countries. The written assurances from third-party suppliers will be costly, especially since most consortia have 100 to 200 suppliers. The contractor, in order to ensure full use of his required technology throughout the contract and subsequent contracts, will be advised to obtain a license or other arrangement from the third-party supplier that allows subsequent transfers to the Enterprise or developing countries. Given the lack of protection for proprietary technology transferred under the treaty and the uncertainty as to timing of performance, these licenses will cost the contractor dearly. The supplier of a key component of the mining system may refuse to provide the written assurance, thus forcing the contractor to use second-best or higher-cost technology. Finally, the definition of technology can be read to contain an implied warranty that the system transferred must work. In any case, the contractor will spend a great deal of time, effort, and money in technical assistance and training to help the Enterprise operate the system in order to protect his position for subsequent contracts.

--The technology transfer obligations could be invoked over a considerable period of time, particularly if the Enterprise does not commence commercial production in the early years. The Enterprise and developing countries would also have access to any technological innovations during that period. If the Enterprise delays commercial production five years after other entities initiate commercial production, the technology transfer obligation would continue at least until the Review Conference is convened, running the risk that the obligations may be extended. In addition, the text is ambiguous as to whether the time limit can be triggered by commercial production by joint ventures, or only commercial production by the Enterprise itself.

The technology transfer provisions discriminate significantly against the industrialized countries and entities sponsored by industrialized countries. The Enterprise and developing countries that apply for reserved sites are not only exempt from the obligations but are the beneficiaries of having direct access to the best mining technology at an advantageous price. Joint ventures with the Enterprise are exempted from the technology transfer obligations (Annex III, Article 5, paragraph 6).

Financial Terms of Contracts

The International Seabed Authority would be the first international organization to collect revenues directly from private and state companies, states, and other entities. The current text establishes a multitude of financial terms of contracts. The contractor may choose to pay either a production charge (which is based on the value of processed metals) or a combination of a lower production charge (based on the value of processed metals) and a share of net proceeds from sale of the metals (Annex III, Article 13, paragraph 4). In addition, the financial terms of contracts are potentially more stringent for industrialized states and entities sponsored by industrialized states than for the Enterprise and joint ventures.

The production charge system contains the following elements:

--The operator is required to pay a fee of $500,000 to finance the processing of his application (Annex III, Article 13, paragraph 2).

--The operator shall pay a fixed annual fee of $1 million from the date of entry into force of his contract. From the commencement of commercial production, the operator shall pay either the production charge or the annual fixed fee, whichever is greater (Annex III, Article 13, paragraph 3).

--Production charges amounting to 5 percent in the first ten years of commercial production and 12 percent thereafter are applied to the gross value of the metals produced from the seabed nodules (Annex III, Article 13, paragraph 5).

The combined system of payments is designed to deal with two basic issues--the valuation of the ore and the sharing of risks and profits from resource development. The text adopts the proportional costs formula to determine the value of the seabed ore and thus the revenue-sharing base of the Authority. This formula allocates profits among the different stages of an integrated operation (mining, transportation, processing) in accordance with the development costs of each stage. Thus, the profits attributed to the ore for each project (whether fully integrated or partially integrated) would be the product of the total net proceeds of the operation and the ratio of the development costs of the mining stage to the total development costs of the operation (Annex III, Article 13, paragraph 6.e.). In order to assure the Authority of a minimum revenue-sharing base, the text puts a floor of 25 percent under this ratio, which is roughly consistent with estimates that mining development costs are between 23 percent and 27 percent of the total development costs of a fully integrated project.

The combined system created in the treaty has the following elements:

--An applicant is required to pay a fee of $500,000 to finance the processing of his application (Annex III, Article 13, paragraph 2).

--The operator shall pay a fixed annual fee of $1 million from the date of entry into force of his contract. From the commencement of commercial production, the operator shall pay either the production charge or the annual fixed fee, whichever is greater (Annex III, Article 13, paragraph 3).

--Production charges (royalties) amounting to 2 percent in the first period of production and 4 percent in the later period are applied to the gross value of the metals produced from the seabeds. If the annual return on investment (the ratio of profits from mining to development costs of mining) in the later period falls below 15 percent, the production charge drops back to 2 percent (Annex III, Article 13, paragraph 6.a.).

-- The Authority's share of the mining profit is based on a progressive schedule tied to the annual return of investment, rather than a flat rate on profits (Annex III, Article 13, paragraphs 6.c. and 6.n.).

-- A higher schedule of rates (both profit-sharing from mining and production charges) goes into effect in the second period of production (Annex III, Article 13, paragraph 6.c.). The higher rates are triggered only when the miner has recovered all his initial investment expenditures plus a 10 percent real profit on that investment (Annex III, Article 13, paragraph 6.d.). The financial terms of contracts are all computed in real terms in order to protect the real value of the miner's profits (Annex III, Article 13, paragraph 13).

The financial terms of contracts contain a number of elements that would deter industrialized countries and entities sponsored by industrialized countries from investing in seabed mining:

--The application fees and fixed annual fees represent a heavy front-end financial obligation that can significantly distort the internal rate of return on capital.

--The production charge in the early period of commercial production is leveled against the gross value of the metals, rather than the ore. This represents an 8 to 10 percent royalty on the gross value of the ore.

--Since the production charges are leveled regardless of the profitability of a mining operation, they significantly undermine the flexibility of the financial terms of contracts, thus threatening the financial viability of the mining project.

The financial terms of contracts discriminate against industrialized nations and entities sponsored by industrialized nations by offering substantial advantages to other entities mining the seabeds. The Enterprise does not pay financial terms of contracts until 10 years after it commences commercial production (Annex IV, Article 10, paragraph 3). The Enterprise is thus exempt from the heavy front-end obligations created by the application and annual fixed fees and from much of the pernicious effect of the production charge. The treaty also instructs the Authority to provide financial incentives for contractors to undertake joint arrangements with the Enterprise and developing countries (Annex III, Article 13, paragraph 1.d.; Annex III, Article II, paragraph 2).

Operational Requirements

Plans of work also include a number of operational requirements: (1) transfer of data; (2) training programs; (3) performance requirements; (4) mining standards and practices including those related to operational safety, conservation of resources, and the protection of the marine environment; and (5) transfer of rights and obligations. Since most of the operational requirements have been left to be established in the rules and regulations of the Authority, it is difficult to gauge the effect of these operational requirements on access. Under the text, these rules and regulations would be negotiated in the Preparatory Commission prior to ratification, would provisionally enter into force, and could only be amended by a consensus decision of the Council (Article 162, paragraph 2.n.; Article 161, paragraph 7.d.) and a two-thirds vote of the Assembly (Article 160, Article 159, paragraph 6). This procedure, although it allows the United States to block adverse amendments to the rules and regulations, creates a rigid regulatory structure that would not respond to changing circumstances.

(1) The treaty requires operators to transfer to the Authority all data necessary and relevant to the effective implementation of the powers and functions of the principal organs of the Authority in respect to the area covered by a plan of work (Annex III, Article 14, paragraph 1). Such information, which may include proprietary data, is transferred in accordance with the rules and regulations and conditions of the plan of work (Annex III, Article 14, paragraphs 1-2). All data, except equipment design, required for the promulgation of environmental rules and regulations, shall not be deemed proprietary (Annex III, Article 14, paragraph 2.)

These provisions create additional risks for the operator. The Authority is granted broad discretion in the collection of data, particularly data necessary for environmental regulations. The text does not specify which organ of the Authority will request and evaluate the data, placing the issue in the hands of the Assembly. The positive feature of allowing the operator to determine which data is proprietary is partially offset by the blanket statement that data necessary for environmental and safety regulations are, by definition, nonproprietary.

(2) The treaty requires all contractors to draw up practical programs for training personnel of the Authority and developing states, including the participation of such personnel in all activities covered by a contract (Annex III, Article 15). The central objective of this provision is to

promote the transfer of relevant technology and scientific knowledge to the Enterprise and developing countries (Article 144, paragraph 2). The provision discriminates against industrialized states and entities sponsored by industrialized states:

--The costs of the training program will be borne by the contractor, thus increasing his operating costs. These costs could be significant, since space onboard ship would be at a premium.

--Industrialized states and entities sponsored by industrialized states will in effect be training their competition, the Enterprise and developing countries.

--Since the training program must plan for participation in *all* seabed activities, the contractors' proprietary data and technology may be subject to disclosure.

--The Enterprise and developing countries are not subject to the provision.

(3) The performance requirements, in particular assurances that the contract will be carried out in good faith, will be developed in the rules and regulations (Annex III, Article 17, paragraph 1.b. iii). Nonetheless, these rules and regulations must fully reflect certain objective criteria (Annex III, Article 17, paragraph 2.c.):

--The Authority shall require, during the exploration stage, that the operator make periodic expenditures that would be expected of a bona fide operator who intended to bring the area into commercial production within time limits established by the Authority.

--The Authority shall establish a maximum time interval after the exploration stage is completed and the exploitation stage begins to achieve commercial production. The interval to bring an area into commercial production should take into account the time necessary to construct large-scale mining and processing systems after the exploration stage.

--Once commercial production is achieved in the exploitation stage, the Authority shall within reasonable time limits and taking into account all relevant factors require the operator to maintain commercial production throughout the period of the plan of work.

The major purpose of these criteria is to ensure that operators granted a plan of work diligently develop seabed minerals rather than tie up commercially exploitable areas of the seabed for speculative or political purposes. Such diligence requirements, as long as they do not result in arbitrary discretion for the Authority, are an important element for efficient development of seabed minerals. The text, however, does not provide a mechanism for enforcing diligence requirements to adequately protect bona fide miners:

--No particular organ of the Authority has responsibility for enforcing diligence requirements, therefore, the Assembly is empowered to assign this function by a two-thirds majority.

--Since the composition and voting rules of the various organs of the Authority are prejudiced against industrialized nations and in favor of the Enterprise and the developing world, the application of the diligence standards is not likely to be consistent and objective.

--The text does not specify which types of sanctions can be brought against an operator who does not comply with the diligence requirements. At best, noncompliance would trigger the dispute settlement process in which implementation would ultimately be made and penalties imposed by the Assembly (by a two-thirds vote) or by the Council (by a three-quarters vote), both of which are dominated by developing countries. Under the current text, the Enterprise would not be subject to such penalties.

(4) Operators must also conform to mining standards and practices, including those related to operational safety, conservation of resources, and the protection of the marine environment (Annex III, Article 17, paragraph, 1.b.xii). The context and enforcement of these standards and practices, however, are left to rules and regulations.

(5) The rights and obligations arising out of a contract can only be transferred with the consent of the Authority (Annex III, Article 20). The Authority can not withhold consent to the transfer except if the transferee is unqualified or if the transfer would violate the antidensity and antimonopoly provisions (Annex III, Article 6, paragraph 3.d.). Since the transferee would have to overcome all the hurdles in the contract approval process described earlier, the contractor is thus not totally free to transfer his rights. Since the Enterprise is not covered by this provision, it may be able to transfer its mining rights without interference.

Institutional Decisions

The Assembly and the Council share a number of institutional powers and functions of the Authority. A number of other institutional decisions are divided between the Assembly and the Council. The United States has little or no control over the institutional decisions made by the Authority. Although some of these decisions are not particularly important, other institutional decisions could be of critical importance to the United States. Potentially critical institutional decisions include (1) the Assembly's power to determine which organ should handle a question not specifically assigned to an organ; (2) the interrelation between the "general policies" of the Assembly and the "specific policies" of the Council; (3) the Council rules of procedure; (4) the initiation of proceedings in the Seabeds Disputes chamber; (e) suspension of members; (6) election of the Governing Board and Director-General of the Enterprise; and (7) entering into agreements with other international institutions.

Decisions of the Assembly

The Assembly has sole responsibility for institutional decisions such as (1) establishing the general policies of the Authority; (2) electing the members of the Council; (3) establishing, as appropriate, subsidiary organs necessary for the performance of its functions in accordance with the treaty; and (4) deciding which organ shall deal with any question or matter not specifically entrusted to a particular organ of the Authority, consistent with distribution of powers and functions among the organs of the Authority. These questions would be decided by a two-thirds majority. Each of these powers and functions can be performed over the objections of the United States and other major industrialized countries.

The Assembly's control over the election of members of the Council has been diluted considerably by the chamber criteria and by the requirement that those states eligible for a particular chamber should nominate their representatives (Article 161, paragraph 2.c.). The United States could be excluded from the Council because it would be unable to control its own caucuses, not because of the electing powers of the Assembly. Similarly, the power to establish subsidiary organs poses little threat to the United States.

The Assembly's power to establish the general policy of the Authority could threaten U.S. interests since contractors must operate in accordance with the general policies of the Authority (Annex III, Article 4, paragraph 6.a.), and the specific policies of the Council must be in conformity with the general policies of the Assembly (Article 162). The extent to which this provision endangers U.S. interests cannot be measured, however, because the term "general policy" is so ambiguous.

The most pernicious of the powers and functions granted solely to the Assembly is its right to determine which organ of the Authority should handle a question not specifically assigned to a particular organ. The Assembly could use this provision to assign a number of additional powers and functions to itself, at the expense of the Council. For example, the text does not specify which organ of the Authority could suspend or terminate contracts or impose monetary penalties. Presumably, the Assembly could assign this power to itself, thus seriously jeopardizing the secure tenure required by every contractor. Similar examples are sprinkled throughout the text and may be common in the rules and regulations.

Decisions of the Council

The Council has sole responsibility for institutional decisions concerning (1) the specific policies of the Authority; (2) establishment of its own subsidiary organ necessary for the performance of its functions in accordance with the treaty; (3) adoption of rules of procedure including the selection of its president; (4) initiation on behalf of the Authority of proceedings before the Seabeds Disputes Chamber in cases of noncompliance; and (5) establishment of a subsidiary organ for the elaboration of draft financial rules, regulations, and procedures (Article 162, paragraphs 1, 2.d., 2.e., 2.t., and 2.x.). Each of these institutional initiatives would be decided by a three-quarters majority of the Council and could be carried over the objections of the United States and like-minded states in the Seabed Miner and Consumer Chamber.

A number of these institutional decisions could adversely affect U.S. interests. The power to establish specific policies could be abused. Since the details of the consensus procedures are not fully worked out in the text, the adoption of Council rules of procedure may diminish U.S. powers to block consensus decisions. Finally, the right to initiate proceedings before the Seabeds Disputes Chamber could be used to harass contractors or states parties.

Decisions Shared by the Assembly and the Council

The Assembly and the Council share a number of institutional decisions:

--The Assembly elects the Secretary General of the Authority from among the candidates proposed by the Council (Article 160, paragraph 2.b.);

--The Assembly, on the recommendation of the Council, elects the Governing Board and Director-General of the Enterprise (Article 160, paragraph 2.c.; Article 163,2, paragraph);

--The Assembly, on the recommendation of the Council, may suspend members of the Authority (Article 166, paragraph 2.m.; Article 185);

--The Council may enter into agreements with the United Nations or other international organizations on behalf of the Authority and within its competence, subject to approval by the Assembly (Article 162, paragraph 2.f.);

--On a finding by the Seabed Disputes Chamber on proceedings initiated by the Council, the Council should notify the Assembly and make recommendations with respect to measures to be taken unless otherwise decided (Article 162, paragraph 2.u.).

The actual interrelation between the Assembly and the Council on each of these institutional decisions is unclear. For instance, the text does not state whether the Assembly can revise or amend a Council decision or only has a choice of accepting or rejecting it. The text is further complicated by the variety of terms used in describing the relationship between the Council and Assembly.

The United States has little control over these institutional decisions since they are made by a two-thirds majority of the Assembly and a three-quarters majority of the Council. Each decision could have major consequences for the United States. For instance, the Governing Board of the Enterprise disposes of the $250 million financial commitment by the United States to the Enterprise; the United States or an ally could be suspended from the Authority; the Authority could join an international agreement to which the United States is not a party.

Financial Control Over the ISA

States parties to the treaty would be required to finance the Authority's administrative budget until such time as the Authority becomes self-financing. Many forecasts have been made on the duration of this obligation. The annual administration budget of the Authority has roughly been estimated at between $20 million and $40 million. The administrative expenses are high because the text establishes a number of organs to administer the seabed mining system, vests considerable power and numerous functions in these organs, and creates a new international bureaucracy to staff the Authority with the requisite legal and technical expertise.

Financial Structure of the Authority/Enterprise System

Figure 3.2 shows the financial organization of the Authority and its operating arm, the Enterprise.

Funds for the Authority would come from the payments that contractors exploring or exploiting the mineral resources of the seabed must make. A second source of capital would be Enterprise revenues channeled back to the Authority. Capital could also be obtained from voluntary contributions by states.

One potential source of funds would be the borrowing ability of the Authority. Another source that could be utilized, since it is not explicitly prohibited in the treaty, lies in the resale of technology that contractors would have to transfer to obtain contracts to exploit the seabed.

The total net revenue of the Authority, after operating and other expenses, would be reinvested in the Enterprise, distributed to states parties to the convention according to some predetermined formula, or some combination of the two.

Figure 3.2
Capital Flow of Authority/Enterprise

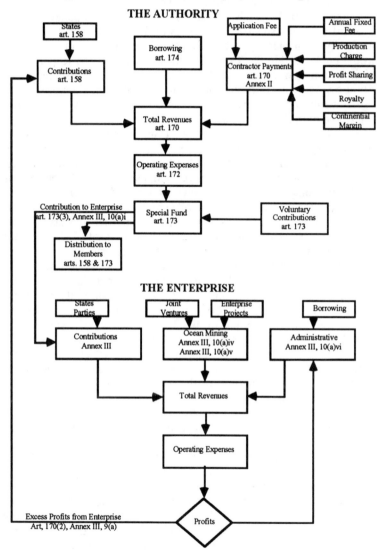

(U.S. GAO 1979)

Figure 3.2 illustrates the numerous revenue-generating activities in which the Enterprise may engage. It would, in the view of developed states at least, be a profit-oriented business, participating in ocean mining either by entering into joint venture agreements with private corporations or by undertaking its own mining operations. The Enterprise could also share in revenues resulting from payments to the Authority mandated by a future treaty. The distribution of revenue would be decided by the Council, which would bear the responsibility of determining what portion of the profits would be transferred to the Authority and what portion would be reinvested in the Enterprise.

Convention procedures give the developing countries the power to determine both the total amount and the individual components of the administrative budget, while the United States and other industrialized countries are expected to supply the bulk of the financial contributions. The Secretary-General of the Authority prepares and submits to the Council the annual administrative budget as part of the overall Authority budget. The Council reviews the budget and, by a three-quarters majority, submits the complete budget to the Assembly for its approval. The Assembly is empowered to consider and approve the budget of the Authority by a two-thirds majority. Finally, the Assembly assesses the contributions of states parties, by a two-thirds majority, in accordance with an "agreed general assessment scale" based on the United Nations scale of assessments. Under this scheme, the United States exerts no control over its financial outlays for the administrative budget. The Council could propose an administrative budget over the objections of the United States and other major contributors, and the Assembly could revise the budget over the objections of the Council. Developing countries, which dominate the Council and the Assembly, could revise the overall amount of the budget, control the operations of the Authority through the individual components of the budget, and even attach political "riders" to the budget. Under the current text, the United States and other major industrialized nations have relinquished financial control over the Authority.

The U.S. financial outlays for the administrative budget would not be cost-effective. With the U.S. share of the administrative budget amounting to approximately 25 percent, the United States would have to contribute between $5 million and $10 million annually. The bureaucracy contemplated to administer seabed mining is considerably larger than necessary to achieve the stated U.S. objectives of assured access to seabed minerals and an investment climate conducive to attracting venture capital.

Finally, the provisions regarding the administrative budget are not consistent with U.S. financial policy. The United States and other major contributors do not control the decision-making procedures and operations of the Authority in a manner commensurate with their financial contributions. In other negotiations and institutions the United States has insisted that financial and political control be commensurate with financial contributions and economic stakes.

The Secretary-General prepares and submits to the Council the annual budget of the Authority (Article 172). The Council "submits the budget of the Authority to the Assembly for its approval" by a three-quarters majority (Article 162, paragraph 2.g.; Article 159, paragraph 6). Under these provisions, the Assembly might well assert a power to alter the budget submitted by the Council, and any challenge to such an assertion would probably not succeed.

The annual budget of the Authority is made up of four major components:

(a) The administrative budget of the Authority, which will include such items as staff salaries and overhead expenses, will be drawn from a special count of state party contributions until such time as the Authority is self-financed (Article 173, paragraph 1; Article 171, paragraph a). The Assembly assesses the contributions of states parties, which can be used only for the administrative budget, in accordance with an "agreed general assessment scale" based on the U.N. scale (Article 160, paragraph 2.e.). Presumably, the Assembly would determine when the Authority was self-sufficient, and the means and timing by which states would make their contributions would be in accordance with the rules, regulations, and procedures of financial management. The administrative budget has first call on Authority funds (Article 173, paragraph 2).

(b) Distribution of the funds of the Authority, "taking into particular consideration the interests and needs of the developing states and peoples who have not attained full independence," must be in accordance with the rules, regulations, and procedures recommended by the Council by consensus and adopted by the Assembly by a two-thirds majority (Article 140; Article 160, paragraph 2.j.; Article 160, paragraph 2.f.i.; Article 162, paragraph 2.n.i.; Article 173, paragraph 2.a.). An additional source of such funds is the revenue from the continental shelf beyond 200 miles (Article 160, paragraph 2.f.i.; Article 162, paragraph 2.n.i.). Presumably the details of the actual distribution of these moneys will be part of the annual budget. Such funds could be distributed to liberation movements or to states that are potential adversaries (Libya, China, Cuba, Iraq, and Iran).

(c) Funds for the Enterprise "shall be provided . . . as it may require to carry out its functions" (Article 170; Article 173, paragraph 2.b.; Annex IV, Article 11, paragraph 1.a.). Presumably, the rules and regulations will include procedures for the transfer of funds to the Enterprise under the aegis of rules and regulations for the "financial management" of the Authority; however, the interpretation is not certain under the current text. Earlier texts were much clearer in that they specified that the "transfer of funds to the Enterprise" would be part of the rules and regulations of the Authority agreed to by both the Council and the Assembly.

(d) The Economic Planning Commission would propose, by a decision-making system to be established in the rules and regulations, a system of compensation or other measures of economic adjustment assistance, including cooperation with specialized agencies and other international organizations, to assist developing land-based whose export earnings or economies may suffer from the reduction in the price of an affected mineral or the volume of mineral exported, to the extent that such reduction is caused by activities in the Area (Article 151, paragraph 4; Article 164, paragraph 2.d.). The Council, by a two-thirds majority, recommends the system of compensation for developing land-based producers to the Assembly, which adopts the system by a two-thirds vote (Article 162, paragraph 2.m.; Article 161, paragraph 7b.; Article 160, paragraph 2.1.; Article 153, paragraph 7). The interrelation of this compensation scheme with the annual budget and the financial rules, regulations, and procedures is unclear, especially since each of these decisions requires a different voting majority.

The sources of Authority revenues play an important role in determining the overall size of the Authority budget. There are apparently six potential sources of revenue for the Authority:

(1) Assessed contributions of states parties will be paid into a special account to be used to meet the administrative budget of the Authority until such time as the Authority is self-sufficient (Article 173, paragraph 1; Article 171; Article 160, paragraph 2.c.). The Assembly assesses the contributions of states parties, by a two-thirds vote, in accordance with an "agreed general assessment scale"

based on the U.N. scale (Article 160, paragraph 2.c.) The United States (25 percent share) and other industrialized countries will be contributing the bulk of funds to be used for administrative expenditures. The annual administrative budget has been roughly estimated at $20 million to $40 million.

(2) The Enterprise will transfer funds to the Authority under the financial terms of contracts after an initial period, not to exceed ten years from the commencement of commercial production. During the initial period, the Enterprise is exempt from such payments (Article 171, paragraph b; Annex IV, Article 10, paragraph 1). Because the Enterprise would not be motivated by the same financial goals and discipline as a private corporation and because it would be exempt from early payments, the Authority is unlikely to receive much revenue from this source.

(3) Income of the Authority arising from activities in the Area in accordance with the financial terms of contracts (Article 171, paragraph c; Annex III, Article 13) consist of the Authority's share of revenues generated from the exploration and exploitation of polymetallic nodules. U.S., European, and Japanese corporations have pioneered the development of seabed mining and therefore will provide most, if not all, of the Authority's revenues from seabed mining. It has been roughly estimated that each twenty-five-year contract will generate between $400 million and $800 million for the Authority, depending on profitability.

(4) The Assembly establishes the limits on the borrowing power of the Authority in its financial regulations "adopted pursuant to Article 160, paragraph 2.f" (Article 174, paragraph 2). The text is ambiguous on a Council role in such financial regulations, but the reference to Article 160.2f. seems to presume such a Council role. The Council exercises the borrowing power of the Authority by a three-quarters vote (Article 174, paragraph 3; Article 161, paragraph 7.c.).

(5) Authority funds also include voluntary contributions made by states parties or other entities (Article 171).

(6) There are important ambiguities on the extent to which "payments and contributions made pursuant to Article 82" (i.e., the share of revenue from the exploitation of nonliving resources on the continental shelf beyond two hundred miles) are part of Authority funds. Article 82 specifies that the payment or contributions should

be made "through the Authority which shall distribute them to states parties to this convention, on the basis of equitable sharing criteria, taking into account the interests and needs of developing states, particularly the least-developed and the landlocked among them" (Article 82, paragraph 4). On the other hand, Article 160 empowers the Assembly, on the recommendation of the Council, to approve rules, regulations, and procedures on the equitable sharing of these payments and contributions, "taking into particular consideration" not only "the interests and needs of the developing states" but also of "peoples who have not attained full independence or other self-governing status." Industrialized countries will provide most of these funds through the Authority because they are likely to lead the development of the outer continental margin and because developing countries that are net importers are exempt from the payments. It is estimated that each petroleum field would generate between $500 million and $700 million in royalties.

The major issue underlying the budget question is control over the International Seabed Authority. Under the current text, the Western industrialized countries have little control over the decision-making mechanism of the Authority, which is based on the one-nation-one-vote principle in both the Assembly and the Council. The Council can propose a budget over the objections of the United States and like-minded nations, and the Assembly probably can revise the budget over the objections of the Council.

Under the existing text, the Assembly is likely to assert the power to revise the budget submitted by the Council. The Assembly could use such discretion to revise the overall amount of the annual budget, to change the individual components of the budget, or to attach "riders" to the budget. Any of these actions could have a serious impact on the United States. First, the discretion to attach riders to the budget could politicize the work of the International Seabed Authority. It takes little imagination to conjure up the political resolutions that the Assembly might be tempted to launch against the international pariahs of the day. The discretion to revise the total amount of the budget could significantly increase the financial commitments of the major contributors to underwrite the administrative budget until such time as the Authority becomes self-sufficient. Combined with the power of the Assembly to set Authority borrowing limits and establish compensation schemes, an uncontrollable budget could bring the creditworthiness of the Authority into question.

Finally, the discretion to change the individual components of the budget could be used to undermine U.S. interests in the seabed mining regime. For example, the staff of the Legal and Technical Commission could be reduced to create a deliberate backlog in its consideration of contracts. Alternatively, the number of inspectors could be significantly increased (to harass seabed miners) or reduced (in order to erode the effectiveness of environmental regulations). An Assembly dominated by Group of 77 ideologies could skew the distribution of Authority revenues so that disproportionate amounts could end up in the hands of the Enterprise (a competitor) or of nations like Cuba, Libya, Iran, or Iraq (politically sensitive for the United States).

Under the text, the Council, by a three-quarters vote, submits the Authority's budget to the Assembly for its approval and exercises the borrowing power of the Authority. In order to block either the budget or unwarranted borrowing, the United States would have to force a coalition of ten Council members, a difficult task in light of the composition of the Council.

The Enterprise

The Enterprise, which is the mining arm of the Authority, is guaranteed the financing for one fully integrated site at an estimated cost of $1.2 billion. The U.S. contribution would be $300 million, one-half in interest-free long-term loans and one-half in debt guarantees. The United States has little or no control over its financial contribution in its amount, timing of the call-up, uses, or repayments. The treaty effectively grants control over Enterprise financing to developing countries.

The composition of both the Council and the Governing Board of the Enterprise ensures developing-country control over Enterprise operations. The treaty enables the developing countries to issue directives to the Enterprise over the objections of *all* industrialized countries. In addition, the treaty offers significant discriminatory advantages and privileges to the Enterprise, which could enable the Enterprise to dominate seabed mining.

Financing the Enterprise

The treaty obligates states parties to finance the Enterprise's initial administrative expenses and a fully integrated mining project (Annex IV, Article 11, paragraph 3.a., 3.h.). The actual amount, and "the criteria and factors for its adjustment," would be determined by the Preparatory Commission in the provisional rules and regulations and would be geared toward providing the Enterprise with enough funds to explore and exploit one mine site and to transport, process, and market the recovered metals, namely copper, cobalt, nickel, and manganese (Annex IV, Article 11, paragraph 3.a.). States parties would provide one-half of these funds in long-term, interest-free loans and would also guarantee the debt incurred by the Enterprise in raising the balance of the funds (Annex IV, Article 11, paragraph 3.b.). The share of each state party in Enterprise financing would be in accordance with the scale of assessments for the United Nations regular budget (Annex IV, Article 11, paragraph 3.b.).

The obligation of states parties to finance the Enterprise would have a considerable impact on the U.S. budget. The capital costs of a fully integrated, four-metal project have been roughly estimated at $1.2 billion (1979 dollars). Annual administrative expenses of the Enterprise have not been determined. The U.S. share under the current United Nations scale of assessments would be $250 million, of which $125 million would be in long-term, interest-free loans and $125 million in loan guarantees. This financial outlay would have to be considered in the context of the administration's and Congress's objectives to control the federal budget, to curtail U.S. contributions to multilateral organizations, and to control off-budget items such as loan guarantees in order to restrain the overall financial liabilities of the United States. The industrialized nations' obligation to finance the Enterprise is a means to win the acquiescence of the developing nations to the current text's system of limited access.   The obligation to finance the Enterprise places the U.S. government in the ironic position of subsidizing the major competitors of a new part of the U.S. mining industry.

The United States cannot fully control the amount, timing, use, or repayment of its financial commitment to the Enterprise. Although the amount of the funds to be made available for mining operations of the Enterprise will be set out in the rules and regulations, these same rules and regulations will also establish the criteria and factors (but not the means) for adjusting this amount (Annex IV, Article 11, paragraph 3.a.) The United States will probably be under considerable pressure during the negotiation of these rules and regulations to accept an adjustment mechanism (such as indexation or a decision of the Authority), which would lead to an open-ended U.S. financial commitment.

The United States will have no control over the timing of its financial commitment to the Enterprise because under the current text, all parties must deposit with the Enterprise "irrevocable, non-negotiable, non-interest-bearing promissory notes" in the amount of their share in the interest-free loans (Annex IV, Article 11, paragraph 3.d.). The Governing Board of the Enterprise, which would be dominated by representatives of the developing nations (Article 160, paragraph 2.c.; Annex IV, Article 5, paragraph 1), would prepare "a schedule of the magnitude and timing of its requirements for the funding of its administrative expenses and for carrying out its activities" (Annex IV, Article 11, paragraph 3.d.).

The Enterprise would encash the promissory notes as required to meet the expenditures outlined in the schedule. Empowering the Enterprise to call up financial commitments would disrupt annual U.S. budget planning and budget flexibility. It runs directly counter to established U.S. financial policy, which has sought to control the timing of financial outlays to international organizations.

The United States and other major industrialized countries, which are the primary financiers of the Enterprise, have no control over the Enterprise's use of their money. Once elected by the Assembly, the Governing Board can be controlled only through directives from the Council, issued by a *two-thirds* vote (Article 162, paragraph i.e.; Article 161, paragraph 7.b.). Under the current text, the developing nations on the Council could issue directives to the Enterprise over the objections of *all* major contributors to the Enterprise, whereas the United States and other major contributors could exert *no* control over Enterprise activities. This decision-making system significantly increases the risk that the Enterprise will flounder and that loan guarantees, the bulk of which are provided by the United States and other major industrialized countries, may be called in by the banks.

Finally, the United States and other major contributors would have little control over the Enterprise's repayment of the interest-free loans. The repayment of the interest-free loans would be in accordance with a schedule adopted by the Assembly (by a two-thirds majority), on the recommendation of the Council (by a three-quarters majority) and the advice of the Governing Board (Annex IV, Article II, paragraph 3.f.; Article 161, paragraph 7.c.). The convention exhorts the Governing Board to "be guided by the relevant provisions of the rules, regulations, and procedures" in the performance of this function (Annex IV, Article 11, paragraph 3.f.). Although the United States and other contributors would know the general standards for repayment, they would not know when their interest-free loans would actually be refunded, if at all. In the context of forgone opportunity costs, inflation, and the likely time horizon for repayment (infinite?), the interest-free loans in effect become grants.

Control Over the Enterprise

The Authority exerts control over the Enterprise in a number of ways:

--The Authority elects the major officials of the Enterprise. Both the Governing Board and the Director-General are elected by a two-thirds majority of the Assembly on the recommendation of three-quarters of the Council (Article 160, paragraph 2.c.; Article 159, paragraph 6; Article 161, paragraph 7.6). Because the Director-General serves a term of five years and the members of the Governing Board serve terms of four years, the Authority can influence the long-term character of the Enterprise by changing Enterprise officials. The United States and like-minded states, however, will be unable to influence this process because they do not control a sufficient number of votes on the Council.

--The Authority sets conditions on interest-free loans and debt guarantees made available by state parties to the Enterprise for its integrated projects. In its rules, regulations, and procedures, the Authority specifies the total amount of funds to be made available, establishes standards for the repayment of the interest-free loans, and sets up procedures for unwinding Enterprise defaults on debts (Annex IV, Article 11, paragraphs, and 3.h.). The Assembly sets the actual repayment schedule by a two-thirds majority on the recommendation by three-quarters of the Council. The United States and like-minded states, however, would be unable to influence the Enterprise's use of these funds.

--The Council reviews the projects proposed by the Enterprise (Annex IV, Article IV, paragraph 1). Under the current text, Council approval of a project would (by accident) require consensus because project reviews fall into the category of decisions that the Council is authorized to take, but without a specified voting majority (Article 161, paragraph 7.f.) The plan of work of the Enterprise, which is applicable only to mining the seabeds, would undergo the same procedures as any other contract. Although the United States could block approval of an Enterprise project, it would have little influence on decisions concerning approval of a plan of work.

--The Authority controls the Enterprise's finances. The Authority is empowered to transfer its funds to the Enterprise, but the mechanism for this transfer is unspecified in the treaty (Article 173, paragraph 2.b). In addition, the Assembly, on the recommendation of the Governing Board, would determine by a two-thirds majority what portion of the net income of the Enterprise should be retained as its reserves (Annex IV, Article 10, paragraph 2). The procedures for such transfers from the Enterprise to the Authority would be specified in the rules, regulations, and procedures of the Authority (Article 160, paragraph 2.f.ii). The developing countries on the

Authority thus control the purse strings of the Enterprise and could leave the Enterprise either flush with or strapped for funds. Under the decision-making system, however, the United States and like-minded States (the major contributors to the Enterprise) will be unable to control Authority decisions on Enterprise finances.

--The Council may control any aspect of Enterprise operations by issuing directives by a two-thirds vote (Article 162, paragraph 2.i.; Article 161, paragraph 7.b.). Such directives could presumably apply to all Enterprise activities, including use of funds, marketing practices, location of facilities, and establishment of joint ventures. Such directives could be issued by the developing countries on the Council, even over the objections of all major contributors (the United States, Western Europe, Socialis Eastern Europe, and China) acting in concert.

The Enterprise does not operate as a semi-autonomous commercial unit but is rather under the complete control of the developing-nation majority of the Authority. The United States and other major contributors, with the exception of a few conditions on initial project financing, have virtually no influence over the Enterprise.

---

[3]Actually there were two "white" papers. The first was a scathing, 127-page critique entitled "The Seabed Mining Regime" made available to Congress and the former Public Advisory Committee on the Law of the Sea; the second, more diplomatically worded paper, "Approaches to Major Problems in Part XI of the Draft Convention on the Law of the Sea," was presented to the Conference and rejected out of hand.

Chapter Four

1994 Treaty Modifications

> . . . [A] treaty is likely to be a highly deceptive document, creating illusory security or a false set of expectations about the way nations party to it are likely to behave in the future.

> . . . I would recall George Kennan's comment that the most fundamental error of United States foreign policy is the belief that international law can actually temper the dangerous ambitions of governments. For the United States to accept a treaty on law of the sea which is less than ideal from the standpoint of protecting substantive national interests because some positive premium value is placed on the treaty itself--on its mere existence--is to make a fundamental error of judgment. The error lies in assigning a positive, premium value to the existence of a law of the sea treaty. Assuming such a positive value stems from a misperception about the role and place of treaties in regulating the conduct of nations. (Knight 1981, 1)

In 1990, U.N. Secretary-General Javier Perez de Cuellar initiated consultations among interested governments aimed at achieving universal participation in the Convention. Since late 1992, pressures mounted to revise or amend what were viewed as unacceptable parts of the Convention. Factors contributing to this renewed pressure included the desire for universal participation in a convention that in most respects was acceptable worldwide, improvements in the international political climate, changes in economic ideology that meant greater acceptance of free-market principles, and the steady increase in the number of ratifications toward the sixty required to bring the Convention into force.

In April 1993, the Clinton administration announced it would actively participate in these consultations on the outstanding issues in the deep-seabed portions of the convention. November 16, 1993, the date when the U.N. Secretary-General received the 60th instrument of ratification/accession, marked the start of the one-year waiting period after which the Convention would enter into force. The consultations led to adoption, on July 28, 1994, by the U.N. General Assembly (by a vote of 121 in favor (including the United States) to 0 against, with 7 (Colombia, Nicaragua, Panama, Peru, Russian Federation, Thailand, Venezuela) abstentions and 36 nations absent) of Resolution 48/263, opening for signature an Agreement relating to the Implementation of Part XI of the United Nations convention on the Law of the Sea. The Agreement amended various seabed-related parts of the convention.

On October 7, 1994, President Clinton transmitted to the Senate the 1982 United Nations Convention on the Law of the Sea and 1994 Agreement relating to the Implementation of Part XI of the United Nations convention (Treaty Document 103-39). The package was referred to the Senate Committee on Foreign Relations. On November 16, 1994, the U.N. Law of the Sea Convention entered into force but without accession by the United States. A primary question facing the Senate is whether the amendments offered in the Agreement sufficiently alter the direction of the Convention's deep seabed mining provisions to make it acceptable to those who oppose U.S. ratification.

The 1994 Agreement relating to the Implementation of Part XI of the United Nations Convention, and its accompanying Annex, is considered an integral part of the Convention package that entered into force on November 16, 1994. In the event of inconsistencies, the Agreement and Annex language take precedence over Convention language. The Annex contains the substantive changes to Part XI and Annexes III and IV of the Convention, while the Agreement defines the legal relationship between the Convention and the Agreement, explains the ways in which states may consent to be bound by the Agreement, and sets the terms of entry into force of the Agreement and its provisional application. However, the legal or binding nature of this agreement is both unprecedented and untested. As a result, the permanence of the changes achieved by this agreement are more a matter of conjecture, or possibly wishful thinking, than definitive judgment.

The four principal areas covered by the Agreement include:

ISA Decision making. The Convention, as originally adopted, lacked adequate influence by the United States and other industrialized countries over the decisions taken by the ISA Assembly and Council and language guaranteeing the United States a seat on the Council. The Annex provides that all substantive decisions of the Assembly shall be taken only on recommendation of the Council and/or Finance Committee; if the Assembly does not accept the Council's recommendation, the matter is returned to the Council for further consideration. The United States is now guaranteed a seat on the Council, in perpetuity. Further, the Annex changes the decision-making structure of the Council to ensure that industrialized states can make up a blocking vote.

Review Conference. Section 4 of the Annex eliminated the Review Conference language in the Convention, providing instead that states parties may decide to review the convention at any time, rather than after fifteen years, and that any amendments resulting from that review will be subject to the normal procedures for amendment set forth in the Convention. The special Review Conference language would have enabled amendments to enter into force after ratification by only three-fourths of the parties.

Technology Transfer. Section 5 of the Annex states that the mandatory technology transfer provisions in Article 5 of Annex III of the convention "shall not apply." Section 5 replaces those provisions with a set of general principles on the issue of technology transfer.

Obstacles to Development. Concerns that the Convention would deter rather than promote future development of deep seabed mineral resources and that assured access to mining by qualified entities would be denied are addressed in the Annex at Sections 2, 6, and 8, respectively, which:

> • terminate the provision on production limits of seabed-based mining in order to protect land-based production;

> • replace elaborate and expensive (including an annual fixed fee of $1 million) financial terms of contracts, with a set of principles, and reduce the $500,000 application fee to $250,000; and

> • modify Annex IV of the Convention so that the Enterprise would become operational only on a decision of the Council. The Enterprise would be subject to the same obligations applicable to other miners, and the Enterprise would conduct its initial operation through joint ventures. The special privileges accorded to the Enterprise under the Convention are eliminated.

DoD and the Navy Support the Treaty

After the Clinton administration participated in the 1993-94 revision negotiations, both the House and the Senate held hearings on the status of the UNCLOS and the prospects of U.S. ocean mining. The administration attempted to convince Congress that participation in the UNCLOS is overwhelmingly in the U.S. national interest, primarily on the basis of sea power and naval mobility issues. The arguments presented by representatives of the Joint Chiefs of Staff, DoD General Counsel, and the Coast Guard, however, essentially stated that the United States would benefit. from the possible reduction in excessive maritime claims by coastal states through lessening the need for a shrinking U.S. Navy to engage in quite so many challenges of coastal state claims. It should be noted that DoD's long-standing support for the treaty has nothing to do with the 1994 Agreement. In fact, DoD has been a consistent treaty proponent since 1982, addressing only the narrow issue of freedom of navigation. In the view of the Joint Chiefs of Staff:

> Remaining outside the LOS convention would have the undesirable effect of placing the U.S. Freedom of Navigation (FON) program "center stage" as the primary U.S. instrument for challenging excessive claims. Although the FON program is intended to be neither provocative nor controversial, some states view it as such. According to a 1992 State Department study of illegal claims, the U.S. was then actively protesting illegal claims by more than thirty states at the rate of 30 to 40 protests per year. This year, more than sixty states are making such claims. Of particular concern to DOD are claims asserting that the rights of transit passage (through an international strait) or innocent passage (through territorial waters) are conditioned on prior notification by warships. We are also concerned with claims of "security zones" or illegal baselines which have the effect of delimiting large ocean areas as territorial sea or internal waters. U.S. policy has been to challenge systematically those claims--both diplomatically and operationally--through the FON program.
> U.S. accession to the Convention should help moderate the proliferation of excessive maritime claims. It is important to note that such claims are not being made by some anti-U.S. bloc, but by virtually all coastal states--including many of our friends and closest allies. They range from Italy's noncompliant historic bay claims, to Canada's excessive baseline claims. Other

examples include Indonesia's restrictive archipelagic sea lanes passage claims and Peru's restriction on aircraft overflight.

This is not to suggest unreasonable unilateral claims which attempt to restrict navigation will cease once the United States becomes party to the LOS convention. Coastal states make excessive claims because they believe such claims to be in their national interest and because they believe they can enforce those claims. With the U.S. as a party, fewer states are likely to view such claims as legitimate or enforceable. With clear support from the U.S., other nations will be more willing to undertake independent or cooperative freedom of navigation operations to challenge such claims. As a party, our diplomatic challenges will clearly carry greater weight. (Adm. Center in U.S. Senate 1994)

This rather weak, one-dimensional argument for acceptance of the treaty pales in significance with the severe problems embedded in Part XI, including the vulnerability of advanced U.S. deep ocean technology to technology transfer which carries with it serious strategic consequences, principally in the antisubmarine warfare (ASW) arena.

In addition, DoD expressions of concern over moving the FON program to "center stage" as the primary means of challenging excessive maritime claims are rather odd as the FON program has been "center stage" since President Carter began it in 1979. Indeed, with or without a UNCLOS a primary peacetime mission of the Navy is, and will continue to be, FON activities, although perhaps on a slightly less frequent basis.

Freedom of Navigation Program

The historic trend is for the commonly shared rights of all users of the seas to be diminished by coastal state claims to exercise rights further from shore. The expansion of the territorial sea breadth from 3 to 12 miles, and the acceptance of the 200-mile exclusive economic zone (EEZ), are prime examples. While the 12-mile territorial sea and 200-mile EEZ have gained international legal acceptance, as reflected in the LOS Convention, many states have asserted claims that exceed the provisions of the Convention. Unless these excessive claims are actively opposed, the challenged rights will be effectively lost. (Roach and Smith, 3-4)

The U.S. government has routinely responded to excessive maritime claims through a program to preserve and enhance navigational freedoms worldwide. This program, named the U.S. Freedom of Navigation (FON) program, was formally instituted during the Carter administration in 1979 to highlight the navigation provisions of the LOS Convention to recognize the vital national need to protect maritime rights throughout the world. The FON program was continued by the Reagan, Bush, and Clinton administrations. It is intended to be a peaceful exercise of the rights and freedoms recognized by international law and is not intended to be provocative. (Negroponte 1986, 41-43) As President Reagan stated on March 10, 1983, it has been U.S. policy to:

> accept and act in accordance with the balance of interests relating to traditional uses of the oceans — such as navigation and overflight. In this respect, the United States will recognize the rights of other states in the waters off their coasts, as reflected in the Convention, so long as the rights and freedoms of the United States and others under international law are recognized by such coastal states.

In addition, U.S. policy has been to:

> exercise and assert its navigation and overflight rights and freedoms on a worldwide basis . . . The United States will not, however, acquiesce in unilateral acts of other states designed to restrict the rights and freedoms of the international community in navigation and overflight and other related high seas. (Public Papers 1983, 378-79)

The FON program operates on a triple track, involving not only diplomatic representations and operational assertions but also bilateral and multilateral consultations with other governments in an effort to promote maritime stability and consistency with international law.

> When addressing other states' specific maritime claims that are inconsistent with international law, the United States uses, as appropriate, the various forms of diplomatic correspondence. These include first- and third-person diplomatic notes, and may take the form of formal notes, *notes verbales* and *aides-memoire*. Since 1948, the United States has filed more than 140 such protests, including more than 110 since the FON program began.

> The United States has more to lose than any other nation if its maritime rights are undercut. Even though the United States may have the military power to operate where and in the manner it believes it has the right to, any exercise of that power is significantly less costly if it is generally accepted as being lawful. If the United States does not exercise its rights freely to

navigate and overfly international waters, international straits and archipelagic sea lanes, it will lose those rights and others, at least as a practical matter.

It is accepted international law and practice that, to prevent changes in or derogations from rules of law, states must persistently object to actions by other states that seek to change those rules. Protest "must, at the very least, be repeated" and "must be supported by conduct which opposes the presentations of the claimant state." Naturally, states are not required to adopt a course of conduct which virtually negates the rights reserved by protest. Consequently, states will not be permitted to acquiesce in emerging new rules of law and later claim exemption from them at will.

Acquiescence is the tacit acceptance of a certain legal position as a result of a failure to make a reservation of rights at the appropriate juncture. For acquiescence to arise, a claim must have been made and accepted. The claim must be made in a manner, and in such circumstances, that the other state has been placed on notice of that claim. The conduct that allegedly constitutes acquiescence, or tacit acceptance of that claim, likewise must be clear and unequivocal. The failure to make a timely protest in circumstances when it reasonably could have been expected to do so may constitute tacit acceptance of the claim.

Operations by U.S. naval and air forces designed to emphasize internationally recognized navigational rights and freedoms complement U.S. diplomatic efforts. FON operations are conducted in a low-key and nonthreatening manner but without attempt at concealment. The FON program impartially rejects excessive maritime claims of allied, friendly, neutral, and unfriendly states alike. These assertions of rights and freedoms tangibly exhibit U.S. determination not to acquiesce in excessive claims to maritime jurisdiction by other states. Although some operations receive public scrutiny (such as those that have occurred in the Black Sea and the Gulf of Sidra), most do not. Since 1979, U.S. military ships and aircraft have exercised their rights and freedoms in all oceans against objectionable claims of more than thirty-five countries at the rate of some thirty to forty per year. (Roach and Smith, 4-6)

Some recent examples of U.S. protests of such claims include:

India and Sri Lanka - Gulf of Mannar and Palk Bay
On June 1, 1979, India claimed as historic the waters of the Gulf of Mannar between the coast and its maritime boundary with Sri

Lanka. The United States protested this claim, among other Indian maritime claims, in a note to the Indian Ministry of External Affairs on May 13, 1983.

Italy - Gulf of Taranto
As part of its 1977 decree establishing straight baselines for portions of the Italian coast, Italy for the first time claimed the Gulf of Taranto as a historic bay. During bilateral discussions with the Italian government in 1984, the United States stated its view that the Gulf of Taranto could not be considered a historic bay since the requirements for such status were not met. The United States noted that "a coastal state claiming such status for a body of water must over a long period of time have openly and continually claimed to exercise sovereignty over the body of water, and its claims must have resulted in an absence of protest of foreign States, amounting to acquiescence on their part."

Libya - Gulf of Sidra
In 1973 Libya's Foreign Ministry circulated a note claiming the Gulf of Sidra as Libyan internal waters. The Gulf was defined by a closing line, approximately 300 miles long, along the 32° 30' parallel of north latitude. The United States first protested this claim in 1974. In a 1985 note to the Secretary-General of the United Nations, the United States reiterated "its rejection of the Libyan claim that the Gulf of Sidra constitutes internal waters to the latitude of 32 degrees 30 minutes north," and rejected "as an unlawful interference with the freedoms of navigation and overflight and related high seas freedoms, the Libyan claim to prohibit navigation" in the Gulf.[4]

Since Libya cannot make a valid historic waters claim and meets no other international law criteria for enclosing the Gulf of Sidra, it may validly claim a twelve-nautical-mile territorial sea as measured from the normal low-water line along its coast. Libya also may claim up to a 200-nautical-mile exclusive economic zone in which it may exercise resource jurisdiction, but such a claim would not affect freedom of navigation and overflight. (The United States has confined its exercises to areas beyond twelve miles from Libya's coast.)

Panama - Gulf of Panama.
In 1956, the United States protested the unilateral declaration contained in Panamanian Law No. 9 of January 30, 1956, purporting to confirm and implement Panama's claim that it exercises sovereignty over the Gulf of Panama as a historic bay.

USSR - Peter the Great Bay.
The former Soviet Union first claimed Peter the Great Bay as historic in a 1957 decree. The United States, and other countries, immediately protested. The 106-mile closing line is, at one point, more than twenty miles from any land. (Roach and Smith, 27-32)

Superficial Changes Are Inadequate

While a number of changes appear to have been achieved by the 1993-94 negotiations, their depth, substance, effectiveness, and legality are highly suspect. The new agreement "does not, even purport to amend the Convention. It establishes controlling 'interpretive provisions' that will control in the event of a dispute. This is not an approach that gives confidence to prospective investors in ocean mining." (Hoyle 1994)

In the view of the U.S. ocean mining industry:

> From an investor's standpoint the biggest problem with the convention as it would be implemented by the "Agreement on Implementation" is that it perpetuates the centrally planned economy model with that system's hostility to private investment. The convention continues to provide for creation of the Enterprise, the "state mining company" of the International Seabed Authority, which will be the U.N. organization set up to administer resource development on 60 percent of the Earth's surface. Each applicant for mining rights must still give half of its mine site to the Seabed Authority to be developed by the Enterprise. An applicant must still provide costly training and services to the Enterprise. As far as technology transfer is concerned, we find that no one, including the United States Patent Office, can understand what the obligations will be under the convention.

> The organization of the system is frightening to investors. The International Seabed Authority will be based on a classic United Nations pattern. The current inability of the United Nations to perform its traditional peace-keeping role effectively does not give us great confidence that a new United Nations-type organization is a prudent model for management and regulation of ocean mining.

> The failure of the convention to provide due process for natural and corporate persons is a major disincentive to investment. In the United States, much of our mineral law has been shaped by Congress and the courts over the past 100 years.

Disputes between the Department of the Interior and miners have often required administrative and judicial remedies. Congressional oversight plays a strong role in ensuring that the Administration does not abuse its discretion. In the Law of the Sea convention, private persons have no right to bring action before the Law of the Sea Tribunal. The convention would prohibit even the United States government from challenging a discretionary act of the Seabed Authority. In land-based mining, discretionary acts of regulatory and enforcement agencies are the main source of contention between governments and mineral investors. Congress crafts legislation very carefully to limit discretion to prevent abuse and provides remedies for abuse of discretion. The Law of the Sea convention provides no such protections.

This lack of due process is enough in and of itself to deprive any investor of assured access and security of tenure. To any investor, assured access and security of tenure are the vital ingredients that must be present. This means not only the ability of a qualified applicant to obtain mining rights, but the ability of the holder of the mining rights to exercise those rights over time without unreasonable interference by the host government. The ability of the International Seabed Authority to nullify the investment by interfering with operations remains a major threat to prospective investors. (Hoyle 1994)

Adherence to the Agreement and the Convention

The Agreement was opened for signature for a twelve-month period, starting July 28, 1994. After that date, any ratification, formal confirmation of, or accession to the Convention is also automatically consent to be bound by the Agreement. Since the purpose of the Agreement is to promote universal participation in the Convention, the Agreement uses several ways to achieve consent to the Agreement. At the same time, the language on consent also had to respond to the legal requirements of the sixty-plus states that had already ratified or acceded to the Convention as well as to accommodate those states that had not ratified or acceded to the Convention. In addition, the Agreement had to take effect as the Convention entered into force so as to maintain the integral link between the two. That link required use of provisional application as a procedure for operation of the Agreement.

Effective November 16, 1994, the Agreement was applied provisionally, pending its entry into force. For each country, provisional application was to be "in accordance with ... national or internal laws and regulations." Provisional application of the Agreement will terminate on its entry into force or on November 16,

1998. States that (1) voted for adoption of the Agreement, (2) signed the Agreement, (3) consented in writing to its provisional application, or (4) acceded to the Agreement will all apply the Agreement provisionally, with certain exceptions. Those exceptions include any state that voted in favor but before November 16, 1994, and notified the United Nations in writing that it would not apply the Agreement provisionally or that it would consent to provisional application only on subsequent signature or written notification and any state that signed the Agreement but notified the United Nations in writing at the time of signature that it would not apply the Agreement provisionally.

The United States announced, when it signed the Agreement on July 29, 1994, that "it intends to apply the agreement provisionally. Provisional application by the United States will allow us to advance our seabed mining interests by participating in the International Seabed Authority from the outset to ensure that the implementation of the regime is consistent with those interests."

Adherence to the Agreement: Provisions

The most curious and potentially most threatening aspect of the U.N. Law of the Sea process is provisional application. We are told that the Administration intends to sign or in some other way commit the United States to the "Agreement Relating to the Implementation of Part XI of the 1982 United Nations Convention on the Law of the Sea" this summer. The Administration does not intend to submit the "Agreement" and the 1982 convention for advice and consent for some years, possibly not until mid-1998. In the meantime, the United States as a signatory of the "Agreement" may become a "Provisional Member" of the Council, the executive organ of the Seabed Authority. We are told by the Administration that United States domestic seabed mining law will continue to control until the United States becomes a full Contracting Party to the United Nations Convention on the Law of the Sea by ratification. At the same time, the convention appears to favor those countries which apply to the Seabed Authority for mining rights in the interim. (Hoyle 1994)

Article 4 (3) of the Agreement sets forth the ways in which a state or entity may express its consent to be bound by the Agreement:

(a) signature that is equivalent to consent to be bound;
(b) signature subject to ratification or formal confirmation, followed by ratification;
(c) signature subject to a procedure set out in Article 5; and
(d) accession.

Article 5 provides an unprecedented "simplified" procedure to be used by any of the sixty states that ratified or acceded to the Convention before the Agreement was adopted in July 1994 and then subsequently signed the Agreement. Upon their signature, such states will automatically be considered parties to the Agreement as of July 28, 1995, unless they notify the United Nations they do not wish to be bound by the Agreement in this way. If a state uses that notification, it may become bound only by specific act of ratification or formal confirmation.

The Agreement will enter into force thirty days after the date on which forty states have established their consent to be bound, provided that at least seven are "pioneer investors with at least five of the seven being developed or [industrialized] states." For each state establishing consent to be bound after entry into force of the Agreement, entry into force takes place thirty days following establishment of the consent to be bound.

Gains and Losses for the U.S. from UNCLOS

In assessing the gains and losses to the range of U.S. ocean interests it becomes clear that the United States has very little to gain but much to lose by accession to UNCLOS. This analysis is drawn from Gary Knight's presentation to the American Enterprise Institute. (Knight, 4-6)

Deep Seabed Mining. Presumably what we want is politically and economically secure access to deep seabed mineral resources for companies or consortia operating from the United States. What we have now (and under a no-treaty regime) is a legal right to mine nodules from the deep ocean floor. That right stems from two factors--first, the *res nullius* character of deep seabed resources, which remain such in spite of General Assembly resolutions on the subject and the UNCLOS negotiations (neither of which has a law-making function), and second, the notion of freedom of the high seas, which gives unrestricted access to ocean space for the purpose of appropriating *res nullius* objects.

What would we obtain under a law of the sea treaty? The proposed treaty would deny nondiscriminatory access and would make it extremely difficult for American and other developed countries' corporations to participate in deep seabed mining.

Navigation. What the United States desires is unrestricted (i.e., freedom of the high seas) navigation in exclusive economic zones

(EEZ) and the right of submerged transit through straits consisting entirely of territorial waters. What we have now is an existing international legal right to engage in all freedoms of navigation more than three nautical miles from the coast.

What would we obtain under a law of the sea treaty? We would have, at best, ambiguous rights of freedom of navigation in EEZ's and submerged transit through straits. Put another way, the difficulty of establishing our legal right to EEZ navigation and submerged straits passage would be no more difficult under an existing customary international law argument than under the convoluted text of the proposed UNCLOS.

The issue then becomes--what will this nation gain or lose in the rest of the treaty? As noted above, we lose substantially on the deep seabed mining issue, and we are probably better off under a no-treaty regime for continental shelf resource exploitation, scientific research, and fisheries purposes. Thus, to suggest that the treaty provisions on navigation are somehow worth trading away a preferred position on other issues is nonsense--there simply is no enhanced value for navigation in the treaty to trade away.

---

[4] In December 1986, the U.S. Department of State's Bureau of Public Affairs published "Navigation Rights and the Gulf of Sidra," in *CIST*, a reference aid on U.S. foreign relations. The study discussed the history of U.S. responses, dating from the eighteenth century, to attempts by North African states to restrict navigation in these waters.

Chapter Five

U. S. and World Supplies of
Manganese, Copper, Nickel, and Cobalt

It is often forgotten that resource insecurity led to World Wars I and II. In both instances, the "have-not" nations (Germany in 1914, and Germany, Italy, and Japan in the 1940s) resorted to war in order to achieve a greater measure of material self-sufficiency. And both times Britain and the United States, which as late as 1939 controlled 75 percent of the world's mineral resources, were the targets of opportunity, although Germany also sought to gain at the expense of Russia and her smaller independent neighbors.

In World War I, Germany's war aims included specific raw-material deposits in Europe and overseas. Some of these were iron from French Lorraine; iron, coal, and manganese from the Ukraine; and other materials from Belgium, Turkey, and certain African colonies. The war aims included, as one might imagine, the rich mines of Katanga in the Belgian Congo. A generation later, in 1939 another German leader, Adolph Hitler, made war in order to achieve tangible resource objectives, most of them on the continent of Eurasia. "The definitive solution," Hitler said in reference to his foreign policy goal, "lies in an extension of our living space, that is, an extension of the raw materials and food basis of our nation." He looked to Southeastern Europe for bauxite, oils chromite, antimony, and copper; he saw Sweden as a supplier of iron, Finland of nickel, and most of all the Soviet Union as a minerals storehouse. With the addition of Soviet resources, Hitler said that Germany would be "the most self-supporting State . . . in the world. . . . We shall swim in" abundance, he asserted.

In retrospect, the astonishing thing is how close the Axis came to achieving their goals. In less than three years --by early 1942- - the aggressors increased their holdings of mineral resources from 5 percent to a third of the world total. The Bureau of Mines calculated that a pincer-like strike into the Middle East and India might leave the Axis with 55 percent of the world's iron-ore production, 22 percent of its energy resources, and two-thirds of the global supply of manganese, chrome, and tungsten. Fortunately, the U.S. Navy halted the Japanese advance in the summer of 1942, and on the Eastern front the Soviets began to turn the tide. During the summer of 1942, Germany and Italian ambitions in the Middle East also suffered severe setbacks. (Agnew 1983, 156-57)

As mentioned earlier, the possession of rich natural resources does not make a state prosperous, but it is essential to great national power. Advantageous geography, fertile soil, or mineral deposits can contribute to economic power, for they can create dependence by other states. By producing the wealth which permits investments, by supplying essential goods, or by affording a remunerative market, a state may gain economic power, and its power to do so is vastly enhanced by, if not entirely dependent on, natural resources of one kind or another. The aggregate area underlain by mineral deposits of economic importance is only an insignificant fraction of 1 percent of the earth's surface, and the geographic position of the individual deposits is fixed by some accident of geology. Since no second crop may be expected, rich diverse mineral deposits are a nation's most valuable but ephemeral possession. Much of history has been made by men who have successively gained wealth and power in different countries through the liquidation of these assets.

Economically the United States seems to dominating and almost impregnable position. With only about six percent of the population and seven percent of the land area of the globe, she has some forty percent of the entire world's productive capacity. With the possible exception of the Soviet Union, the U.S. is more nearly self-sufficient in vital minerals and raw materials than any other nation.

There is, however, another side to this picture. The United States is in reality far from self-sufficient in the vital materials of modern industry.[5] The U.S. is wholly deficient in such essentials as tin, industrial diamonds, natural rubber, and quartz crystals. The U.S. has to rely on foreign sources for virtually all of its manganese, chromium, nickel, and cobalt. The U.S. now has to import several vital materials which it once possessed in sufficient supply: copper, zinc, and lead.

Something like seventy materials are now classed as "critical and strategic". Of these materials "over 40 are not produced in the U.S. in sufficient quantities to mention; of those produced in this country in any significant amounts, only eight are available to meet one-half of . . . peace time requirements are not available in the entire Western Hemisphere." (Padleford and Lincoln, 33-34)

Defining Strategic Materials and Dependence

The Department of Defense (DoD) determines what materials are strategic and critical under statutory guidance in the Strategic and Critical Materials Stockpiling Act (50 U.S.C. 98 et seq.). This act creates a National Defense Stockpile of these materials based on estimated needs in a national emergency. This act also authorizes research and development of substitutes and conservation measures.

Under the act, DoD determines the U.S. dependence on strategic materials in three areas: the requirements of our military ($2.3 billion in January 1991 prices), requirements of the industrial sector ($11 million), and essential civilian needs ($1.0 billion) under mobilization conditions, including civilian austerity measures (DoD, 1992). These demands are then compared to U.S. production of these materials (if any) and to anticipated imports based on foreign production adjusted for projected war damage, shipping losses, reliability of suppliers, and U.S. market share. Materials for which the United States has been found in need are considered strategic and have been authorized by Congress to be included in the National Defense Stockpile. If the strategic materials were not available in sufficient quantities when needed, the ability of the United States to produce essential equipment would be impaired, especially in a time of war. (Allen and Noehrenberg 1992, 7)

The strategic stockpile list currently consists of 66 materials, as shown in Table 5.1. The size of the stockpile for each material is defined as a function of an assumed threat for planning purposes. The planning guidance is based on a statutorily mandated three-year conventional war and a warning period, which is based on intelligence estimates. Although the likelihood of this type of threat has significantly decreased due to the recent world events, the Congress has not altered the three-year-war planning requirement However, DoD has plans to lengthen the warning period beyond the one year used in recent estimates. In addition, reduced threats have led to reductions in the estimated force structure needed; thus, estimates of stockpile requirements are declining.

Projecting Demand for Strategic Materials

Accurately predicting the demand for strategic materials is a very difficult task. Defense-related equipment results from a long series of production steps far removed from the original raw materials. To determine which materials would be in demand for projected military equipment production would require gathering information not only from the major manufacturers but also from every sub-subcontractor. Unfortunately, information on new trends in the demand for strategic materials is not currently gathered in any single location. The same problem of data availability applies to whether substitutes for current strategic materials would be available and used widely by the end of the decade.

However, the following three factors suggest that the composition of demand for strategic materials will not change significantly by the end of the decade. First, the magnitude of the demand in the military, industrial, and civilian sectors for each strategic material makes it unlikely that the composition of strategic materials will change quickly. For example, the magnitude of steel production in the United States is between 75 and 100 million tons annually, and manganese is required to produce all of it. Similarly, 1 million tons of stainless steel are produced annually, and chromium is required for all of that. Furthermore, many of the potential substitute materials are only laboratory experiments at the moment. Even if a breakthrough is achieved, it will take years to translate a laboratory process into a production-level technology. So far, the increased use of composites in airframes has not had an apparent impact on the large quantity of steel produced annually in the United States.

Second, some major industries, such as steel, electronics, and superalloys, have very precise methods of operation, making changes in the process very difficult, time-consuming, and expensive. Third, as the military's budget decreases, the demand to produce new types of assets requiring a change in the composition will be significantly smaller than in the past. (Allen and Noehrenberg, 8-9)

Table 5.1
Strategic Materials List
(as of 1991)

Aluminum metal group	Mica, phlogopite, block
Aluminum(abrasives)	Mica, phlogopite, split
Antimony	Molybdenum group
Asbestos, amosite	Morphine
Asbestos, chrysotile	Natural insulation fiber
Bauxite, refractory	Nickel
Berylliummetal group	PGMs, iridium
Bismuth	PGMs, palladium
Cadmium	PGMs, platinum
Chromite and ferrochromium	PGMs, rhodium
Chromite, refractory grade	PGMs, ruthenium
Cobalt	Pyrethrum
Columbium group	Quartz crystals
Copper	Quinidine
Cordage fiber, abaca	Quinine
Cordage fiber, sisal	Rayon fiber, aerospace grade
Diamond, industrial	Ricinoleic acid
Fluorospar, acid	Rubber
Fluorospar, metal	Rutile
Germanium	Sapphire and ruby
Graphite, Ceylon	Silicon carbide
Graphite, Malagasy	Silver, fine
Graphite, other	Talc, block and lump
Indium	Tantalum group
Iodine	Thorium nitrate
Jewel bearings	Tin
Lead	Titanium sponge
Manganese, battery grade	Tungsten group
Manganese, chemical and metal grade	Vanadium group
Mercury	Vegetable extract, chestnut
Mica, muscovite, block	Vegetable extract, quebracho
Mica, muscovite, film	Vegetahlc extract, wattle
Mica, muscovite, split	Zinc

(Allen and Noehrenberg, 8-9)

Chart 5.1
U.S. Mineral Imports

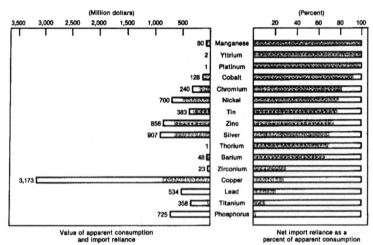

Value of apparent consumption and import reliance

Net import reliance as a percent of apparent consumption

The United States is reliant on imports of a number of critical minerals that are known to occur on the seafloor within the 200-mile U.S. EEZ.

(U.S. OTA 1987, 9)

What all of this obviously means is that the U.S., along with all of Western Europe and Japan, find themselves dangerously dependent on external sources of raw materials which are vitally needed to support their industrial base. And in the case of raw materials, such as this paper is concerned with, the dependence appears to be increasing. As stated earlier, dependence itself erodes a significant portion of a nation's power, but this erosion is vastly exacerbated when the nation, in whose possession the vital materials lie, happens to comprise some of the most politically unstable nations in existence. Therefore, the problem which confronts the United States, along with the other nations spoken of, is what to do in a situation where you are becoming increasingly dependent on a politically unstable supplier for materials basic to your industrial success and hence your way of life.

As will be shown on the following pages, concerning the future supply of manganese, copper, nickel and cobalt, the United States' resource wealth of these minerals is negligible, her use of the resources is constantly rising, and her dependence increases.

Manganese

Although manganese oxides are common in nature and small concentrations are geologically ubiquitous, large high-grade deposits are relatively rare. (Flawn, 295) The United States possesses none. (Landsberg, 435) Current domestic production is almost nonexistent and about two million tons of ore is imported each year primarily from South Africa, India, Brazil, and Mexico. Domestic potential ore is of such low grade that, assuming no change in the present inability to utilize the potential ore, U.S. imports through the remainder of the century can be taken to equal U.S. requirements. (Landsberg, 436)

> There are no economic substitutes for manganese in the metallurgical and chemical industry. About 93 percent of the manganese consumed in the U.S. was for metallurgical purposes steel production), 5 percent was for chemical and other miscellaneous purposes, and 2 percent was for manufacture of dry-cell batteries. (Flawn, 296)

Due to its hardening effects, manganese is important as an alloying element for both ferrous and non-ferrous metals, and as a reagent in the steel making process, it is considered essential. (Landsberg, 304) Inasmuch as about 35 pounds of manganese ore are used to make a ton of steel, and more than 90 percent of all manganese is consumed for such metallurgical purposes, it seems clear that manganese is tied firmly to steel. (Flawn, 296) Chart 5.2 represents future world demand projections for manganese up to the year 2005. This demand projection follows very closely the expected future demand for steel owing principally to the direct relationship between manganese and steel.

Roughly 90 percent of the combined total usage of the EEC and Japan occurs in iron and steel production alone. Counteracting the effects of sulfur by increasing the malleability of crude steel is the single most important application of manganese. This is an essential function in crude steel production and no other metal can compete with manganese on a cost basis in this application. As a consequence, all crude steel contains manganese as a result of standard steel production procedures. Moreover, in addition to its desulfurizing properties, manganese has useful cleansing and deoxidizing characteristics in raw steel. Most manganese consumed for this purpose is used in the form of one of the ferro alloys--ferromanganese, silicomanganese, and speigeleisen. Of these, ferromanganese is by far the most important, comprising about 90 percent of the total in the U.S. and similar proportions in other major steel producing countries. In addition to its use as a desulfurizing additive in crude steel, manganese is also utilized as an alloying element in a number of special purpose steels. (U. N. Doc. TD/B/483/ADD.1, 3)

Chart 5.2
Manganese:
Projected Demand

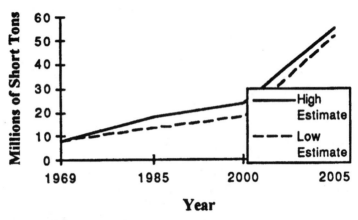

(U.S. Depot. of Interior, <u>Minerals Yearbook</u>)

As seen in Chart No. 2, the developing countries account for an increasing share of world manganese trade. The principal suppliers of manganese among the LDC's are Brazil, Gabon, and India. Although the former U.S.S.R. is by far the largest single producer of manganese, very little manganese leaves the Warsaw Pact nations and enters the world market.

Table 5.2
World Production of Manganese Ore
(Thousands of Tons)

	1982	1992
World	24,217	20,718
Developing Countries	6,450	3,765
Brazil	2,225	2,472
Gabon	1,485	1,556
Ghana	160	362
India	1,468	1,500
Morocco	94	33
Zaire	4	---
Developed Countries	6,450	3,765
Australia	1,127	1,300
Japan	78	---
S.Africa	5,216	2,462
U.S.A.	15	---
Eastern Europe	10,005	6,500
U.S.S.R.	9,821	6,500

(United Nations. UNCTAD Commodity Yearbook Various Issues)

As steel production is generally accepted as one measure of industrial growth and power, and as seen, manganese production is essential for a modern steel industry, manganese itself thus becomes a mineral vital to a nation's industrial base. The linkage effects occasioned by a sudden curtailment in the flow of manganese to the United States, or some other large steel producer, can entail serious disruptions in that nation's economic stability.

Copper

Copper, one of the first, if not the first, metal used by man and certainly the first used for tools and weapons, (Lucretius, 210) is still one of the most important industrial metals. (Flawn, 306)

> Several features make copper a very useful metal. It combines the properties of withstanding corrosion, excellent malleability, and first-class conductivity both of electrical current and heat. The main use of copper in earlier periods was in places where corrosion was a problem. The development of stainless steel and the decreasing costs of aluminum have reduced the importance of copper as an anti-corrosion material. In recent decades, more than half of all copper consumption has been in the electrical industry, but here too, substitution by aluminum, a less efficient, but increasingly cheaper electrical conductor, has been considerable over time. Another major use of the red metal is in construction (piping). The durability and ease with which it is handled make copper superior to such substitutes as plastics and aluminum in construction work. The transport industry is a further large-scale copper consumer. Attempts to substitute for copper in car radiators have proved commercially unsuccessful. The ease with which it can be fashioned into complicated shapes, and its superiority as a heat conductor, have so far allowed copper to remain unchallenged in this field. (Radetzki, 124)

The bulk of the world's reserves are in large deposits in copper-rich parts of the crust. About 85 percent of known reserves are in the six principal producing areas: in order of their magnitude of reserves, these are:

    (1) Andean Western Slope - Chile and Peru,
    (2) Central African Copper Belt - Zambia and Zaire,
    (3) Western United States,
    (4) Former U.S.S.R. - Ural Mountains and Kazakstan
    (5) Central Canada, and
    (6) the Lake Superior region of the U.S. and Canada. (Flawn, 307)

Other significant deposits occur in Bolivia, Cuba, Cyprus, Finland, India, Mexico, Norway, Sweden and Turkey.

A very rough estimate, by the World Bank, suggests that in 1970, the developing countries, representing about half of the world's land area, accounted for less than 40 percent of the global reserves of all minerals. This is the result not of nature, but of the unequal spread of exploration. The search for minerals has had a much lower priority in the developing world. (Flawn, 128)   As a result of the relatively thorough prospecting activities to which North America, Western

Europe and Japan have for long been exposed, as newly-discovered ore deposits are unlikely to be much above a grade of, say, 0.5 percent metal content. Not so for developing nations. (Flawn, 128) The increasing knowledge of hitherto unexplored areas in these countries is gradually revealing substantial deposits of a much richer metal content.

Projections of future copper demand which extend up to the year 2000 are found on Chart 5.3. Over the thirty year period, medium estimates put future demand rising from approximately 7 million short tons, in 1970, to approximately 18 million short tons in 2000.

Chart 5.3
Copper:
Projected Demand

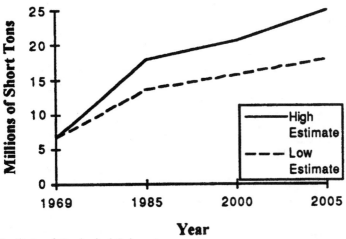

(Institute of Geological Science)

It is quite possible that the intensification of mineral exploration in developing countries will arrest or even reverse for some time the long term declining path of cut-off grades in economic copper ores. More importantly, the copper-mining industries in some developed countries could become uneconomical, and might have to be closed down, as a result of the rapidly expanding exploration activities in Africa, Asia and Latin America.

In this way, depletion of economic mineral reserves may occur on a national level. The U.S. Japan, and several European countries have already used up their best copper deposits. Careful geological surveys and mineral explorations during long periods of time make it increasingly unlikely that new high-grade deposits will be found. Given a world market price of copper, production from the remaining low-grade resources becomes increasingly uncompetitive, (Radetzki, 130) and has to be closed down to avoid losses as richer deposits are discovered and brought into exploitation in other parts of the world. (Stewardson)

Table 5.3
World Production of Copper Ore
(Thousands of Tons)

	1982	1992
World	8,067	9,236
Developing Countries	3,807	4,234
Chile	1,242	1,933
Mexico	230	291
Peru	356	369
Zaire	483	144
Zambia	567	433
Philippines	292	124
Developed Countries	2,440	3,367
Canada	613	746
Australia	245	378
Japan	51	12
S.Africa	207	198
U.S.A.	1,147	1,761
Eastern Europe	1,516	1,209
U.S.S.R.	1,010	800
Poland	376	332

(United Nations. UNCTAD Commodity Yearbook Various Issues)

Nickel

Nickel is used mainly as an alloying metal and is found in a wide variety of both producer and consumer goods, to which it imparts strength and a resistance to corrosion and heat. Total alloy use of nickel accounts for about 80 percent of all nickel consumption, with most of the remainder going to electroplating, a process in which nickel constitutes a basic material; other, nonmetallic uses of nickel are small in terms of the quantity of nickel consumed. (U.N. Doc. TD/B/C.1/172,2)

While its principal application is in ferrous metallurgy, the use of nickel is ubiquitous and growing. "Over 3,000 alloys, ferrous and non-ferrous, are at present estimated to contain nickel, in amounts varying from a mere fraction to 99 percent." (Lansberg, 306) Typical applications are as monel metal, in food processing, paper, and textile machinery; nickel silver, in plated silverware and marine hardware; nickel condenser tubes and resistance wire; Inconel, in exhaust manifolds or combustion chambers of aircraft and in chemical industry and heat-treating equipment.(Lansberg, 306) Strength, hardness, corrosion resistance, resistance to deformation at high temperatures, and pleasing appearance are among its qualities - and it often takes the addition of very little nickel to impart them. (Lansberg, 306)

As seen by Table 5.4 on the following page, the world's nickel requirements are supplied by a relatively small number of ore-producing countries and territories: Canada, the USSR, New Caledonia, Australia, Cuba and, more recently, the Dominican Republic, which together supplied nearly ninety percent of the world mine production in 1973. (U. N. Doc. TD/B/C.1/172, 3) As a group, the developing countries currently produce slightly less than one-third of the world's nickel, although they hold more than two-thirds of total land-based reserves, and are among the fastest growing ore producers.

As a group the LDC's experienced a 9.6 percent average rate of growth in nickel production between 1960-1973, as compared with a 3.8 percent growth rate for the DC's. The 9.6 percent rate for the LDC's was well above the 5.5 percent world total. These figures indicate that the LDC's are increasing their share of the world market for nickel at a rate far in excess of either the Developed Market Economies, or the Socialist Countries of E. Europe and Asia.

Entry to the nickel mining industry is limited by the large scale nature of production and by the consequently heavy initial investments required for plant and infrastructure. In addition, most of the world's nickel reserves, including nearly all reserves in developing countries, are laterite ore deposits which, while relatively easy to mine, are more complex to process and require higher energy inputs than the sulfide deposits found in temperate-zone countries. Nevertheless, as the price of nickel has more than doubled, in current terms, during the last two decades, it has become possible to produce from some of the more difficult laterite deposits and the geographical distribution has consequently altered. The developing countries and territories have markedly increased their share of world production, mainly at the expense of Canada whose share has fallen from 60 percent at the end of the 1950's to 36 percent in 1973, although Canada still remains the largest producer of nickel ore. (U. N. Doc. TD/B/C.1/172, 3)

As seen in Chart 5.4, below, nickel consumption is expected to experience a long-term pattern of growth through the year 2000. Over this period (1970-2000) demand for nickel is expected to almost triple from a 1970 total of 550,000 short tons to some 1,500,000 in 2000.

Chart 5.4
Nickel:
Projected Demand

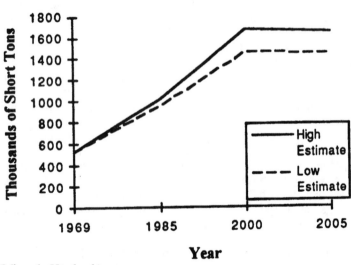

(Minerals Yearbook)

U. S. nickel consumption which is projected to rise from the 1960 level of over 100,000 tons to more than 550,000 tons in 2000, would constitute a cumulative demand of nearly 12 million tons in the 40 years. Demand in the rest of the non-communist areas of the world, if it were to grow at 6 percent (International Nickel Co) would accumulate to some twenty-five million tons, for a total of 37 million tons for the non-communist world as a whole. (Lansberg, 445)

Table 5.4
World Production of Nickel Ore
(Thousands of Tons)

	1982	1992
World	624	835
Developing Countries	219	311
Colombia	5	20
Cuba	38	30
Indonesia	42	78
Developed Countries	97	195
Canada	89	189
Australia	88	55
N. Caledonia	60	99
U.S.A.	3	6
Eastern Europe	179	183
U.S.S.R.	170	180

(United Nations. UNCTAD Commodity Yearbook Various Issues)

Cobalt

Cobalt is at present a relatively scarce, expensive metal which is nevertheless used in a wide variety of industrial products, both metallic and non-metallic. Its special properties make it particularly suited to a number of rapidly-expanding advanced technology industries, and in these uses there are few other metals which could be substituted for it. "At considerably lower prices, cobalt itself could probably be substituted for various other nonferrous metals." (U.N. Doc. TD/B/449/ADD.l, 2-37, Lansberg, 307) Cobalt has a wide variety of applications of which about three-fourths are metallic and about equally divided among three principal groups: permanent magnet alloys, high temperature steels, and a miscellany composed mostly of tool steels. (Lansberg, 307) The non-metallic uses are principally as chemicals used in the enameling of metals, in pigments, and in salts and driers. See Chart on following page.

At present U.S. production is minimal after a brief period of growth and then decline during the 1950's and 1960's, due to a period of high Government purchase contracts. Production in 1953 jumped from .7 million pounds per year (in 1948) to 1.3 million and in 1958 hit 4.8 million. When the period of stockpiling ended during the 1950's, production dropped to only .5 million tons in 1963. "In the United States, cobalt mines were viable only with Government support." (U.N. Doc. TD/B/449/ADD.l, 2) Reserves are small: 43,000 tons with an additional 107,000 tons of potential ore. (Lansberg, 451)   Even when taken together they amount to only a small part of projected use. "Forty years of consumption at 1960 levels would more than exhaust them." (Lansberg, 451, Burrows)[6]

> Although the stages of cobalt metal production are fairly straight forward (ore extraction, concentration, refining), most cobalt ore is found in conjunction with other metallic ores and in the majority of mining operations cobalt is recovered as a byproduct, mainly as an adjunct to the production of copper or nickel. In these cases the amount of cobalt recovered is largely a function of the quantities of copper or nickel produced and cobalt production cannot generally be varied independently. For Zaire, (U.N. Doc. TD/B/449/ADD.l, 5) however, although cobalt is recovered from what are essentially copper deposits, it does not appear to be, strictly speaking, a by-product. The deposits vary in cobalt content and it is possible to produce additional cobalt-bearing ores without comparable increases in copper output. (U.N. Doc. TD/B/449/ADD.l, 5)
>
> Cobalt has come into increasing use as a catalyst in the

desulfurization of petroleum and coal. This is a rapidly growing use but not one which is likely to be highly price sensitive. The use of cobalt in desulfurization catalysts depends principally on the construction of desulfurization plants. The catalyst can apparently be re processed after use. The potentials of cobalt catalysts in afterburners for automotive exhaust gases are being considered. This use could open up a large new market if the desired technical performance can be attained and if cobalt is sufficiently low in cost. The cobalt content in the catalyst would account for only a small amount per vehicle, but in view of the large numbers of cars on the road and the need to replace the catalyst after some period of use the automotive market could account for a substantial and growing demand. (U.N. Doc. TD/B(XIII)/Misc.3, 5)

Chart 5.5 illustrates an expected doubling of world cobalt demand between 1970 and 2000. Medium estimates place 2000 demand at somewhere near 44,000 short tons compared with 1970 totals of 23,000 short tons.

Chart 5.5
Cobalt:
Projected Demand

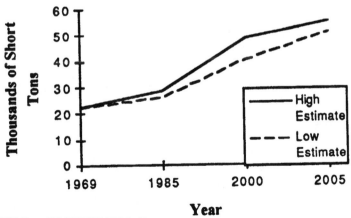

(U.N. Doc. TD/B/483/ADD.1, 3)

The principal uses of cobalt in the United States are as magnet alloys, high temperature alloys, high speed steels, and tool steels. In addition, at least 80 percent of world cobalt demand is accounted for by the United States which, as stated earlier, possesses little cobalt of any economic value.

On the whole, cobalt consumption can be expected to grow in line with the expansion in the principal end uses except where technological substitution occurs. The relatively faster rate of growth of world cobalt consumption outside the United States can largely be attributed to the faster pace of industrial growth in countries such as the EEC nations and Japan. (U.N. Doc. TD/B/483/ADD.1, 5)

Table 5.5
World Production of Cobalt Ore
(Thousands of Tons)

	1989	1992
World	29,714	24,444
Developing Countries	14,800	12,136
Brazil	200	88
Zaire	9,311	6,547
Zambia	4,488	4,610
Cuba	1,000	765
Developed Countries	7,365	6,893
Canada	6,167	5,102
Australia	1,100	1,670
N. Caledonia	165	121
Eastern Europe		
U.S.S.R.	5,600	4,400

U.N. Doc. UNCTAD Commodity Yearbook

By far, the largest use of cobalt is in nickel-base alloys for gas turbine engines. Cobalt enhances the stability of a strengthening feature in alloys called "gamma prime." These alloys are indispensable for engine vanes and blading, disks, seals, casings, shafts, and virtually all hot-section components. Replacing or modifying these alloys in the event of a disruption or severe shortage of cobalt would be possible but with performance penalties.

In addition to the use of cobalt in gamma prime alloys, cobalt-base alloys also play a large role in jet aircraft engines.

High cobalt content combustors gave the Pratt & Whitney F100 engine a 300 °F temperature advantage over other hot section alloys. Since power and speed are directly related to the turbine inlet temperature, this was a major breakthrough. The F100 is the power plant for the McDonnell Douglas F-15 fighter which has broken nearly every existing rate-of-climb record. The PWA F100 is also used on the General Dynamics F-16, air-superiority fighter. (Edwards, 126-28)

High cobalt content alloys are also used for combustors for air- and sea launched cruise missiles, auxiliary power units (APUs) and in civilian airliner engines such as the General Electric CF6-80 engine that powers many of the world's jumbo jets.

47 components of the space shuttle's main engine are made of high cobalt content alloys. Here the alloy was selected both for high-temperature resistence and for its resistance to hydrogen embrittlement at cryogenic temperatures.

While over three-quarters of the cobalt alloys used in the United States go into gas turbine engines, there are other important uses of cobalt alloys.

> Cobalt alloys also have an unsurpassed resistance to a phenomenon known as cavitation erosion. Cavitation erosion occurs on the surface of very high-speed components operating in fluids such as water, mercury and liquid sodium. The theory is that cavitation erosion is caused by tiny bubbles collapsing on the metal surface with great rapidity. One prime example of the problem is at the condensing end of steam power turbines in electric power plants. The solution for many years has been to inlay, or braze. metal sheet of a 58Co-30Cr-4W-1C alloy, on the leading edge of turbine blading. Practically every condensing-type turbine in the Western world is so outfitted. High-speed pumps and air- and hydrofoil surfaces can be protected in a similar manner. (Edwards, 128)

During the Vietnam war, helicopter main rotors and tail rotors were also fitted out with high cobalt alloy erosion shields. The cobalt alloy protected the metal from the scouring of abrasive propwash when the copters landed and took off from unpaved strips in remote areas. Unprotected rotors usually failed in less than 500 hours in this service, but the cobalt alloy gave many times this life.

An interesting sidelight that illustrates the strategic importance of cobalt alloys occurred in 1966. With a shortage of these erosion shields imminent in December of that year because of a strike at the Kokomo plant, President Johnson invoked the Taft-Hartley Act to order management and workers back on the job to assure a continuing supply of these and other alloy helicopter components. Historically, this is the only instance where action of this nature was taken. (Edwards, 129)

Other Uses for Manganese Nodules

Manganese nodules, in addition to being a direct source of raw manganese, copper, nickel, and cobalt have economic potential as a commodity in their natural state.

Flue Gas Desulfurization

In 1967, the U.S. Patent Office issued a patent to the Kennecott Corporation for a process in which manganese nodules were used to remove sulfur dioxide effluent from flue gas with a 98 percent or greater efficiency. In 1972, Stanford University conducted a study for the EPA investigating the sulfation kinetics of various porous solid materials for use as dry sorbents of sulfur dioxide in flue gases. This study included the examination of Blake Plateau manganese nodules, noting an extremely high unit surface area (170m2/g) available for sorption. At temperatures and pressures typical of power plant flues, the nodules were successful in achieving high sorption rates of sulfur dioxide, with complete sulfation of the primary constituents.

Additional findings of the Stanford University study concerned the extraction of metals from the completely sulfated nodules. Although metallurgical processing of nodules in their oxide form is complex, the sulfated compounds are amenable to metals extraction by traditional metallurgical procedures. During the study, boiling water was used to leach completely sulfated nodules, resulting in the extraction of 97 percent of the cobalt, 82 percent of the nickel, and 99 percent of the copper. The experimental work by Stanford University provides a sound chemical basis for the use of manganese nodules in dry sorption flue gas desulfurization, with the added possibility of the economic extraction of metal byproducts. (NOAA. Workshop Report 1994, 31-35)

Additional Economic Possibilities

Another possible application for the manganese nodules would be the development of secondary filters for the removal of nitrogen oxide from effluent of coal-fired power plants. Nitrogen oxides are a major pollutant resulting from combustion of fossil fuels and a primary contributor to acid rain. Secondary filters would consist of ground nodules (manganese oxide) saturated with chlorine dioxide. The chlorine dioxide would act as an oxidizing agent, yielding NO2 when added to NO and making absorption more efficient. A final backup electrostatic filter and possible dust collector cyclone could be considered for retention of any fine particulate metals.

Other options worthy of further study are based on industry investigations of the late 1960s and 1970s. Of particular interest to industry was the fact that the manganese nodules can be used in their natural state, as they have a very high porosity and require little processing. Mobil Research and Development Corporation conducted experiments on Pacific Ocean nodules (similar in composition to Blake Plateau nodules) to determine the effectiveness of the material as an oxidation catalyst for reducing combustible trace materials in automobile emissions. Crushed nodule particles sized at 16-20 mesh were tested against commercially available CuO and Pt/Al2O3 catalysts and were found in all cases to have activities greater than the commercial oxidation catalysts. Reynolds Aluminum Company expressed an interest for using Blake Plateau nodules for the removal of unwanted metals and sulfur from crude petroleum. The nodules have a limited useful life as a desulfurization or demetallization material, experiencing a loss of activity as they take up metals and sulfur. Nevertheless, they take up significant amounts of metals of value and could be processed for the recovery of such commodities as cobalt, nickel, molybdenum, and vanadium. (NOAA. Workshop Report 1994, 31-35)

---

[5] Owing to higher industrial growth rates and a smaller resource base, the nations of Western Europe and Japan are considerably worse off in these terms.

[6] "Ample cobalt reserves exist in the laterite ores of Cuba, together with nickel and chromium, but the program to exploit these ores has received a serious setback through the Castro revolution. Nevertheless, in the perspective of four decades the 370,000 tons of cobalt estimated to be contained in Cuban deposits of reasonably commercial quality, and another 700,000 tons in low grade ores (between 0.07 and 0.1 percent cobalt content) are bound to have an effect on availability." (Lansberg, 451)

Chapter Six

Resource Wealth of Deep Seabed Areas

> If it [the United States] signs a treaty like the present draft,
> American companies can be expected to cut their losses and
> either get out of this business altogether, or to rent out their
> technology to the new masters of the seabed, as oil companies
> do in the OPEC countries. But while individual companies can
> save themselves to some extent in this manner, the American
> public cannot. The hard minerals of the deep seabed offer our
> last chance to convert a resource, discovered and produced by
> American technology, into a reserve of critical minerals, free of
> foreign domination. One OPEC is enough. (Ely 1982, 31)

Resource Shortages and National Responses

If, in fact, there will be shortages of certain commodities vital to
industry in the future, what will be the likely U.S. response to such
scarcities? The options open to the United States in such an eventuality
are twofold. They are to: reduce their consumption of these materials
by recycling, inhibiting the nation's rate of growth, or by decreasing
the nation's living standard; or the problem can be either avoided or
solved by an expansion of the nation's overall resource base. This
second alternative can be accomplished through the development of
substitutes or the securing of alternative sources of supply for the
resources which have become, or are becoming inaccessible.

Since a reduction in either a nation's growth rate or living standard
are the most remote owing to a myriad of economic, social and
political implications, and since recycling alone cannot possibly solve
the massive problem of resource scarcities, the most likely alternative

to be pursued will be to develop alternative sources of supply through the expansion of the nation's overall resource base. As explained earlier, this is not a novel answer to such a problem, but rather, one that has been used throughout the ages to enhance a nation's economic or political position. Unfortunately, in the past, it has almost invariably been accomplished through the use of warfare or some other act whereby one nation either dominates or annexes portions of another's territory in order to achieve its objectives.

What makes the current era unique, is that owing to massive technological achievements in numerous fields, we are now on the verge of an expansionist period into uninhabited and unclaimed areas - an expansion which promises the potential of achievement without the unpleasantness of direct human suffering, characteristic of national, tribal, or territorial expansion throughout history.

Future U.S. shortages of certain commodities are expected, not by the cutoff of foreign supplies, but rather by economic inaccessibility due to rising prices. The possibility of very large price increases arbitrarily imposed through the political actions of resource-rich countries can only be reduced if alternatives are available to the user. In recent years, it has become apparent that the most likely alternative that the U.S., Western Europe, and Japan will opt for in quest of a more stable mineral supply will be to exploit the vast potential mineral wealth represented in the form of manganese nodules on the ocean floor. As shown in Table 7, with the exception of copper, the oceans possess greater reserves of the four principal nodule metals than can be found on land.

Table 6.1
Distribution of Metal Resources: Ocean vs. Land

Metal	Ocean (%)	Land (%)
Manganese	56.4	43.6
Copper	31	69
Nickel	83.8	16.2
Cobalt	95.2	4

(Singh 1994, 19)

Manganese nodules generally range in size between 0.5 - 25 cm in diameter, but average about 3 cm if those nodules which have no nucleus or only a relatively small one are considered.

This apparent size range may be somewhat influenced by the sampling devices that have been used to recover the nodules. No object much larger than 1 ft. in diameter can enter the 1x3 Ft. mouth of the chain bag dredge and nodules less than 1 cm. in diameter would tend to filter through the openings in the net of the dredge. (Mero 1965, 132)

Manganese nodules are formed by the precipitation of metallic compounds from solution and the process of particle agglomeration. The mechanism is believed to be one of precipitation of electrically charged, hydrated iron and manganese oxide from saturated sea water. These charged particles then attract other metal ions from the water and attach themselves to objects such as shark's teeth or rock fragments on the ocean floor to form manganese nodule nuclei. A continuous supply of charged colloidal particles allows the nuclei to grow, layer by layer, until they are buried in sediment at which time growth ceases. Deep ocean currents play an important role in nodule development as they are responsible for bringing colloidal materials into the areas of deposition and sweeping sediment from or over nodule surfaces, enhancing or retarding accretion. (Bollow, 30)

As seen in the following photographs, the nodules are irregular in shape, and knobbly and round like potatoes.

Figure 6.1
Manganese Nodules

(Welling 1976, 7)

Figure 6.2
Nodules on the Sea Floor

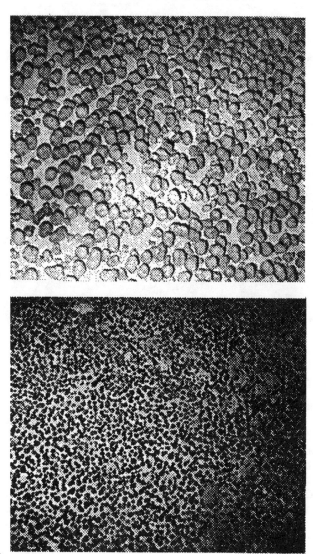

(Welling 1976, 8)

Figure 6.3
Nodules on Deck

(Government of Japan, DOMA, 7)

The composition of the nodules varies greatly according to the areas of the ocean in which they are found. For example, nodules found in the area off of New Zealand have a high concentration of iron as compared to those with a high nickel content found off the western coast of Mexico. The following map illustrates the location of these nodules, while the chart immediately following gives the mineral breakdown of the nodules by area. For the purposes of this study, the minerals: copper, manganese, nickel and cobalt, are the most important as they form the largest percentage of the nodule's mass, and since they are the minerals most likely to be sought after though the commercial recovery of the nodules. (Mero 1965, 161)

Figure 6.4
Nodule Distribution in the Pacific Ocean

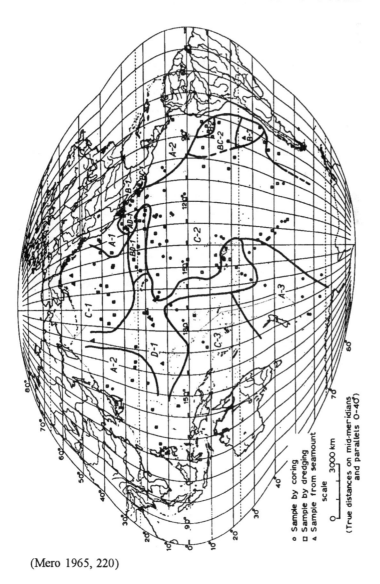

(Mero 1965, 220)

Nodule Distribution in the Pacific Ocean

Figure 6.4 shows the compositional regions of the manganese nodules in the Pacific Ocean. "Nodules from the 'A' regions are high in iron; from the 'B' regions, high in manganese; from the 'C' regions, high in nickel and copper; from the 'D' regions, high in cobalt. Also indicated on this map are the locations of points where samples of nodules have been obtained on which chemical analyses have been performed." (Mero 1965, 226)

As seen in column 3 of Table 6.2, the potential of manganese nodules as a long term source of supply for the minerals under study is tremendous. Mero in dividing the mineral content of the nodules by the 1960 rate of world consumption arrives at figures which indicate a 400,000 year supply of manganese, 200,000 year supply of cobalt, 150,000 year supply of nickel, and a 6,000 year supply of copper. Of course these figures are based on 1960 data and assume that the exploitation of all manganese nodules is economically and technically feasible. In addition, column 7 estimates the rate of accumulation of the nodules in millions of tons per year. This column is particularly interesting if looked at in conjunction with column 8. These two columns indicate that, using 1960 U.S. consumption figures as a measure, manganese in the nodule is accumulating at a rate three times the U.S. consumption rate, indicating that at 1960 rates of use the supply of manganese from these nodules is inexhaustible. As far as the other minerals are concerned, cobalt accumulation is 4.5 times consumption, nickel equal to consumption, and copper only .05 of consumption.

Table 6.2
Metal Content of Mn Nodules

METAL CONTENT AND RATIO STATISTICS OF THE VARIOUS COMPOSITIONAL REGIONS OF MANGANESE NODULES IN THE PACIFIC OCEAN

Region	Statistic	Reduced weight percentages						Mn/Fe	Weight percentage ratios			
		Mn	Fe	Co	Ni	Cu	Pb		Mn/Ni	Mn/Pb	Ni/Cu	Fe/Co
A	Maximum	35.6	39.5	0.82	0.91	0.61	0.40	1.25	94.3	420	5.0	517
	Minimum	7.6	19.7	0.06	0.08	0.07	0.047	0.22	30.0	21	0.46	37
	Average	21.7	28.3	0.35	0.46	0.32	0.21	0.79	53.8	146	2.21	168
AD	Maximum¹ Minimum	22.3	26.4	0.69	0.30	0.43	0.28	0.85	74.4	80	0.68	38
	Average											
B	Maximum	57.1	3.5	0.20	0.83	0.43	0.089	61.8	870	9,500	5.7	318
	Minimum	40.6	1.1	0.008	0.06	0.013	0.006	11.6	69	540	1.0	7
	Average	49.8	2.3	0.055	0.26	0.14	0.047	29.8	356	2,200	3.0	106
BC	Maximum	50.4	13.5	0.36	2.18	1.40	0.12	9.87	45.8	3,360	1.92	185
	Minimum	40.0	5.1	0.045	1.52	0.72	0.038	2.82	18.7	333	1.42	37
	Average	43.6	10.7	0.15	1.67	0.04	0.070	4.94	28.2	1,178	1.61	103
C	Maximum	45.3	25.8	0.75	2.37	2.92	0.52	6.21	59.4	608	2.58	260
	Minimum	15.0	7.3	0.076	0.54	0.44	0.049	0.97	11.3	51	0.64	19
	Average	33.3	17.7	0.39	1.52	1.13	0.18	2.14	23.7	261	1.51	60
CD	Maximum	38.3	24.4	1.22	1.94	1.46	0.54	3.41	45.5	860	1.74	38
	Minimum	23.4	10.1	0.47	0.59	0.34	0.04	1.09	15.9	43	0.97	8
	Average	31.7	17.5	0.69	1.45	1.09	0.29	1.96	25.4	201	1.36	27
D	Maximum	33.2	27.4	2.09	0.97	0.39	0.41	1.84	65.0	232	6.1	39
	Minimum	20.2	16.6	0.70	0.37	0.13	0.10	0.90	27.7	60	1.4	8
	Average	28.5	22.6	1.21	0.66	0.21	0.30	1.31	45.6	109	3.4	22
Statistics on all the samples	Maximum	57.1	39.5	2.09	2.37	2.92	0.54	61.8	870	9,500	6.1	517
	Minimum	7.6	1.1	0.008	0.06	0.013	0.006	0.22	11.3	21	0.46	8
	Average	32.4	18.5	0.47	1.14	0.80	0.19	4.11	60.0	431	1.95	74

¹ Only one sample point in region AD-1.

(Mero 1965, 227)

Table 6.3
Reserves of Metals in Mn Nodules

RESERVES OF METALS IN MANGANESE NODULES OF THE PACIFIC OCEAN

Element	Amount of element in nodules (billions of tons)[1]	Reserves in nodules at consumption rate of 1960 (years)[2]	Approximate world land reserves of element (years)[3]	Ratio of reserves in nodules/ reserves on land	U.S. rate of consumption of element in 1960 (millions of tons/year)[4]	Rate of accumulation of element in nodules (millions of tons/year)	Ratio of rate of accumulation/ rate of U.S. consumption	Ratio of world consumption/ U.S. consumption
Mg	25.0	600,000	L[6]	—	0.04	0.18	4.5	2.5
Al	43.0	20,000	100	200	2.0	0.30	0.15	2.0
Ti	9.9	2,000,000	L	—	0.30	0.069	0.23	4.0
V	0.8	400,000	L	—	0.002	0.0056	2.8	4.0
Mn	358.0	400,000	100	4,000	0.8	2.5	3.0	8.0
Fe	207.0	2,000	500[5]	4	100.0	1.4	0.01	2.5
Co	5.2	200,000	40	5,000	0.008	0.036	4.5	2.0
Ni	14.7	150,000	100	1,500	0.11	0.102	1.0	3.0
Cu	7.9	6,000	40	150	1.2	0.055	0.05	4.0
Zn	0.7	1,000	100	10	0.9	0.0048	0.005	3.5
Ga	0.015	150,000	—	—	0.0001	0.0001	1.0	—
Zr	0.93	100,000	100	1,000	0.0013	0.0065	5.0	2.0
Mo	0.77	30,000	500	60	0.025	0.0054	0.2	—
Ag	0.001	100	100	1	0.006	0.00003	0.005	
Pb	1.3	1,000	40	50	1.0	0.009	0.0009	2.5

[1] All tonnages in metric units.
[2] Amount available in the nodules divided by the consumption rate.
[3] Calculated as the element in metric tons. (U. S. BUREAU OF MINES STAFF, 1956).
[4] Calculated as the element in metric tons.
[5] Including deposits of iron that are at present considered marginal.
[6] Present reserves so large as to be essentially unlimited at present rates of consumption.

(Mero 1965, 228)

The area of greatest commercial interest lies in the Clarion/Clipperton Fracture Zone in the eastern-Pacific in a belt stretching from southeast of Hawaii to an area approaching Baja, California. Nodules in this area have particularly high concentrations of nickel and cobalt and would prove the most lucrative to mine. Numerous claims to mine sites in this area have been filed with national governments and/or the International Seabed Authority's Preparatory Commission. At present, seven nations have filed claims within the Clarion/Clipperton Zone, they are: U.S., Germany, Japan, France, the United Kingdom, South Korea, and the People's Republic of China.

Figure 6.5
Nodule Mining Area

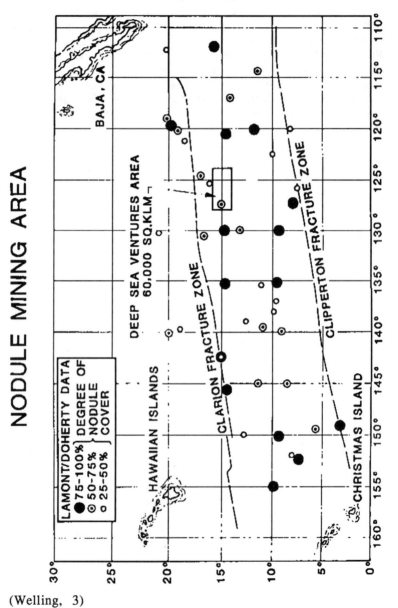

(Welling, 3)

Figure 6.6
Mine Site Claims Map

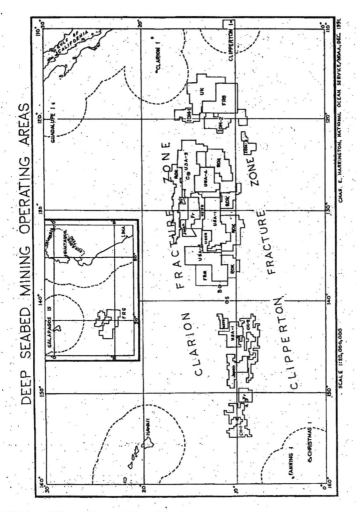

(NOAA. Office of Ocean Minerals)

Mineral Resources and Reserves

A general classification for describing the status of mineral occurrences was developed by the U.S. Geological Survey and the U.S. Bureau of Mines in 1976. The so-called "McKelvey Box" named after the then director of the USGS. Vincent McKelvey, further simplified the understanding of the economic relationships of the mineral-resource classification system:

Figure 6.7
McKelvey Box

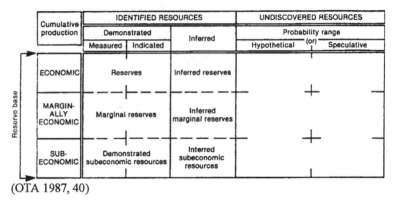

(OTA 1987, 40)

The system is based on the judgmental determination of present or anticipated future value of the minerals in place according to the opinions of experts. Below are the economic definitions on which the resource classification system is based:

Resource: Naturally occurring mineral of a form and amount that economic extraction of a commodity is potentially feasible.

Identified Resource: Resources whose location and characteristics are known or reliably estimated.

Demonstrated Resource: Resources whose location and characteristics have been measured directly with some certainty *(measured)* or estimated with less certainty *(indicated)*.

Inferred Resource: Resources estimated from assumptions and evidence that minerals may occur beyond where resources have been measured or located.

Reserve Base: Part of an *identified* resource that meets the economic, chemical and physical requirements that would allow it to be mined, including that which is estimated from geological knowledge (inferred reserve *base).*

Reserves: Part of the reserve *base* that could be economically extracted at the time of determination.

Marginal Reserves: Part of the *reserve base* that at the time of determination borders on being economically producible.

Undiscovered Resources: Resources whose existence is only postulated.

Under this scheme, manganese nodules would currently fall into the category of *Reserve Base* but with a political climate and price structure conducive to commercial operations nodules would quickly reclassified as *Reserves.*

Manganese Nodule Research and Development

Although shallow marine (Baltic Sea) and lake ferromanganese nodules have been known for hundreds of years, deep sea nodules were unknown until they were dredged at many sites throughout the world ocean during the H.M.S. *Challenger* Expedition (1872-1876). J.Y. Buchanan, the expedition chemist, must be credited with being the first person to recognize the commercial possibilities of manganese nodules. In a letter to his father he wrote: "Manganese is a mineral of great commercial importance and it is one of the principal substances used in the manufacture of bleaching powder and although of course the bottom of the sea at present could never be made a paying source of supply, its occurrence there with the certainty of having been formed there may turn out to be an important fact in geology." (Glasby 1977, 1-9)

> But after the initial excitement generated by the discovery of nodules, scientific interest in them waned, and they received only sporadic attention for the next 80 years. The principal exceptions to this relative neglect were provided by Agassiz, who reported limits of nodule occurrence in the eastern equatorial Pacific, based on dredging during *Albatross* expeditions, and Pettersson (1943, 1945), who considered the source of metals in nodules and their rate of accumulation.

> However, published research has accumulated at an increasing rate during the past two decades, and in particular the past five years. Expanded oceanographic research subsequent to World

War II, along with the International Geophysical Year (1957-58) spurred renewed interest in manganese nodules. Pioneering studies by Russian scientists (e.g., Bezrukov, 1960; and Skornyakova, et al., 1962), by representatives of the Scripps Institute of Oceanography (e.g., Goldberg, 1954; Dietz, 1955; Arrhenius, 1963; and Menard, 1964) and by John Mero (see below) were among the initial results of this renewed interest. The recent acceleration of nodule research, such as that sponsored by the State of Hawaii Office of the Marine Affairs Coordinator, NOAA-Sea Grant, and NSF-International Decade of Ocean Exploration, as well as the formation of deepsea mining consortia, can be attributed to a possibility repeatedly emphasized by Mero, i.e., certain deposits of marine nodules appear economically attractive as metal ores. Much of the recent research has been directed toward an understanding of the origin of nodules. (State of Hawaii 1978, A-1)

Origins of Ocean Mining

In late 1962, began a study of the hardware aspects of nodule exploitation. Less than two years later they acquired a vessel and converted it to the R/V *Prospector* to be used for nodule exploration. The man in charge of the Newport News Shipbuilding and Dry Dock Co. efforts in the field of marine mining was Jack Flipse, and he become president of the corporate subsidiary known as Deepsea Ventures when Tenneco acquired NNSDDC in 1968. Kennecott Copper also began studies of nodule mining in 1962, recovering 10 tons of nodules for their initial assessment work.

Several other industrial groups became actively interested in deep ocean mining within a few years after the initial NNSDDC and Kennecott studies. John Mero founded Ocean Resources, Inc. in 1965, and shortly thereafter began cooperative studies with Japanese groups. During 1968, the year in which Deepsea Ventures became a corporate entity, the International Nickel Co. (Inco) is reported to have begun feasibility studies of nodule mining. The following year, 1969, West German commercial interest in nodules began. Summa Corp., with Lockheed and Global Marine, commenced its own program in the same year, later to be revealed as a guise for attempts to recover a sunken Russian submarine, although genuine nodule research was carried out simultaneously. French groups, most prominently CNEXO (Centre National pour l'Exploitation des Océans), entered the field of marine mining in 1970.

Two types of mining systems (bucket dredging and airlifting) have undergone preliminary testing. The first test of the continuous line bucket dredge (CLB) system was conducted by a Japanese group in shallow water near Japan during 1968. Two more CLB tests during

1970 in water depths up to 3,600 m were followed in 1972 by a partially successful large scale test aboard the *Kyokuyo Maru No. 2* in water depths around 4,500 m in the northeastern Equatorial Pacific. Deepsea Ventures reported that during the summer of 1970 it had successfully tested a prototype airlift mining system in water depths approaching 1,000 meters on the Blake Plateau (LaMotte, 1970), after having tested the system in 250 meters of water in a flooded Virginia mine shaft during August, 1969. Deepsea Ventures tested a larger scale airlift system with *Deepsea Miner II* in 1,000 meters of water off Southern California during June, 1977, and in November of 1977 began testing components of the system in the deep waters of their claim area west of Mexico. The *SEDCO 445* of the Inco consortium commenced at-sea testing in November, 1977.

Figure 6.8
Three Basic Ocean Mining Systems

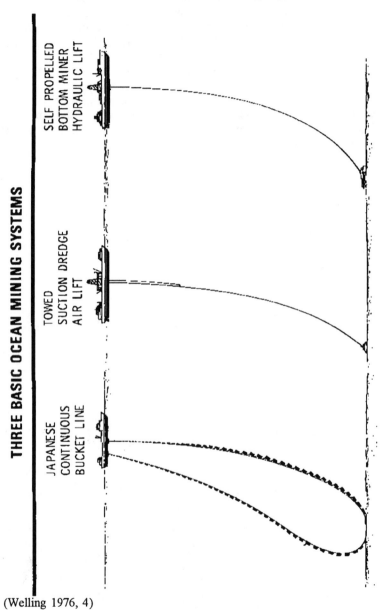

(Welling 1976, 4)

Figure 6.9
Two Major Ocean Mining Concepts

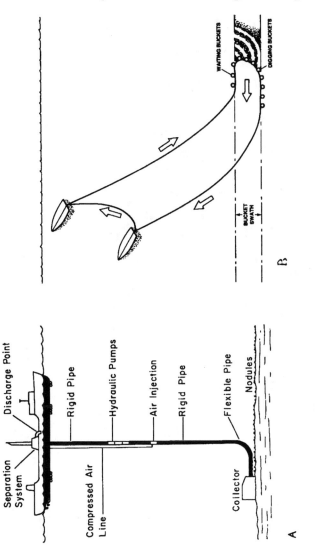

Figure 24.—Diagrams of two major mining systems. (A) Hydraulic pumping and compressed air lifting (both have been used) (Burns, et al. 1980); (B) continuous line bucket (conceptualized by NOAA).

Figure 6.10
German Bottom Crawler - Front

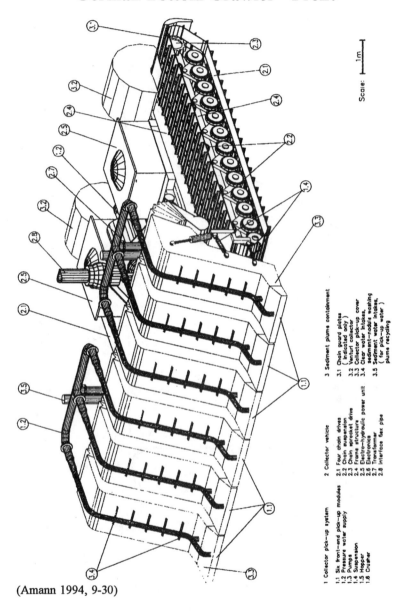

(Amann 1994, 9-30)

Figure 6.11
German Bottom Crawler - Rear

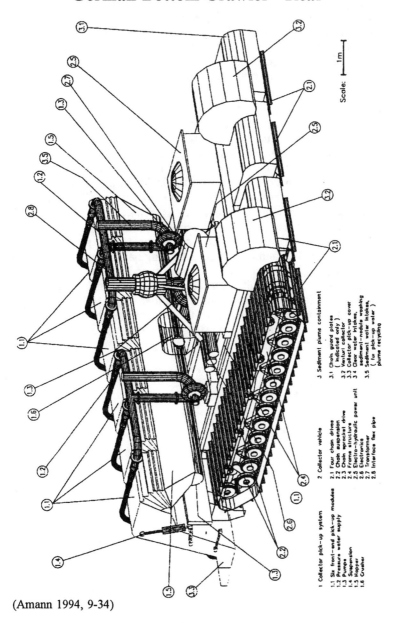

(Amann 1994, 9-34)

Both Deepsea Ventures and Kennecott have successfully operated pilot processing plants for separation of metals from nodules. Taylor (1971) reported that Deepsea Ventures had operated a processing plant in Gloucester, Virginia, with a throughput of one ton of nodules per day. Kennecott is reported to have operated three processing pilot plants (Rothstein and Kaufman, 1973). Inco and Lockheed have also investigated metal separation techniques.

Nodule Mining Technology

Several enterprises in Japan, North America and Western Europe are at different stages of design and testing of nodule mining systems. At present the most advanced mining system has been developed by the Hughes Tool Company and is embodied in the Glomar Explorer.

The Hughes system operates on the hydrolift principle. The major components of the system are the 36,000 ton Hughes Glomar Explorer and a seafloor mining vehicle which is connected to the ship by a string of 16 inch pipe and an umbilical cable that supplies electric power and control circuits. A large submersible barge plays a key role in the system. The mining vehicle is too large and heavy to be handled by the ship's gear in a conventional manner and must be installed from beneath the ship. The unit is loaded onto the submersible barge which meets the ship in calm waters of a specified depth. There, the barge submerges and the docking legs of the ship engage the mining vehicle which is then connected to pipe string lowered from the ship's rugged derrick. (Ocean Science 1974, 1)

Figure 6.12
Heavy Lift Capabilities

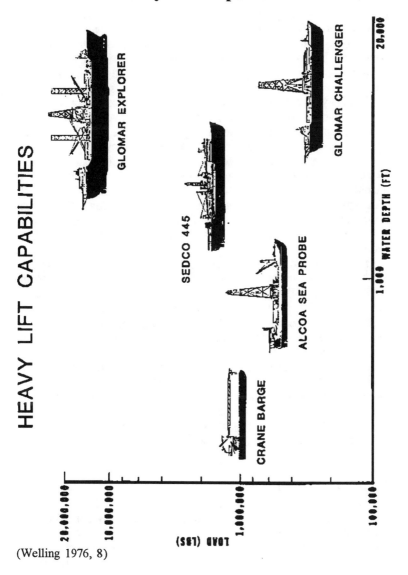

(Welling 1976, 8)

Further developmental work was undertaken on the airlift system developed by Deepsea Ventures. The Demag Co., of Germany, designed a hydraulic mining system which could operate at water depths up to 15,000 feet. This system would have a pumping station, engine room and primary nodule processing facilities installed in a 22 meter long submerged compartment. The nodules would be collected from the seafloor by special equipment mounted on crawlers and pumped up to an intermediary submerged processing station from where they would be lifted to the mining ship. (Ocean Industry 1971, 18; U.N. Doc. A/AC 138/73, 7) Aside from the hydrolift system, the other system which shows the most promise is the Continuous Line Bucket (CLB method) which is depicted on the following page.

This system was conceived and developed by Commander Yoshio Masuda of Japan. It consists of a continuous loop of cable to which is attached a series of dredge buckets. The loop of cable is sufficiently long that it is able to reach from a surface vessel and down to the ocean floor. It was tested during the summer of 1970 at several depths (up to 3,500 m) in locations near Tahiti where nodule deposits had been found.

The production capacity of the CLB system is a function of the size of the buckets, the spacing of the buckets on the dredge cable, the velocity at which the cable loop is operated and the filling efficiency of the buckets. The filling efficiency of the buckets depends on their design and on operational conditions, namely, the lateral velocity of the surface ship in relation to the vertical velocity of the cable and the length of line with attached buckets is allowed to drag on the ocean floor. The appropriate operational practice (i.e., synchronization of cable speed, lateral ship velocity and bucket drag on the sea floor), is intended to prevent the buckets from passing over the same area of the sea floor continuously. The results of the 1970 tests seem to indicate that filling efficiency could be maintained at over 50 per cent of bucket capacity with appropriate operational practice. (U.N. Doc. A/AC 138/73, 7)

Metallurgical Processing

For some time, the processing of nodules was thought to be an even more difficult problem to solve than the recovery of nodules from the ocean floor. In the last few years, however, several announcements have been made indicating that a number of different procedures for the economic extraction of metals from nodules have been successfully tested.

The most promising of these various processes is being carried out by Deepsea Ventures. Deepsea Ventures is continuing developmental work on a hydrometallurgical process which was tested in 1971 in a 1-ton/day pilot plant. The company is reported to be preparing additional process tests on a 10-ton/day pilot plant. The process starts with the crushing and drying of the nodules to expose a larger surface area to promote reactiveness. The ground nodules are then reacted with hydrogen chloride in furnaces, and the soluble metal chlorides are subsequently leached with water. The leach liquor is then processed with solvent extraction liquids to separate copper, cobalt and nickel, which are recovered by electrolytic precipitation. The remaining manganese chloride solution is stripped of residual metals such as cadmium, zinc and chromium, and then converted into manganese metal. (Caldwell 1971, 54-55) High rates of metal recovery - over 95 percent - are claimed for this purpose.

The U.S. Bureau of Mines Research Station at Salt Lake City has announced the successful experimental processing of nodules by an acid and ammonia leaching system. High recoveries of all metals in the nodules was achieved in this rather conventional approach to nodule processing. The Kennecott Copper Co., after some 10 years of research on all aspects of nodule mining and processing indicated the development of a pyrometallurgical process technique. Although pyrometallurgical processes generally involve rather high investment and operational costs, recovery of nickel, cobalt and copper in the Kennecott process is reported to be above 90 percent. (U.N. Doc. A/AC 138/73, 9)

Additional experimental work is underway at the University of California at Berkley, to develop a technique of differential leaching of metals from nodules. "This oxide heap leaching process permits the separation of nickel, copper and cobalt without getting either manganese or iron into the solution." (U.N. Doc. A/AC 138/73, 9)

This process would allow nodule processing with comparatively lower initial plant capital and operating costs than that required by the previously mentioned processes. To date these experiments have permitted the recovery of only 60 percent to 80 percent of the metal content in the nodules, but it is hoped that further development might increase processing efficiency. (U.N. Doc. A/AC 138/73, 9)

Chapter Seven

Effect of Nodule Exploitation on Current and Future Markets

Much concern has been expressed over the effect that large scale mining of manganese nodules will have on the prices of constituent metals. Because of the disparity between the ratio of constituent metals in the nodules and the ratio of their world demands, this concern is warranted. With many different groups of nodules available the extent of the disparity will be dependent on the type of nodule mined. In order to determine the effect that extensive exploitation of manganese nodules may have on future prices of the constituent metals, one must compare expected metal yields with actual world production. Chart 7.1 depicts the relative dollar value of nodules over time while Charts 7.1-7.5 show anticipated yields from increments of one million tons of mined nodules as a percent of world metal production.[7] The data which follows includes metal contents from average assays of these nodules, plus the composition of nodules from the proposed Deepsea Ventures' mine site. Dollar values of metal yield per ton of nodules are also shown. All figures assume a 98 percent processing yield figure claimed by Deepsea Ventures. (Taylor 1971, 27-38)

Chart 7.1
Value of a Ton of Nodules
(In Constant Dollars and Francs)

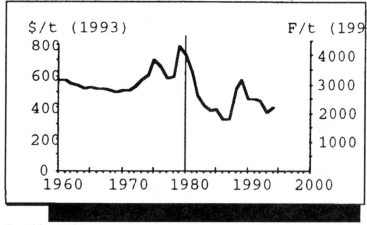

(Lenoble, 4-15)

Projected Constituent Metal Demand

Table 7.1 shows that nodules with high copper and nickel or high cobalt content are the most lucrative commercially at current market prices. High manganese content nodules, on the other hand, are typically poorer in the other metals and have the lowest commercial value of the types shown.

Table 7.1
Dollar Value of Nodule Types

Metal	1992 Price p/lb. $	High Mn %	High Ni & Cu %	High Co %	Deepsea Ventures %
Mn	.13	.50	.33	.29	.26
Cu	1.21	.026	.015	0.07	.013
Ni	6.15	.014	.011	0.02	.01
Co	22.25	.006	.004	.012	.024
$ per Ton		189	474	627	332

(Hoagland, 293 and Mero 1965, 227)

Metal Content and Values of Nodule Types

According to these estimates, high cobalt content nodules ($627 p/ton) are the most valuable at current market prices but as will be seen, the introduction of oceanic derived cobalt should be expected to result in a drastic lowering of the price of cobalt. Due to a more stable price structure for nickel and copper, these nodules high in these minerals should be the most valuable in the long run, with an expected price of $474 per ton of nodules. This is compared with high manganese nodules bringing an expected price of just $189 per ton.

The following charts (7.2-7.5) illustrate the possible impact on current and future markets that various nodule mining scenarios would entail. These graphs highlight the effects of harvesting the various classifications of nodules in particular years, by the magnitude of mining operations, and by their mineral yield as a percent of total demand for the selected years. These graphs are very useful in relating gross effects of nodule exploitation operations for illustrative purposes.

For example, as seen in Chart 7.2 (manganese yield), given a productive capacity of 15 million tons of nodules from the proposed Deepsea Venture's mine site in 1985 approximately 45 percent of world manganese demand can be satisfied from this one production area. If given the same production scenario, high manganese content nodules are mined, then approximately 90 percent of 1985 world demand can be satisfied. Although the mining of high manganese nodules is unlikely owing to their lower dollar value, viz. other types of nodules, almost any production scenario entails disruptive effects on the world manganese market.

The effects that nodule mining would have on the world copper market would be quite different from the case of manganese production. For example, even if 25 million tons of high copper content nodules are extracted in 1985, oceanic supplies would account for only 2.5 percent of world demand. This is due to the much smaller incidence of copper occurrence in the nodules, between .07 and 1.46 percent of the nodules' mass as compared with a 7.6 - 57.1 percent for manganese.

Nickel Yield

The impact of oceanic-derived nickel on the world nickel market is quite similar to the manganese scenario. If high nickel and copper nodules were mined at the rate of 15 million tons per year at projected 1985 rates of consumption, then nodules would have accounted for approximately 30 percent of world demand. Due to expected increases in world demand for nickel in the year 2000, it would take a mining rate of 25 million tons per year to retain that 30 percent market share. In spite of the rapid increases expected in nickel demand (Figure 7.4), nodule exploitation will result in a serious alteration of the traditional sources of supply.

Cobalt Yield

The cobalt market will suffer the most extreme disruptions owing to the exploitation of cobalt bearing manganese nodules. Due to the relatively high occurrence of cobalt in nodules of all types, a rate of occurrence much greater than any projected increase in world demand, any mining scenario will create a glut of cobalt on the world market and is likely to result in the lowering of the world market price of cobalt.

As seen in Chart 7.5, if high nickel and copper nodules are recovered at a rate of 15 million tons per year in 1985, over 400 percent of world demand for cobalt in that year would have been provided for as a by-product of nickel and copper exploitation.

It appears that the scenario which the investors in nodule mining technology expect to develop is one where terrestrial mining will not expand as rapidly as world demand and that the introduction of nodules into the world market will not have a great affect on metal prices. The underlying assumption is that the nodules will serve to supply only a portion of the world's greater mineral needs and the result of nodule mining will be to maintain constant prices in order to preserve the economic desirability of the nodules. Another basic assumption is that nodule mining is characterized by constant returns to scale owing to the vast untapped potential of the seabed and to the favorable occurrence of the nodules. This is quite different from the case of terrestrial mining where depletion is a very real constraining factor.

It is clear that all constituent metals, with the exception of cobalt will fit into this scenario. And it appears certain that copper will fit particularly well as a ten million ton per year recovery capacity, could satisfy a maximum of only 1 percent of 1985 demand.

As seen in Charts 7.2-7.5, seabed mineral production can be expected to displace a considerable proportion of land-based mineral supplies which currently account for 100 percent of world mineral demand.

Chart 7.2
Theoretical Impact of Ocean Mining as a
Percentage of Manganese Demand

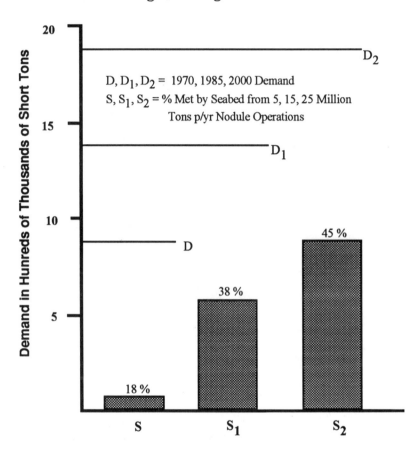

Chart 7.2 illustrates the effect of nodule sources on the focus of manganese supplies for the years 1985 and 2000. If 15 million tons from the proposed Deepsea Venture's mine site were recovered in 1985, 38 percent of world demand for that year would have been met by oceanic sources. If 25 million tons per year are recovered in 2000, despite increases in demand, the market share will rise to 45 percent.

Figures for 1970 are only meant as comparative indicators to further illustrate this relationship.

Chart 7.3
Theoretical Impact of Ocean Mining as a
Percentage of Copper Demand

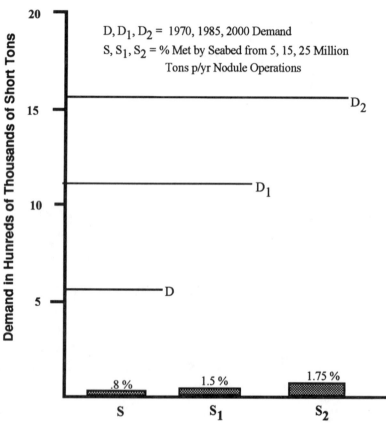

As seen in Chart 7.3, the copper market will experience virtually no effects due to the introduction of nodule derived copper into the world market. As stated earlier, this is due to the reduced magnitude of copper occurrence in the nodules compared with world demand, a situation very different to that of manganese as seen on the preceding pages.

Chart 7.4 illustrates the increasing role of oceanic nickel in the overall world nickel market. The trends shown in these charts are quite similar to those which characterized the manganese market spoken of earlier. Although the impact will not be as extreme as in the case of manganese, nickel from nodules can be expected to supply 24 percent of 1985 demand and 27 percent of 2000 demand according to the mining scenarios envisioned here.

Chart 7.4
Theoretical Impact of Ocean Mining as a
Percentage of Nickel Demand

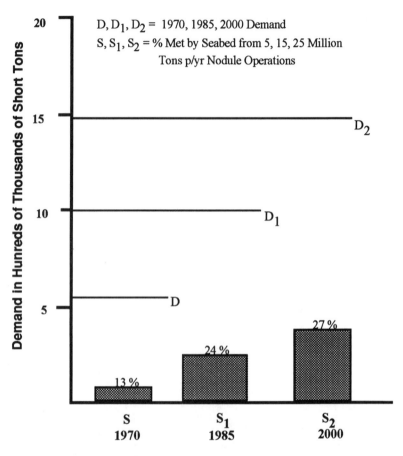

D, D_1, D_2 = 1970, 1985, 2000 Demand
S, S_1, S_2 = % Met by Seabed from 5, 15, 25 Million
      Tons p/yr Nodule Operations

Chart 7.5 reveals that the market which will suffer the greatest disruptions will be the cobalt market. Given a 15 million tons per year mining capacity, in 1985, the Deepsea Venture's mine site alone would have supplied some 225 percent of world demand. This impact is exacerbated in 2000, when in spite of increases in world demand, oceanic sources provide some 250 percent of demand for that year. It should be expected that extensive disruptions would be created in the location of cobalt supplies which will result in virtually all cobalt originating as the by-product of nodule exploitation.

Chart 7.5
Theoretical Impact of Ocean Mining as a Percentage of Cobalt Demand

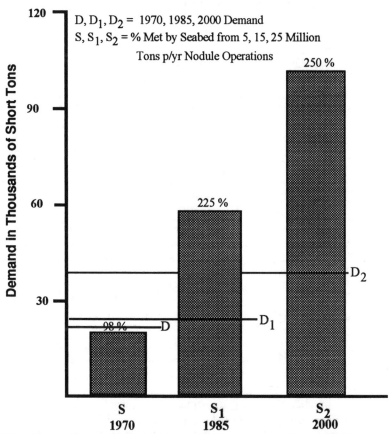

The direct effects of this development is interesting. For example, five million tons of nodules of a high cobalt content would have supplied over 200 percent of 1985 demand, and 10 million tons would have provided 458 percent of total demand, thereby causing a dramatic fall in prices. Due to this likelihood of a drop in value, the economic desirability of exploiting this type of nodule is questionable, making the high nickel and copper content nodules the optimum type to mine.

It should be expected that seabed production will gradually account for an increasing share of the overall world market for the constituent metals. The set of assumptions behind these figures are that the number of mining operations will increase to represent an overall capacity of 25 million tons (m/t) per year (p/y); for illustrative purposes the incremental capacities used are 5 m.t. p/y, 15 m.t. p/y, and 25 m.t. p/y. Had seabed production begun in the 1970's, as originally predicted, it would have displaced marginal land-based production; the rate of development of land-based supplies would have been slowed due to the transfer of development capital into seabed production which in the long run is assumed to be more cost effective per unit of investment.

Since the developing countries consume relatively minor amounts of the metals concerned, their position as net providers of these raw materials to the industrialized world constitutes the appropriate criterion for the analysis of the economic interests of these countries as a group in the foreseeable future." The impact of seabed production may be expected to be particularly adverse for the developing producing countries, because they typically depend more heavily on the minerals concerned for their export earnings and government revenues than developed producing countries and for other reasons. (U.N. Doc. TD/B/C.1/120, 5)[8]

The chief consequence of such production for land based producers of the minerals concerned would be that their total export earnings from these minerals would grow less rapidly than they would have done otherwise, and might in some circumstances decline from previously achieved levels.

For example, oceanic manganese production should be expected to have its most pronounced effect on Gabon where 18.5 percent of that nation's per capita Gross National Product is derived from the export of manganese ore.

The next largest single producer of manganese is India, but manganese production accounted for only 2.2 percent of their per capita gross national product. Hence, Gabon will suffer a severe loss of income by any drastic drop in the world price of manganese.

A number of nations are extremely dependent on copper exports for much of their gross national product but, as stated earlier, owing to the limited impact of oceanic exploitation on the world copper market, the possible impact on these nations should be considered as insignificant.

As far as nickel is concerned, only a limited effect on the incomes of LDC's should be expected owing to the widely scattered nature of nickel production. Nations which will be effected to some degree are Cuba and Zimbabwe, but the share of nickel in the gross national product of either nation accounts for only 2.1 percent. Therefore, even these effects will be minor. The most severe disruption will be felt by New Caledonia whose gross national product is almost exclusively derived from nickel exports.

Although the most extensive disruption will be found within the cobalt industry, the magnitude of the effects will be minimal in terms of any one nation. For example, Zaire is by far the largest producer of cobalt, but cobalt production only accounted for 3.6 percent of their Gross National Product. Since Cobalt is mainly a by-product of copper production, it is likely that even if the price of cobalt drops drastically, Zaire can still sell it at a profit. Hence, there will be an impact on cobalt producers, but one which will not prove disastrous in and of itself.

The introduction of seabed production could be expected to result in lower market prices for the minerals concerned than would otherwise have prevailed. Moreover, because output from the seabed is likely to be relatively low cost, it would tend to displace marginal land based production[9] (or such land based output as was previously marketed in the country which the new supplies emanating from the seabed would be consumed).[10] In addition, the momentum which nodule production would undoubtedly impart to the existing technological trend in favor of the direct processing of mineral concentrates, and the possible elimination of intermediate processes which are now partly carried out in developing countries, would exacerbate the loss of potential export income on the part of the developing producing countries. (U.N. Doc. TD/B/C. 1/170, 4) "The overall consequence of the price and volume effects would be that the total earnings of land based producers from the minerals concerned would be smaller than in the absence of production from the seabed." (U.N. Doc. TD/B/C. 1/170, 4)[11]

Table 7.2 illustrates the magnitude of the displacement of land-based mineral producers by comparing rates of growth of demand, oceanic supplies, and land based supplies. As seen, manganese demand is expected to grow at an annual rate of growth of 2.69 percent. While land production will grow at only 1.33 percent, the remaining 1.36 percent difference between land production and world demand will be made up by oceanic sources. These figures reflect the same patterns of displacement spoken of on the earlier pages. As far as copper production goes, the difference between world demand and land supply is only .09 percent which indicates that land-based mines will remain as the predominant source of future copper supplies and land-based nickel suppliers will suffer a reduction in their rate of growth of .73 percent per year. This small reduction is made possible in the face of oceanic sources increasing their market share, due to the tremendous increases in nickel demand which one expected. The annual growth of nickel demand is expected to be 3.54 percent up to the year 2000. As seen by the figures for cobalt, it is expected that the huge amounts of cobalt from oceanic sources will virtually replace the entire land-based cobalt industry.

The magnitude of the impact would vary among nations, production areas, and producing enterprises according to relative efficiencies, patterns of trade and market structures.

Table 7.2
Projected Displacement of Land-based Mineral Suppliers

Mineral	Projected Demand (000's of Tons)				Proj. Seabed Production				Proj. Land Production (000's of Tons)			
	1970	1985	2000	Growth Rate	5 m.t. 1970	15 m.t. 1985	25 m.t. 2000	Growth Rate	1970	1985	2000	Growth Rate
Mn	8160	13700	18265	2.69	1468	5206	8219	4.96	6692	8494	10046	1.33
Cu	6612	11200	15700	2.96	528	1680	2747	4.66	6084	9520	12953	2.87
Ni	530	960	1464	3.54	68	230	395	5.11	462	730	1069	2.81
Co	22	25	40	2.01	20	57	101	4.54	2	---	---	---

Effects of Deep Seabed Mining on Developing Country Mineral Producers

Some attempts have been made to answer the extremely important question of whether or not developing country land-based producers will be significantly affected by deep seabed mining. (Leipziger and Mudge 1976) Quite apart from the problem of forecasting, however, is the problem of defining exactly what constitutes lost revenue. Is it the difference between that amount of revenue an exporter might earn in the absence of nodule mining and the amount actually earned in the presence of seabed mining? This measures the absolute difference in earnings at some future point in time. Or is it the difference between actual earnings in a milieu including seabed producers compared to the trend of past earnings? This would adjust an earnings difference by the average of past earnings or account for a historical trend line in earnings. Or perhaps one should include "losses" associated with a decision not to exploit newly discovered mineral reserves because of the threat of seabed competition. This would include the loss associated with the foregone opportunity to mine a deposit.

The objective here is to concentrate on actual losses in the export earnings of traditional land-based producers which are clearly ascribable to seabed mining. Those developing country producers are identified whose export earnings are substantially dependent on affected minerals and where reductions in earnings are significant in magnitude.

Setting such limitations involves a decision to exclude certain possible cases. It excludes the cases of mineral exporters whose economies are not crucially dependent on affected minerals, e.g., say affected mineral exports are less than 5 percent of total exports. (In these cases, it is to be expected that adjustment to a reduction in revenue from a minor export will be manageable.) And finally a decision to limit the inquiry into metal markets in which additional supplies from seabed sources are a significant proportion of total supply excludes cases in which a small addition to net supply (e.g., say 5 percent or less) can have significant effects on land-based mineral producers. Additional mineral sources—land-based or from the seabed—can always affect producers, and the international community should not be expected to guarantee mineral export earnings. What should concern the international community, however, is the future impact on traditional, undiversified LDC mineral exporters of an internationally agreed on effort to extract minerals from a new, large source of supply. We examine the cases of copper, cobalt and manganese.

To begin with, looking at the case of copper, the seabed mineral of most interest to LDCs because copper exports play a vital role in the economies of developing country producers, especially Zambia, Chile and Peru. Total copper exports from the largest six LDC producers were valued at $2 billion in 1992. Given the magnitude of developing country copper exports as sources of foreign exchange, slight price or output variations can result in sizable differences in foreign exchange earnings. Calculations indicate that copper from seabed sources in 1985 would have accounted for 1.9 percent of total world copper production. An UNCTAD study on the effect of deep seabed mining on the copper market concluded that such an increase in supply would be well below the average annual fluctuations of copper mining output in recent years. (U.N. Doc. TD/B/484, 7) Therefore, it is difficult to argue that seabed supply would add a significant new degree of uncertainty into the determination of market prices for copper. The United Nations Secretariat Report on the economic implications of deep seabed mining, prepared for the Law of the Sea Conference, concludes that "production from nodules is expected to have a very minor impact on copper markets by 1985." (U.N. Doc. A/Conf. 62/25, 36)

Any such prognosis, however, is sensitive to the base year and future year selected for analysis. Therefore, one cannot say that in the year 2000, for example, seabed mining might not be a major source of copper, with concomitant effects on land sources of supply. What can be said, though, is that knowing what we do now about first generation mining given reasonable assumptions, it is highly unlikely that land-based copper producers will be adversely affected to any appreciable degree by deep seabed mining.

The case of manganese is a rather difficult one to examine, since present indications are that firms will not extract manganese ore from nodules but that if all firms did decide to do so, the manganese ore market would be affected to some extent. Were all firms to extract manganese ore, the net addition to total supply would be approximately 10 percent. This increase in supply might exert some downward pressure on prices and might affect the export earnings of LDC land-based producers. As reported earlier, only Gabon is currently dependent on manganese ore exports for more than one percent of its total foreign exchange earnings, and Gabon's export profile was recently radically improved with the discovery of onshore and offshore oil deposits. Therefore, the outlook for Gabonese export earnings is rather optimistic with or without nodule mining.

The latest information available suggests that Deepsea Ventures will extract manganese in its metallic form; the Kennecott and INCO consortia had not indicated whether they will extract manganese ore, stockpile it or discard it. At first glance, the last course does not appear likely considering the high cost of recovering nodules from the deep ocean floor and the first course does not seem likely given the current and future projected low prices of manganese ore. The decision of whether to sell, discard, or stockpile tailings (i.e., mineral residue perhaps containing recoverable amounts of metals) depends on the costs of storage, costs of extraction, price of the metal and expectations of future metals prices. (U.N. Docs. TD/B/483 and TD/B/483/Add. 1)[12]

Estimates concerning the effects of manganese nodule mining on land-based producers of manganese ore are therefore rather uncertain. It does not appear, however, that the maximum 10 percent addition to the supply of manganese ore that occurs if all nodule miners were to extract manganese ore is likely to affect prices radically. To the extent that ore is stockpiled, however, nodule mining firms will gradually be building stocks of manganese ore which by their very existence constitute a threat to the price of manganese ore past 1985. If all producers except Deepsea mine and stockpile manganese ore, the stockpile by 2000 would be sufficient to interfere substantially with the market. (U.N. Doc. TD/B/C.1/185)

---

[7]The Deepsea Ventures proposed mine site is in an area of the Pacific, to the west of the southern tip of Baja, California, bounded by: Lat. 15 44' North, Long. 124 20' West to where line drawn west to Lat. 15 44' North, Long. 127 46' West and South to Lat. 14 16' North, Long. 126 46' West and East to Lat. 14 16' North, Long. 124 20' West. (U.S. Senate 1975)

[8] "Thus, developing countries, which are increasingly processing minerals produced from land sources before export, would lose such potential export income to the extent that minerals produced from the seabed were processed on the mainland of the producing enterprise 's home country '" . (U.N. Doc. TD/B/C.1/120, 5)

[9]This is not meant to suggest that prices would fall below current levels, only that they will not rise to the levels they may have achieved had nodule recovery not come about .

[10]"Because aggregate demand for many minerals is not very responsive to falls in their prices, output from the seabed would tend to displace marginal land production (or such land output as was previous ly marketed in the country in which the new supplies emanating from the seabed were consumed). This adverse quantitative effect would be compounded by the restrictive effects on land production of its diminished profitability and the accompanying decline in investment resources. " (U.N. Doc. A/AC. 138/73, 29)

[11]"...the need for large-scale capital investments for the exploration and mining of seabed resources might adversely affect the flow of private investment into similar activities in developing countries. Because fewer alternative investment and employment opportunities exist in the developing countries, compared with the developed countries, particularly heavy economic and social costs will be incurred in any re-allocation of resources that may be necessitated as a result of competition from seabed production." (U.N. Doc. TD/B/C. 1/170, 5)

[12]Our conclusions are rather different from those presented by UNCTAD which

reported a possible reduction in LDC manganese export earnings of as much as 30 percent from their normal levels in 1980. UNCTAD assumed that mining would begin in 1974 possibly reaching 10 million tons by 1980 and that all firms extract manganese ore, which is 30 percent of the nodule material. This analysis is in part based on an econometric model of the manganese ore industry which is highly suspect.

Chapter Eight

Critical Technologies at Risk

On the shore, dimly seen through the mists, the mists of the deep,
Where the foe's haughty host in dread silence reposes . .
The Star Spangled Banner

Although the 1994 treaty modifications have toned down some of the most direct mandatory technology transfer requirements, the treaty still places at risk some very sensitive, and militarily useful, technology which may readily be misused by the Navy's of ocean mining states. The military application of these technologies would provide new anti-submarine warfare (ASW) capabilities, strategic deep-sea salvage abilities, and deep-water bastions for launching sub-surface ballistic missiles (SSBM's).

Three classes of technology would be placed at risk by U.S. accession to UNCLOS: 1) deep-water bathymetric and high-resolution mapping systems including advanced deep ocean visual surveillance systems; 2) sophisticated vessel station-keeping and navigation systems critical to ASW and strategic salvage operations; and 3) state-of-the-art robotics and remotely operated vehicle technology. Much of the data associated with these technologies is classified for national security reasons and is also at risk.

With or without the mandatory technology transfer provisions contained in the UNCLOS U.S. participation would provide a "legal" conduit and cover to justify the acquisition of state-of-the-art deep ocean devices and technology which have profound national security implications. Ocean mining activities by the Enterprise or third world nations, such as China or India, can provide plausible justification for successfully purchasing technologies which, in the absence of ocean mining, would likely be denied on national security grounds.

In 1995, for instance, the PRC--a nation self-sufficient in the domestic production of the principal metals derived from manganese nodules--sought and obtained sophisticated micro-bathymetry equipment from the United States, along with 6,000 meter capable video and side-scan sonar systems. This equipment may easily be misapplied by the PRC to help advance its meager ASW capability (see capability Charts 8.2 and 8.3) in support of its attempts to develop a "Blue Water" navy. This equipment can also be used to help the PRC locate undersea bastions, even within the U.S. EEZ, for their missile launching submarines.

The justification used by the PRC is its pioneer investor status awarded by the UNCLOS PrepCom in 1993. Ostensibly the equipment will be used for manganese nodule exploration within the Clarion/Clipperton fracture zone. Unfortunately, such surveys should only take for several months at sea to accomplish. In part this is due to the rapid wide-swath capability of the system they purchased and to their choice of minesite locations on, or adjacent to, heavily prospected and claimed nodule fields.

How will the PRC choose to utilize this equipment over the 95 percent of its productive life when it is not involved in nodule exploration? ASW and military submarine mapping are overwhelmingly the most likely applications. An additional factor to consider is the U.S. government's policy of imposing security classifications on many types of microbathymetry data while indiscriminately selling the equipment which is used to generate such data.

Mapping and Bathymetric Issues

Improvements in seafloor mapping have resulted from the development of multi-beam bathymetry system, the application of heave-roll-pitch sensors to correct for ship motion, the improved accuracy of satellite positioning systems, and improved computer and plotter capability for processing map data. (Andersen in Lockwood and Hill, 63-67) These improvements make possible:

-- much higher resolution for detecting fine scale bottom
   features;
-- a significant decrease in time required for making area surveys;
-- nearly instantaneous automated contour charts, eliminating the
   need for conventional cartography; (Farr, 88-89) and

-- the availability of data in digital format.

Deep Water Systems

Swath bathymetric systems are of two types: those designed to operate in deep water and those designed primarily for shallow water. The principal deep-water multi-beam systems currently in use in the United States are Sea Beam and SASS. Sea Beam technology, installed on NOAA's NOS ships to survey EEZ waters deeper than 600 meters, first became available from (General Instrument (GI) Corp. in 1977. GI's original multi-beam bathymetric sonar, the Sonar Array Sounding System (or SASS) was developed for the U.S. Navy and is not available for civilian use. Sea Beam is a spin-off from the original SASS technology.

Sea Beam is a hull-mounted system, which uses 16 adjacent beams. 8 port and 8 starboard, to survey a wide swath of the ocean bottom on both sides of the ship's track. Each beam covers an angular area 2.67° square. The swath angle is the sum of' the individual beam width angles. or 42.67 °. With the swath angle set, the swath width depends on the ocean depth. At the continental shelf' edge, i.e., 200 meters, the swath width is about 150 meters at the bottom; in 5,000 meters (16,400 feet) of water, the swath width is approximately 4,000 meters. Therefore, Sea Beam's survey rate is greater in deeper waters. By carefully spacing ship tracks, complete (or overlapping) coverage of' an area can be obtained. The contour interval of bathymetric charts produced from Sea Beam can be set as fine as 2 meters. (U.S. OTA 1987, 126)

Figure 8.1
Frequency Spectra

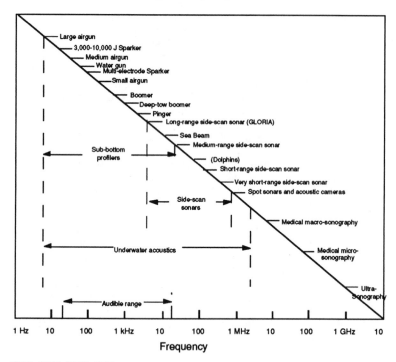

(U.S. OTA 1987, 133)

Figure 8.2
Sea Beam Patterns

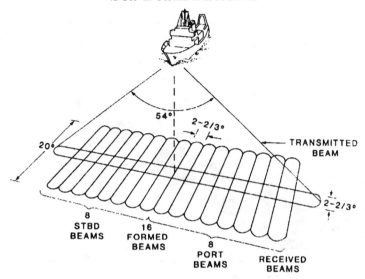

The Sea Beam swath width at the seafloor depends on water depth. In 200 meters of water the swath width is about 150 meters; in 5,000 meters of water, the swath width is approximately 4,000 meters.

(U.S. OTA 1987, 127)

Figure 8.3
SeaMARC vs. Sea Beam

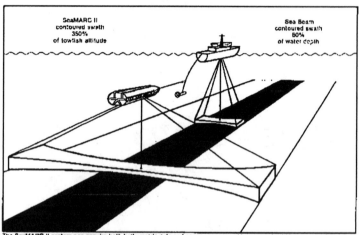

The SeaMARC II system can acquire both bathymetric data and sonar imagery and has a swath width more than four times that of the Sea Beam system. The Sea Beam system, however, produces more accurate bathymetry.

SOURCE: International Submarine Technology, Ltd., Redmond, WA.

(U.S. OTA 1987, 130)

The Navy's older SASS model uses as many as 60 beams, providing higher resolution than Sea Beam in the direction perpendicular to the ship's track (Sea Beam resolution is better parallel to the ship's track). In current SASS models, the outer 10 or so beams are often unreliable and not used. (U.S. OTA 1987, 126-27)

Improvements in Sea Beam, which has performed very well but which is now considered to be old technology, have been proposed. One proposed modification is to develop a capability to quantify the strength of the signal returning from the bottom.'' With such information. it would be possible to predict certain bottom characteristics. Nodule fields. For example. already have been quantified using acoustic backscatter information. Another proposed modification is to build a towed Sea Beam system. Such a system could be moved from ship to ship as required.

All bathymetric systems have resolution and range limits imposed by wave front spreading, absorption, and platform noise. However, by reducing Sea Beam's current beam width. its resolution can be improved. There are limitations to using the immense amounts of data that would be collected by a higher resolution system. Only a small fraction (2 percent) of existing Sea Beam data are used in making bathymetric charts (except for charts of very small areas), and generating charts with a 1- meter contour interval is impractical. Sea Beam. unlike SASS, may be installed on small ships. In order to build a Sea Beam with a 1° beam width an acoustic array 2.5 times longer than current models would be required. To accommodate such an array, one must either tow it or use a larger ship. The Navy has found that the current Sea Beam system is capable of producing contour charts of sufficient quality for most of its needs and is currently considering deploying Sea Beam systems for several of' its smaller ships.

It is important to match resolution requirements with the purpose of the survey. Use of additional exploration technologies in conjunction with Sea Beam data may provide better geological interpretations than improving the resolution of the Sea Beam system alone. For instance, combined bathymetry and side-looking sonar data may reveal more features on the seafloor.

Improving swath coverage is probably more important than improving resolution for reconnaissance surveys. Wider swath coverage, for example. could increase the survey rate and reduce the time and cost of reconnaissance surveys. Sea Beam's swath angle is narrow compared to that of GLORIA or SeaMARC; thus the area that can be surveyed is smaller in the same time period. It may be possible to extend Sea Beam capability from the current 0.8 times water depth to as much as 4 times water depth without losing hydrographic quality. The current limit is imposed by the original design; hence, a small amount of development may produce a large gain in survey coverage without giving up data quality.

Another factor that affects the survey rate is the availability of the Global Positioning System (GPS) for navigation and vessel speed. Currently, NOAA uses GPS when it can; however. it is not vet fully operational. When GPS is inaccessible, NOAA survey vessels periodically must approach land to maintain navigational fixes accurate enough for charting purposes. This reduces the time available for surveying. Ship speed is also a factor, but increases in speed would not result in as great improvements in the survey rate as increases in swath width.

SASS data acquired by the U.S. Navy is classified. NOAA neither knows what the bathymetry is in areas surveyed by SASS nor what areas have been surveyed. More optimistically, once the Global Positioning System becomes available around the clock thereby enabling precise navigational control at all times it may be possible for NOAA to utilize multi-beam surveys conducted by others. (U.S. OTA 1987, 126-28)

Reflection and Refraction Seismology

Seismic techniques are the primary geophysical methods for acquiring information about the geological structure and stratigraphy of continental margins and deep ocean areas. Seismic techniques are acoustic. much like echo sounding and sonar. but lower frequency sound sources are used. Sound from low-frequency sources. rather than bouncing off the bottom, penetrates the bottom and is reflected or refracted back to one or more surface receivers (channels) from the boundaries of sedimentary or rock layers or bodies of different density. Hence, in addition to sedimentary thicknesses and stratification, structural characteristics such as folds. faults. rift zones. diapirs, and other features and the characteristic seismic velocities in different strata may be determined. Ninety-eight percent of all seismic work supports petroleum exploration: less than 2 percent is mineral oriented. (U.S. OTA 1987, 132)

Magnetic Methods

The most important problem in acquiring high quality data at sea is not technology but accurate navigation. The Global Positioning System, when available, is considered more than adequate for navigation and positioning needs. Future data. to be most useful for mineral exploration purposes. will necessarily need to be collected as densely as possible. It is also important that magnetic (and gravity) data be recorded in a manner that minimizes the effects of external sources, such as of the towing platform, and that whatever data are measured be incorporated into larger data sets. so that data at different scales are simultaneously available to investigators. (U.S. OTA 1987, 137)

Optical Imaging

Optical images produced by underwater cameras and video systems are complementary to the images and bathymetry provided by side-looking sonar's and bathymetry systems. Once interesting features have been identified using long-range reconnaissance techniques, still cameras and video systems can be used for close-up views. Such systems can be used to resolve seafloor features on the order of 10 centimeter to 1 meter. The swath width of imaging systems depends on such factors as the number of cameras used, the water characteristics, and the height of the imaging system above the seafloor. Swaths as wide as 200 meters are currently mappable.

ANGUS (Acoustically Navigated Underwater Survey) is typical of many deep-sea photographic systems. Basically, ANGUS consists of three 35 millimeter cameras and strobe lights mounted on a rugged sled. The system is towed approximately 10 meters off the bottom in water depths up to 6,000 meters

(19,700 feet), and is capable of taking 3,000 frames per sortie. It has been used in conjunction with dives of the submersible Alvin. A newer system, currently under development at the Deep Submergence Laboratory (DSL) at Woods Hole Oceanographic Institution, is Argo. On her maiden voyage in September 1985 Argo assisted in locating the Titanic. Like ANGUS, Argo is capable of operating in water depths of 6,000 meters. Argo, however, is equipped with a wide area television imaging system integrated with sidelooking sonar. It currently uses three low-light level, silicon-intensified target cameras (one forward-looking, one down-looking, and one downlooking telephoto), extending the width of the imaged swath to 56 meters (184 feet) when towed at an altitude of 35 meters. (U.S. OTA 1987, 152)

Rona and others have used the concept of "closing range to a mineral deposit" to describe an exploration strategy for hydrothermal mineral deposits. With some minor modifications this strategy may be applicable for exploration of many types of offshore mineral accumulations. It is analogous to the use of a zoom lens on a camera which first shows a large area with little detail but then is adjusted for a close-up view to reveal greater detail in a much smaller area. The strategy of closing range begins with regional reconnaissance. Reconnaissance technologies are used to gather information about the "big picture." While none of these techniques can provide direct confirmation of the distance size, or nature of specific mineral deposits, they can be powerful tools for deducing likely places to focus more attention. (U.S. OTA 1987, 115)

- Bathymetric profiling yields detailed information about water depth, and hence, of seabed morphology .
- Midrange side-looking sonar's provide acoustic images similar to long-range sonar's but of higher resolution.
- Seismic reflection and refraction techniques acquire information about the subsurface structure of the seabed.
- Magnetic profiling is used to detect and characterize the magnetic field. Magnetic traverses may be used offshore to map sediments and rocks containing magnetite and other iron-rich minerals .
- Gravity surveys are used to detect differences in the density of rocks, leading to estimates of crustal rock types and thicknesses.
- Electrical techniques are used to study resistivity, conductivity, electrochemical activity and other electrical properties of rocks.

- Nuclear techniques furnish information about the radioactive properties of some rocks. (U.S. OTA 1987, 118)

Many of these reconnaissance technologies are also useful for more detailed studies of the seabed. Most are towed through the water at speeds of from 1 to 10 knots. Hence, much information may be gathered in relatively short periods of time. It is often possible to use more than one sensor at a time, thereby increasing exploration efficiency. Data sets can be integrated, such that the combined data are much more useful than information from any one sensor alone. Generally, the major cost of offshore reconnaissance is not the sensor itself, but the use of the ship on which it is mounted.

Indirect methods of detection give way to direct methods at the seabed. Only direct samples can provide information about the constituents of a deposit. their relative abundance. concentration. grain size, etc. Grab sampling, dredging, coring and drilling techniques have been developed to sample seabed deposits, although technology for sampling consolidated deposits lags behind that for sampling unconsolidated sediments. If initial sampling of a deposit is promising, a more detailed sampling program may be carried out. In order to prove the commercial value of a mineral occurrence. it may be necessary to take thousands of samples.

Remotely Operated Vehicles

ROVs are unmanned vehicle systems operated from a remote station, generally on the sea surface. There are five main categories of ROVs:

1) tethered, free-swimming vehicles (the most common);
2) towed vehicles:
3) bottom crawling vehicles:
4) structurally-reliant vehicles; and
5) autonomous or unteathered vehicles. (U.S. OTA 1987, 146)

The environmental limits within which a vehicle can work are determined by such design features as operating depth. speed, diving duration and payload. These factors are also an indication of a vehicle's potential to carry equipment. The actual working or exploration capabilities of a manned or unmanned vehicle are measured by the tools. instruments, and/or sensors that it can carry and deploy. These capabilities are, in large part, determined by the vehicle's carrying capacity (payload), electrical supply, and overall configuration. For example, Deep Tow represents one of the most sophisticated towed vehicles in operation. Its equipment suite includes virtually every data-gathering capability available for EEZ exploration that can be used with this type of vehicle. On the other hand, there are towed vehicles with the same depth capability and endurance as Deep Tow but which cannot begin to accommodate the vast array of instrumentation this vehicle carries, due to their design. Towing speed of these vehicles ranges from 2 to 6 knots.

Tethered, free-swimming ROVs offer another example of the wide range in exploration capabilities available in today's market. Vehicles with the most basic equipment in this category have at least a television camera and adequate lighting for the camera (although lighting may sometimes be optional). However, there is an extensive variety of additional equipment that can be carried. The ROV Solo, for example, is capable of providing real-time observations via its television camera, photographic documentation with its still camera, short-range object detection and location by its scanning sonar, and samples with its three-function grabber (i.e., manipulator). The vehicle is also equipped for conducting bathymetric surveys. Assuming it is supported by an appropriate sub-sea navigation system, it can provide:

• a high-resolution topographic profile map on which the space between sounding lanes is swept and recorded by side-looking sonar,
• a sub-bottom profile of reflective horizons beneath the vehicle,
• a chart of magnetic anomalies along the tracks covered,
• television documentation of the entire track.
• selective stenographic photographs of objects or features of interest, and
• the capability to stop and sample at the surveyor's discretion.

With adequate equipment on the vehicle and support ship and the proper computer programs. the entire mapping program, once underway, can be performed automatically with little or no human involvement. At least a dozen more competitive models exist that can be similarly equipped.

Untethered, manned vehicles are, for the most part, equipped with at least one television camera. still camera, side-looking sonar, and manipulator. and with pingers or transponders compatible with whatever positioning system is being used. The absence of an umbilical cable has an advantage that received little attention until the Challenger space shuttle tragedy in 1986. Challenger's debris was scattered under the Atlantic Ocean's Gulf Stream, which flows at maximum speed on the surface but decreases to less than 0.25 knot at or near the bottom. Once the manned submersibles used in the search descended below the swift flowing surface waters (upwards of 3 knots), they worked and maneuvered without concern for the current. The ROVs used, on the other hand, were all tethered, and, even though the vehicle itself might be operating within little or no discernible current, the umbilical had to contend with the current at all times. This caused considerable difficulty at times during the search operation.

Hard mineral exploration, however is a task well-suited for manned vehicles and tethered, free swimming ROVs. A wide array of manipulator held sampling equipment for these vehicles has been developed over the past two decades. This sampling capability ranges from simple scoops to gather unconsolidated sediment to drills for taking hard-rock cores. Present undersea vehicles cannot. however collect soft sediment cores much beyond 3 feet in length or hard-rock cores more than a few inches in length.

A recent example of a vehicle application was the search for and subsequent examination of the RMS Titanic. which sank in the Atlantic in 1912. The vessel was thought to be somewhere within a 120 square-nautical-mile area. A visual search with an undersea vehicle could literally take years to complete at the 4.000-meter (13,000-foot) depths in which she lay. Instead, the area was searched using a side-looking sonar which detected a target of likely proportions after about 40 days of looking. To verify that the target was the Titanic, the towed vehicle ANGUS was dispatched with its television and still cameras. The next step, to closely examine the vessel, was done with the manned vehicle Alvin and the tethered, free-swimming ROV Jason Junior W) Alvin provided the means to "home on" and board the vessel, while JJ provided the means to explore the close confines of the vessel's interior.

> The search for the space shuttle Challenger debris is another example of the division of labor between undersea vehicles and over-the-side techniques. Since the debris was scattered over many square miles and intermixed with debris from other sources, it would have taken months, perhaps years, to search the area with undersea vehicles. Instead, as with the Titanic, side-looking sonar was used to sweep the area of interest and likely targets were plotted to be later identified by manned and unmanned vehicles. The same vehicles were subsequently used to help in the retrieval of debris. Once again, the large area was searched with the more rapid over-the-side techniques while precision work was accomplished with the slower moving undersea vehicles. (U.S. OTA 1987, 151)

These two examples suggest that the main role of undersea vehicles in the EEZ is and will be to provide the fine details of the bottom. A typical exploration scenario might begin with bottom coverage with a wide-swath side-looking sonar, like GLORIA, progress to one of the midrange sidelooking sonar's or a Sea Beam-type system, and end with deployment of a towed vehicle system or a tethered, free-swimming ROV or manned submersible to collect detailed information.

Submersible Vehicles

Four categories of submersible vehicles are considered: manned tethered, manned untethered, unmanned tethered, and unmanned untethered. Tethered, unmanned vehicles are commonly called ROVs (remotely operated vehicles); untethered, unmanned vehicles are AUVs (autonomous underwater vehicles). Unmanned vehicles, including those that are tethered (ROVs) and those that are not tethered (AUVs) are identified by the Navy as UUVs (unmanned underwater vehicles). A range of UUVs, whose basic sensor and video systems are a high resolution sonar and a low light level television, respectively, have evolved from the early use of manned submersibles and divers for the offshore oil and gas industry. The umbilical by which tethered submersibles are connected to a support platform, which could be a surface ship or a submarine, provides power, communications, and, in some cases, life support in the form of oxygen for breathing and a means to expel carbon dioxide.

In order to work underwater the submersible platform needs an ability to navigate, an ability to detect and visualize, and, for many tasks, the ability to manipulate tools and/or a target object. These technology areas are interdependent. Without one ability, the others are not useful; a degradation in one technology area, however, may be partially compensated by an increased capability in another.

Searching for small objects, particularly if they are nonmetallic, in a cluttered environment requires the use of vision systems. Detection at long range enables submersible vehicles to quickly acquire a target and, thus, reduce search time.

Small, manned, untethered submersibles of the 1960s were built or sponsored by the U.S. Navy for deep-ocean research, deep submergence rescue of submarine crews, and deep-sea retrieval of military objects (e.g., hydrogen bombs). While manned submersible missions arc still important, advances in technologies related to submersible vehicles have precipitated the use of UUVs for a greater variety of missions. The current or potential ability of submersible vehicles in conjunction with underwater vision systems includes: searching for and locating objects in the ocean or on the ocean floor, delivering and/or retrieving personnel, mines, or sensors; and attacking ships or submarines. These

186   *Reforming the Law of the Sea: Opportunities Missed*

abilities make the vehicles important for several areas of naval warfare: submarine warfare, anti-submarine warfare, mine warfare, counter-mine warfare, and special operations (clandestinely directed at harbors, ports, or landing areas). When robots and manipulators are added, the abilities of submersible vehicles arc extended to implant and recovery of seafloor-mounted measurement equipment; intervention of adversary measurement equipment; and retrieval of combat and non-combat objects from the ocean floor. These systems of submersible vehicles, vision systems, robots, and manipulators allow large objects, such as military vessels or aircraft, to be recovered at depths exceeding 1,000 m and in Sea State 3 conditions. Smaller objects, such as warheads or sensors, can be recovered or manipulated at much greater depths.

Chart 8.1
Ocean Depths

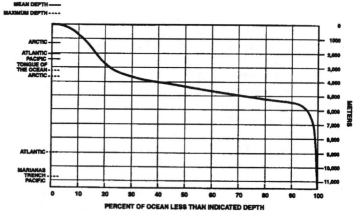

(Gillmer 1970)

Manned tethered vehicles can be connected overtly to a surfaced mother ship with the tether over its side and a deck crane for lifting the vehicle into and out of the water. Covert operation can be achieved by a surfaced mother ship that is equipped with a trap ("moon pool") below the waterline (clandestine operation), or by a submarine that deploys and recovers the vehicle while submerged (covert operation).

Manned untethered vehicles are more power limited than the tethered vehicles, but they can travel further—both horizontally and vertically—from the mother ship from which most operate. Few of these manned, untethered vehicles operate without a mother ship. Most manned, untethered vehicles are launched and recovered from a surface vessel or are towed out to sea and supported by a surface vessel. And few of these have dual power systems; most use simple lead acid batteries that are inexpensive, long lived, and capable of numerous recharges.

Unmanned tethered vehicles are the least expensive submersibles and the most numerous in both the military and commercial sectors. Like the manned vehicles, they can be operated overtly from surface ships or covertly from surface ships or submarines. Except for transport and insertion of personnel ashore, unmanned tethered vehicles can do most tasks done by manned vehicles, and they can do tasks that are too dangerous for manned vehicles (e.g., locating and disabling mines).

Unmanned untethered vehicles are the most sophisticated submersibles. They are equipped with their own power supply and their own navigation and control systems. They are small, quiet, and capable of operating at long distances from their home facility. Commercial and research uses include seafloor exploration, resource exploitation (mining), biological and geological reconnaissance, environmental monitoring, and mapping unexplored areas.

Strategic Uses.

Equipment and technology associated with ocean exploration and resource exploitation are much like equipment and technology usable to perform covert activities such as harbor mining; sensor implantation and removal; delivery of combat swimmers into shallow water areas; gathering intelligence on seafloor-mounted systems; and monitoring clandestine terrorist-type activities that might involve implanting underwater explosives. Exploitation of submersible vehicles and related technology for such activities has taken place in the former Soviet Union, North Korea, and other countries. There are ongoing programs in a number of countries to obtain these vehicles for their military. The cost of these vehicles is relatively low, but the covertness and difficulty in detecting them are very high.

The potential for covert launch and recovery from a compartment hidden below a surface ship's waterline or from a submarine makes the manned tethered vehicle a clandestine military threat.

A similar threat is posed by manned untethered vehicles, which can operate at distances of hundreds of miles without surfacing, thus making them difficult to detect and intercept. Because of their use to insert combat swimmers, limitations in range and underwater endurance have been established in order to exclude military applications that are within the domain of most non-military applications.

The unmanned untethered vehicles are the underwater equivalent of air-delivered cruise missiles, and they are much more covert. And, like cruise missiles, they can be launched from ships, submarines, or aircraft.

Military missions for UUVs, tethered or untethered, are numerous. In submarine warfare, UUVs could perform area search and reconnaissance, and thus expand the search horizon of a mother submarine. They can collect intelligence from stationing near a port or in a transit area. They can be used as offboard platforms to detect wakes and acoustic emissions. They can lay mines, although mine dispensing from the surface appears much more plausible. And they could act as communications relays or as decoys. In ASW, UUVs could perform barrier surveillance by towing an acoustic array through an area and automatically transmitting detection's to another platform. Ocean surveillance would be an extension of the ASW mission: UUVs could patrol wide areas with passive sensors; or they could be employed to provide an active sound source whose reflected pulses would be monitored by fixed and towed underwater surveillance systems like the SOSUS (sound surveillance system) and the SURTASS (surveillance towed array sensor system), respectively.

In mine warfare, UUVs could be especially useful countermeasures. Mines are effective because they are difficult to detect. In the Korean War, North Korean sampans and junks laid a field of mines in Wonsan harbor in 1951, delaying a U.S. amphibious operation by several weeks. In the Vietnam War, Haiphong harbor was closed by a small number of U.S. air-laid mines. In another part of the world in 1984, a small mine field (less than 20 bottom mines) laid by a Libyan cargo ship closed the Suez Canal and the Red Sea for about six weeks. In the Persian Gulf War, the presence of Iraqi mines frustrated Coalition plans for an amphibious operation in the liberation of Kuwait and resulted in significant damage to two U.S. warships, the guided missile cruiser Princeton and the amphibious assault ship Tripoli.

Besides being difficult to detect, mines are a major problem because of their proliferation in the third world: over 45 countries have a mining capability; 21 countries produce mines; and 13 countries export mines. The mine problem is further aggravated by the large variety of types of mines. Figure 19 depicts mine placement: bottom mines, moored mines, and rising mines. Mine fusing can be mechanical (pressure plate or tilt rod) or by influence (magnetic, acoustic, or pressure). And the mine case can be metallic or non-metallic.

Figure 8.4
The Mine Threat

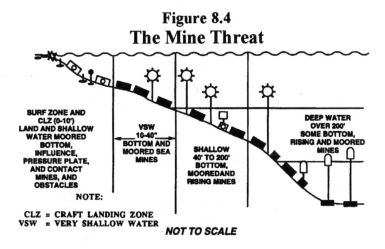

SURF ZONE AND
CLZ (0-10')
LAND AND SHALLOW
WATER MOORED
BOTTOM,
INFLUENCE,
PRESSURE PLATE,
AND CONTACT
MINES, AND
OBSTACLES

VSW
10-40"
BOTTOM AND
MOORED SEA
MINES

SHALLOW
40' TO 200'
BOTTOM,
MOOREDAND
RISING MINES

DEEP WATER
OVER 200'
SOME BOTTOM,
RISING AND MOORED
MINES

NOTE:

CLZ = CRAFT LANDING ZONE
VSW = VERY SHALLOW WATER

NOT TO SCALE

(U.S. Navy 1993)

Mine countermeasures (MCM) must be a top-priority item for naval forces that would be involved in littoral operations against countries of concern. Active MCM involves mine hunting and mine disposal. To be effective against modern sophisticated influence mines, the mine hunter — quite possibly a UUV—must be equipped with highly sophisticated sonar and video systems. Mine detonation, by UUVs deployed from a mine hunter, is accomplished by positioning a remotely detonated charge next to the mine or by severing the tethering wire of moored mines so they float to the surface where they can be destroyed. The desire to keep the MCM platform as far removed as possible from danger zones leads to the requirement for remote-controlled or autonomous surface and subsurface platforms for mine hunting and mine disposal. The UUV makes MCM operations possible under conditions too dangerous for mine clearance divers.

Fiber Optics

Because of its high data rate transmission capability, fiber-optic cable (vice coaxial cable) and associated parts, viz., fiber-optic connectors and hull penetrators, are increasingly being adopted by both commercial and military groups involved in underwater search, inspection, and reconnaissance with submerged vehicles. The submerged vehicles can transmit large amounts of video to a mother ship or submarine, where the video can be stored and/or read in real time.

Commercial applications of fiber-optic cable involve (1) exploration for oil, gas, and strategic metals (e.g., manganese nodules) and (2) laying, inspecting, and repairing underwater cables. Military applications involve reconnaissance by submersible vehicles that search for sensors and mines implanted on the seafloor and for military items that have sunk to the seafloor (viz., weapons, vessels, and aircraft).

The use of such penetrators and connectors—whether the link to the submersible vehicle is from a submarine or the submerged hull of a surface vessel—cannot be observed externally. And, thus, clandestine operations of submersible vehicles by countries of concern would not be detected.

In conflicts with countries that currently cause international concern, our Navy would operate in littoral waters listed below with the average depths indicated. These operations would very likely include implanting sensors at selected seafloor locations to detect and track adversary submarines. Adversaries would be motivated to locate and destroy or damage these sensors. Video via fiber optic cable would facilitate their search.

Table 8.1
Selected Ocean Depths

Country of Concern	Littoral Water	Average Depth, m
Iraq, Iran	Persian Gulf	100
Iran	Gulf of Oman	>1000
Iran	Arabian Sea	>1000
North Korea	Yellow Sea	40
North Korea	Sea of Japan	>1000

(IDA Doc. Addendum 1995, 8.2-23)

The principal technologies in fiber optic connectors are maintaining alignment and, more recently, mating connectors underwater by man or robot. Connectors advertised to withstand pressures at 20,000 ft+ depths are producible, but they are not yet off-the-shelf items. For shallow waters like the Persian Gulf and the Yellow Sea, the use of fiber-optic cable (rather than copper coaxial cable) could be finessed by (1) foregoing the use of connectors and (2) using good engineering design practice to ensure that hull penetrators are strong enough to withstand the pressure difference across the hull wall.

Most commercial and military seafloor mapping systems are mounted on surface ships. They determine their geographic positions from satellite or radio-positioning data. By measuring the sonar return reflected from features on the seafloor, the Position of those features is calculated and plotted on a chart. As the ship moves across the sea, the map of seafloor features below the ship is plotted.

A newly developed system works differently from present systems in that it detects features on the seafloor and measures the distance to, and the height of, these features. The system builds up a map of the seafloor from these measured distances without reference to the position of the platform making the map. The system is a more expensive way of mapping the seafloor and it would not be used when more conventional mapping systems, which are used today, would suffice. Its commercial application would be where, because of surface conditions such as ice cover or weather, conventional mapping with its required surface link to a navigation positioning system is not available. It is used militarily on a submerged platform, manned or unmanned, to map the ocean bottom or to follow a map.

This technology allows a small underwater vehicle to travel long distances without surfacing to reset navigation and to arrive within a few feet of a designated objective point. Currently available systems lose their position accuracy with time and distance traveled, requiring the carrying platforms to surface to reset their navigation systems, at which time the vehicles become susceptible to detection and attack.

The system would be useful for manned submersible vehicles operating covertly in shallow water. It would be useful for unmanned vehicles to implant strategic or tactical equipment (e.g., mines or bombs) in harbors or other choke points; the underwater delivery system could be an undersea cruise missile. The underwater acoustic seafloor mapping system can be used by submersibles in the same way terrain avoidance radar systems are used by low-flying aircraft.

Deep Salvage Technology

Deep salvage technology covers integrated systems used for searching for, locating, identifying, marking, attacking, retrieving, and implanting objects on the ocean floor. The integrated systems include technologies and equipment required for recovery or salvage of objects from depths greater than 1,000 m and objects weighing more than one ton at depths greater than 100 m. The systems and technologies are also incorporated in salvage systems that operate and are entirely supported below the surface. An integrated salvage system is one that involves two or more of these technologies: motion-compensated ship platforms, hydraulic systems, constant-tension devices, heavy lift winches, navigational positioning systems, torque-balanced synthetic cable, automatic dynamic positioning systems, sensor systems, and/or buoyancy systems. Technologies covered in this section also include deep sea drilling and implanting sensors beneath the ocean floor.

Navy salvage missions have long included Sea Line of Communications (SLOC) Control (towing and debeaching), Amphibious Support (debeaching and underwater repair), Battle Damage Repair (towing, fire-fighting, and damage control), and Harbor Clearance (damage control, heavy lift, and demolition). The salvage mission, Deep Object Recovery, has been formulated by the confluence of several technological advances: Manned and unmanned submersibles replaced man-divers; sonar and computer advances provide efficient and reliable acoustic search systems; and dynamic vehicle positioning can be done with such accuracy that mooring is not required. With increasing awareness of the possibilities of deep ocean recovery, demands have grown for human remains recovery, aircraft accident investigation, and removal of classified or dangerous objects. Recovery of objects is sometimes time critical—before an adversary can either intervene or make the recoveries himself.

With their associated technologies, integrated salvage systems provide the capability to recover or manipulate large objects such as sunken military vessels or aircraft at depths exceeding 100 m and in Sea State 3 conditions. The integrated salvage systems enable the military to recover small objects, such as warheads and sensors, at much greater depths.

The applications of deep sea drilling technologies include the ability to implant surveillance equipment on the ocean floor. The equipment comprises the sound surveillance system (SOSUS), whose Navy mission has been to track ships and submarines of Cold War adversaries. The SOSUS has been used by other agencies to monitor earthquakes and volcanoes at sea, to track whales, to detect illegal fishing, and to look for ocean temperature shifts (sound speed changes with water temperature) that are signs of impending climatic trouble.

Currently, there is an increased military concern with potential regional conflicts, perhaps protracted, that require naval presence in littoral areas and a corresponding decrease in the likelihood of open ocean battles between naval task forces. But equipment and technologies related to ocean implant and ocean salvage still need to be controlled. While SOSUS operations are being greatly reduced, for example, the U.S. Navy may find it necessary to implant microphone arrays that target countries of concern that have submarines and other submersible vehicles. And the capability to implant sensors and transponders to detect, locate, and track submarines directly affects the strategic nuclear balance as well as tactical anti-submarine warfare.

Military Acoustic Systems

Most marine sensing systems employ acoustic signals (sound waves) to locate underwater objects and features. Systems that use underwater sound generally are called sonar's. Sonar systems are termed "active" when sound is generated by the system for the purpose of echo ranging on a target. In contrast, "passive" sonar systems only listen to the sound radiated by the target.

Most advanced acoustic systems technologies are developed for military purposes. Since commercial acoustic systems are often a spin-off from a military system, many have potential for effective military application. Acoustic systems technology is a primary ingredient in element 5 under "Military Superiority" of the U.S. major long term goals articulated by the National Military Strategy.

Sonar systems are the principal sensors used in all areas of Undersea Warfare (USW), including antisubmarine warfare (ASW), torpedo defense, mine warfare, deep sea salvage and for swimmer warfare. Sonar's are used militarily for detecting, classifying, identifying, locating and tracking potential underwater targets, for undersea mine and torpedo homing and activation, for countermeasures, for underwater navigation, for depth sounding and for bottom mapping. Sonar's are used commercially for locating fish and other objects in the ocean, for seismic exploration at sea, for petroleum and mineral exploitation and for academic studies. These uses also involve the detection, classification, localization and tracking of underwater objects and features, for navigation and for depth sounding and bottom mapping. Obviously there is a sizable amount of overlap between the military and commercial applications but with lesser overlap in design; with specifics delineated in the critical elements. Likewise, many terrestrial (land based) systems employ sound waves to locate geological features in the earth's crust. Such systems used for geophysical prospecting are called seismic systems. All acoustic seismic systems are "active," but have passive implications for ASW. Passive terrestrial systems are designed for intruder detection and the detection and location of direct fire weapons. Acoustic vibrations are also a critical issue for space platform stability.

The U.S. as a maritime nation is economically and militarily dependent on freedom of the seas. Historically, over 95 percent of U.S. peacetime and wartime transport of material has been by sea. This figure held for the recent Persian Gulf War. The fact that a relatively few cheap sea mines can effectively hold a major sea power at bay was also reaffirmed. Considering these facts along with the Former Soviet Union (FSU) advanced and prolonged mine and submarine building programs and the realization that many potential adversaries have or are likely to acquire modern mines and submarines, dictates that the U.S. maintain ASW and mine warfare as high war fighting priorities. ASW and mine warfare are also expected to remain a high priority mission of both the Eastern and Western worlds for the foreseeable future; although the emphasis is shifting from deep ocean to littoral warfare and the potential adversary from the FSU to undesignated third world countries. Other undersea warfare roles, such as swimmer warfare and deep sea salvage and rescue, are also high priority. In each of these areas, the civilian and military needs, techniques, and applications are very similar. Therefore, the areas covered under air, marine, space platform and terrestrial acoustic systems remain of great importance to the security of the Western world and must be carefully considered. (IDA Doc. D-1404 1994, 182)

If the control of militarily applicable acoustic systems is lessened, then the exploitation by potential adversaries could seriously diminish the U.S. operational advantage in ASW, mine warfare and space platform utilization. Prolonged release could offset the stealth advantages of U.S. submarines that we obtained at great cost, reduce the effectiveness of U.S. acoustic barriers and ASW screens for battle groups and convoys, and reduce the effectiveness of U.S. mines, torpedoes and countermeasures.

The major concern with commercial marine acoustic systems is not as much with the potential application in major naval combatants, as for: (1) installation on auxiliary vessels for rapid mobilization needs, (2) "use" in ocean measurements and research and development on the data bases for evaluating and improving USW systems, and (3) for use in developing more effective operational scenarios for current and future USW systems.

Foreign Technology Assessment

The U.S. has maintained a significant lead in acoustic systems technology over the FSU and a comfortable lead over the major western producing countries. The proclaimed FSU gain in ASW capability during the 1980s came more from improved submarine quieting than from improved sensors. The UK and France clearly pace the remainder of the western world, and though smaller in size, still lead the FSU in many technology areas. Germany and Japan come next in size and quality of acoustic systems technology capability, followed by Australia and Canada. All of the above have reasonably complete capability in acoustic sensors and weapons; largely sustained by competent government laboratories and industry. Japan has obtained a large portion of their capability by licensing arrangements with the U.S. Navy. Italy, Netherlands and Norway have acoustic capability in limited niche areas. Other countries . . . have a very limited acoustics capability. All countries are listed that have a known acoustic capability. (IDA Doc. D-1404 1994, 184)

Chart 8.2
Foreign Technical Capabilities
(Part 1)

	Sec. 8.2 Subsurface & Deep Submarine	Sec. 8.3 Ocean Salvage & Deep Sea Implant
Argentina	No capability	No capability
Australia	Some critical elements	Limited
Austria	No capability	No capability
Brazil	Limited	Some critical elements
Canada	Majority of critical elements	Some critical elements
China	Limited	Limited
Czech	No capability	No capability
Egypt	No capability	No capability
Finland	Extensive	Some critical elements
France	Majority of critical elements	Some critical elements
Germany	Majority of critical elements	Some critical elements
Hungary	No capability	No capability
India	Limited	No capability
Iran	No capability	No capability
Iraq	No capability	No capability
Israel	Limited	Limited
Italy	Majority of critical elements	Some critical elements
Japan	Extensive	Majority of critical elements
Korea, N.	Limited	Limited
Korea, S.	Some critical elements	Some critical elements
Netherlands	Majority of critical elements	Extensive
Norway	Majority of critical elements	Some critical elements
Pakistan	No capability	No capability
Poland	Limited	Limited
Spain	No capability	No capability
Sweden	Majority of critical elements	Some critical elements
Switzerland	Majority of critical elements	Some critical elements
Turkey	No capability	No capability
Taiwan	Limited	No capability
UK	Extensive	Majority of critical elements
US	Extensive	Extensive
USSR (Former)	Some critical elements	Some critical elements

LEGEND:

- Extensive capabilities in all critical elements
- Capabilities in majority of critical elements
- Capabilities in some critical elements
- Limited capability
- No capability or none identified

(U.S. DoD 1992 Militarily Critical Technologies List)

The United States pioneered the development of advanced fixed, deployed, hull mounted and towed passive sonar's. France and the UK have developed some innovative techniques for their unique platforms. Their capability is equal to the U.S. in limited niche areas. Most other countries import or manufacture run-of-the-mill systems designed from data available to them.

The United States has also paced the world in the "development" and "use" of seismic systems. France, Germany, .Norway and the UK are approaching an equal capability. A fledgling seismic industry has appeared in the former PACT countries and the PRC; probably anchored from the FSU which lags the West by about 10 years. This lag is probably due to lack of national priority as well as the lack of an innovative industrial base. Most systems seem to be retained for long periods of time or updated based on a western system design with innovation being secondary to development cost.

Chart 8.3
Foreign Technical Capabilities
(Part 2)

	Sec. 6.1 Acoustics	Sec. 6.2 Optical Sensors
Argentina	▨	☐
Australia	▨▨	▨▨
Brazil	▨	▨
Canada	▨▨	▨▨
China	▨	▨
Czech	☐	▨
Egypt	▨	☐
Finland	▨	☐
France	▨▨▨	▨▨▨
Germany	▨▨	▨▨▨
Greece	☐	▨
Hungary	☐	☐
India	▨	▨
Iran	☐	☐
Iraq	☐	☐
Israel	▨	▨▨
Italy	▨▨	▨
Japan	▨▨	▨▨▨
Korea, N.	▨	☐
Korea, S.	▨	▨
Neth	▨	▨▨▨
Norway	▨	☐
Pakistan	▨	▨
Poland	▨	▨
Portugal	▨	☐
New Zealand	▨	☐
S. Africa	☐	▨
Spain	▨	▨
Sweden	▨	▨▨
Switzerland	☐	▨▨
Turkey	▨	▨
Taiwan	▨	☐
UK	▨▨▨	▨▨▨
US	▨▨▨▨	▨▨▨▨
USSR (Former)	▨▨	▨
Yugoslavia	▨	▨

LEGEND:

▨▨▨▨ Extensive capabilities in all critical elements	▨▨ Capabilities in some critical elements
▨▨▨ Capabilities in majority of critical elements	▨ Limited capability
	☐ No capability or none identified

(U.S. DoD 1992 Militarily Critical Technologies List)

Active Acoustic Systems

Such systems are used militarily for ASW, torpedo defense, mine warfare, swimmer warfare, deep sea salvage, and underwater communications and navigation. Functions performed are the detection, classification, identification, location and tracking of underwater targets and features; undersea mine and torpedo homing and activation; depth sounding; and bottom mapping. Commercial uses of active systems are locating fish and other objects in the oceans, tracking pipelines, petroleum and mineral exploitation, academic studies and seismic exploration at sea. Functions performed are the detection, classification, identification, location and tracking of underwater objects and features; depth sounding; bottom mapping; and the detection, location and identification of specific features of the earth's crust under the ocean floor. Obviously, there is a sizable amount of overlap between the commercial and military applications but a lesser overlap in the designs. Most commercial sonar's are designed to operate monostatically in the direct path mode from medium size fishing or work boats or from submersibles; all in limited environmental conditions. Commercial systems are as simple and as economical as possible to perform the specified job, though they are often current state-of-the-art. Navy sonar's operate monostatically or multistatically from a variety of surface ships, submarine and aircraft, from a moored or bottom mounted location and in all environments. Navy systems are designed to operate reliably for diverse applications and in widely varying situations; therefore are much more complex, expensive and incorporate the latest state-of-the-art. Perhaps the major difference between commercial and military systems is that the military systems must have a very high probability of correct response in order to succeed in their warfare role. (U.S. DoD 1992 Militarily Critical Technologies List, 186-87)

Mine detection and deep sea salvage active sonar's are generally high frequency, 30 to 750 kHz, in order to provide the resolution to discriminate and identify the desired targets from background clutter. The search mode starts with the lower frequencies of 30 to 80 kHz for faster area coverage and changes to higher frequencies of 100 to 750 kHz for classifying and identifying a detected target. Forward-looking and side scan active sonar's are both used for these purposes. (U.S. DoD 1992 Militarily Critical Technologies List, 187-88)

Marine seismic systems use a towed, 8 to 200 Hz frequency source and a long towed hydrophone array (streamer) to receive the sound signals bounced off the ocean bottom and other features in the earth's crust. The purpose of this procedure is to locate underground, or surface, areas that have a potential for petroleum or hard mineral exploration exploitation. Marine seismic data is recorded at sea and later processed at a land based analysis center. Seismic streamer data gathering systems are of strategic concern because they are very similar to and have a direct application as ASW passive sensors. (U.S. DoD 1992 Militarily Critical Technologies List, 189)

Critical Elements

1. Active sonar for area surveillance has reportedly been under development to supplement the SOSUS network in order to counter the newer generation of quiet threat submarines. Low frequencies and very high power are required for the ranges desired. All aspects of such sonar's are sensitive and incorporate many critical technologies.

Active sonar systems with real-time, automatic or computer aided detection, classification, discrimination, identification or localization of targets are considered militarily critical because of the potential for large numbers of targets processed with correct response. The use of neural network techniques for the above functions is likewise critical. Real-time adaptive beam-forming for interference suppression, reverberation suppression and signal processing gain of over 20 dB all improve the system figure-of-merit for both longer ranges and increased correct response. Such techniques are required for a successful military sonar, but not often needed for commercial sonar's.

2. Wide swath bathymetric survey systems were developed by the U.S. Navy for efficiently obtaining accurate ocean bottom contour maps for use in strategic navigation. Such maps provide an effective way to absolutely update submarine navigation without surfacing. Modern bathymetric systems provide the capability to cost effectively and somewhat covertly develop bottom contour maps, accurate enough for submarine ballistic missiles to pinpoint U.S. and Allied targets. The accurate contour maps needed for submarine holding areas are not economically possible without such systems. Commercial needs are largely for less than 600 m depth or can be met with less accurate systems.

3. All navies of the world use active sonar object detection systems for some aspects of undersea warfare. The concern with commercial systems is for both use as military sensors and for potential use as a countermeasure/jammer against military systems. This item covers the sonar's used in aircraft, ships, submarines, torpedoes and mines; those that are deployed and bottom mounted and those used for underwater acoustic communications (IIL 6.A.l.a.l.b).

a. Most ASW sonar's operate below 10 kHz. No commercial sonar's operate below this frequency except for sub-bottom profilers which are exempt from control (IIL 6.A.l.a.l.b.l).

b. Some military sonars and weapons operate at frequencies above 10 kHz. Therefore, the source level is also important from 10 kHz to 30 kHz as commercial systems can serve as jammers to the military sonars and weapons. Current fish-finding sonars have been tested and proven effective for several military applications. The concern is with scanning vertical sonar's as well as horizontally operated systems; which can be interchanged to a limited degree. The proposed frequency, source level and range combined, limit these from fully overlapping military application or serving as jammers to such systems.

Some current military sonars require narrow beams of less than one degree for the purpose of finding small military strategic items on the ocean floor. Since there is insignificant commercial justification for such narrow beams below 100 kHz, this capability is controlled. Control of all systems with less than one degree beam was sought but denied by CoCom.

c. Sonars are difficult to build that operate effectively at great depths. The transduction elements must be exposed to the ambient pressure. The 1000 m depth limit is selected as most applications at greater depths have military significance. The depth floor is applied throughout III. 6.A. 1 and this section except for the non-dynamically compensated arrays noted here and the depth sounders and sub-bottom profilers exempted by a note. All commercial sonar applications are for less than 5,120 m range, most much less; while ASW sonars routinely exceed this limit.

4. The most sophisticated active sonars for use on submersibles are military use only but some are now being considered for commercial and academic applications. The strategic value is for rapid localization and identification of military hardware in the ocean with low probability of intercept. The special features are the ability to detect, classify and track multiple small contacts in a cluttered environment and to navigate through hazardous terrain. These features are also appealing to commercial interests and a commercial version is expected with a few years.

5. Channel adaptive processing is a critical technology because it significantly reduces the interference from multiple arrivals and other signal fading phenomena and thereby provides longer range with greater reliability of operation.

6. The U.S. and Allies have dominated the world-wide deep sea salvage arena. At times, this is of the highest priority. Acoustic systems for determining position with an accuracy of 10 m at a range of 1000 m are a crucial element in this capability that has not been otherwise available in the proscribed countries. This capability allows a systematic, high "probability of detection"

search pattern for lost objects or to accurately implant strategic system at great depths. The U.S. anticipates the need for both functions to remain for the indefinite future. There are also numerous commercial application for such acoustic location systems, such as salvage, petroleum and mineral exploitation and academic studies. Most of these applications can be met with the uncontrolled systems where ranges are shorter or the accuracy is not necessary at long ranges. (U.S. DoD 1992 Militarily Critical Technologies List, 195-98)

Full-spectrum processing is necessary in ASW as the threat frequencies vary from platform to platform and with each type of threat weapon system. The processing is an extension of the traditional sonar intercept receiver. The concern for detecting transients requires a new form of processing for short duration signals that are traditionally processed out as noise. Large scale processing is required for the large data base received from the applicable arrays. Computer assistance is necessary as the operator cannot expeditiously handle such a large data base. There is no commercial counterpart. (U.S. DoD 1992 Militarily Critical Technologies List, 212)

Neural network technology is a special approach to the acoustic processing above based on the decision logic of the human brain by utilizing a multiplicity of simple computational devices arranged in large networks that can be trained.

Real-time "data-fusion" for a combination of arrays requires the sorting and combining of the massive amount of data received from each array and passing these in a usable form to an operator or to the control unit of a weapons system. Computer aided pattern recognition and other forms of artificial intelligence processing are often required to reduce a large data base without losing the targets of interest. There is a limited commercial counterpart of this need based on real-time and data volume. The acoustic processing used in seismic exploration approaches this need based on data base size but is largely an off-line process.

All acoustic sensors that are required to move through the water or have current flow by them are hindered by the flow noise. Most acoustic hydrophones that are in varying motions are subject to acceleration generated noise. Often the noise limits sensor performance. New techniques to cancel this noise by countering with out-of-phase type processing have proven successful. This is very important to sensors that travel at high speeds and are impacted by the turbulent flow vibration. There are no commercial acoustic sensors that need to operate with such high speed and low self noise such as to require these techniques.

Adaptive beamforming, null steering and sidelobe suppression are techniques to reduce background noise from directions other than from the target by enhancing the signal beam and reducing all others. Adaptive beamforming allows the operator to limit the signal beams to the area of interest and rejecting interfering noise outside the beam. Adaptive null steering allows the nulling of a loud signal coming from a bearing of less concern such as for a close in escort ship. Adaptive sidelobe suppression is electronic enhancement of the signal beam while reducing the sidelobe noise. Such techniques require large amounts of processing power and are often necessary to succeed in a tactical ASW scenario with multiple targets and a cluttered acoustic environment. There is no commercial counterpart for real-time applications. (U.S. DoD 1992 Militarily Critical Technologies List, 212-13)

Towed hydrophone arrays are the most effective mobile ASW sensors in use today. Continued improvements are required to stay effective against quieter targets.

Long towed arrays used for increased aperture present significant seakeeping challenges. The same aperture can be achieved by towing the same length but divided into multiple, shorter arrays. If a volumetric array is formed, then the bearing ambiguity can be reduced. To use these arrays effectively, there must be an accounting of the relative position of individual elements between arrays; generally achieved in real-time by acoustic methods. Seismic streamers also use acoustic method for the same purpose between their multiple arrays, but the processing is performed off-line. (U.S. DoD 1992 Militarily Critical Technologies List, 224)

There are few commercial applications for passive sonar's except for research. Most areas of concern are with the passive subset of active systems. The major concern is with the passive ASW capability of (active) seismic marine exploration systems which overlap the passive ASW frequency spectrum. ASW towed arrays are the most effective mobile sonar improvement to date. Towed array systems have been carefully controlled, but seismic streamers (towed hydrophone arrays) operating at 35 m or greater depths make an effective substitute. Such systems can detect modern submarines at transit speeds without modification to the seismic system. At less than 35 m depth, seismic arrays are not effective for ASW. Furthermore, 98 percent of the seismic streamers are operated at less than 30 m depths and most passive ASW systems are operated below 30 m. Therefore, seismic systems limited to shallow depth can have more array sensitivity than is tolerable for greater than 35 m depth operation. Other criteria are included to prevent real time signal processing and beamforming which provide significantly greater ASW value.

Hydrophones are the key component for successful underwater acoustic operation. Many techniques developed for military application are being brought into commercial use. This criteria is intended to permit most commercial usage with recommended control of dominantly military applications. Military use requires extra depth, sensitivity, and acceleration compensation capability.

Towed hydrophone arrays are yanked around by the ship motion and weather conditions. Each acceleration motion creates noise in the hydrophones. The better a hydrophone is compensated, the lower the self noise level. This criteria was developed as a demarcation point between commercial and military applications. Seismic arrays operate at less than 5 knots and experience little difficulty with array self noise. (U.S. DoD 1992 Militarily Critical Technologies List, 218)

Hull mounted hydrophones are in continuous changing motion when the ship or submarine is underway, especially in heavy sea state. Each acceleration motion creates noise in the hydrophones. The better a hydrophone is compensated, the lower the self noise level. This criteria was developed as a demarcation point between commercial and military application. Commercial ships can experience similar acceleration, but their systems do not require as high a signal to noise ratio level. (U.S. DoD 1992 Militarily Critical Technologies List, 219)

Security Classification of Bathymetric and Geophysical Data

While some technology has been specifically designed for minerals exploration, much technology useful for this purpose has been borrowed from technology originally designed for other military applications. Some of the most sophisticated methods available for exploration were developed initially for military purposes. For instance, development of multi-beam bathymetric systems by the U. S. Navy has proven useful for civilian charting, oceanographic research, and marine minerals exploration. Much technology developed for military purposes is not immediately available for civilian uses. Some technologies developed by the scientific community for oceanographic research are also useful for minerals exploration .

> The convergence of two advanced technologies— multi-beam echo sounders and very accurate navigational systems— provides the basis for extremely detailed maps of the seabed that are spatially accurate in longitudinal and latitudinal position on the earth's surface as well as precise in determining the depth

and land forms of' the undersea terrain. Multi-beam systems when used in conjunction with the satellite-based Global Positioning System. can produce charts from which either surface craft equipped with the same shipboard instruments or submarines with inertial navigation and sonar systems can navigate and accurately position themselves. If geophysical information, e.g., gravity and magnetic data, is superimposed over the mapped region, its value for positioning and navigation is further enhanced. A 1987 workshop of' Federal, private. and academic representatives concluded that NOAA should acquire geophysical data that would not hinder the timely acquisition of the bathymetric data. Classification stymied NOAA's effort to form a cooperative arrangement with industry and academia. Thus, to date, NOAA has not acquired gravity or magnetic data. (U.S. OTA 1987, 269-70)

While the capability to identify subsurface terrain features and accurately determine their position is a boon to scientists seeking to locate and explore geological features on the seafloor, it presents a potentially serious security risk if used by hostile forces. Because of the security implications, the U.S. Navy, with the concurrence of the National Security Council's National Operations Security Advisory Committee, initiated actions to classify multi-beam data and restrict its use and distribution. (U.S. OTA 1987, 270)

Modern undersea warfare requires that submarines, once submerged, remain submerged to avoid detection. When submarines operate globally, this long-term submergence presents significant navigational problems. Inertial guidance systems and other navigational gear must be occasionally updated with precise location information if the submarine's position is to be determined accurately. One means for doing this is by fixing terrain features on the ocean bottom and triangulating within them to determine the vessel ' s position . With detailed bathymetric maps and precise geodesy, modern acoustical detectors and onboard computers are capable of precisely fixing a submarine's position without having to surface and risk detection. Little imagination is needed to understand the security implications of high-resolution bathymetry. Bathymetric data may also affect other aspects of undersea warfare, including acoustical propagation and mine warfare countermeasures. (U.S. OTA 1987, 270)

Earlier Reviews of Data Classification

In a 1985 report the Naval Studies Board determined that the unrestricted release of accurately positioned, high resolution bathymetric data could result in new and significant tactical or strategic military threats. The Board concluded that 'map matching," i.e., locating one's position by matching identifiable features on the seafloor by using precise bathymetry from broad regional coverage, could afford potentially hostile forces a unique and valuable tool for positioning submarines within the U.S. EEZ.

While the Naval Studies Board supported the Navy's position with regard to classifying and controlling 'processed" survey data. it did not favor classifying raw data until they are processed into a form that provides full geodetic precision and large area coverage. As a further measure, the Board suggested that each processed map be reviewed for distinctive navigational features that would make it valuable for precise positioning and that the sensitive data be "filtered" as necessary to permit its use in unclassified maps. The Board further recommended that the sensitive data be made available on a classified basis to authorized users and that raw data covering a limited area be released without security restrictions for the pursuit of legitimate research.

A second review of the Navy s data classification policy regarding multi-beam data was also undertaken by the National Advisory Committee on Oceans and Atmosphere (NACOA) at the request of NOAA in 1985. NACOA generally supported the Naval Studies Board's conclusions.

Undersea Robots and Manipulators

Robots are used in deep sea environments that are too hazardous or impractical for divers or manned vehicles. Some robots are remotely controlled while others are preprogrammed or can operate without inputs from a human source. Telerobotic systems involve man in the supervisory control loop via telepresence. Robotic techniques can be applied to tethered and untethered, free maneuvering or bottom crawling vehicles to do repetitive underwater work, which includes visual inspection, nondestructive testing, surveying, measuring, welding, and trenching. Undersea robots use the following technologies: real time vehicle position, automatic navigation and hovering control, lighting and viewing systems, and advanced underwater manipulators. (IDA Doc. D-1264)

Remotely controlled, articulated manipulators are used on manned and unmanned, tethered and untethered submersible vehicles to perform underwater work under the pressures found at ocean depths. They are the critical tool for working under water. Advanced manipulators, which have seven or more degrees of freedom and forced feedback, can do more types of work at a higher level of quality and in less time than less sophisticated manipulators. Figure 8.5 illustrates a remotely controlled manipulator with six degrees of freedom (DOF) or degrees of freedom of movement (DFM). A more advanced manipulator with nine DOF/DFM is shown in Figure 8.6. In both figures, the function of claw opening and closing is not counted as a DOF/DFM. Besides forced feedback—which is a tactile sensor between the manipulator and an underwater object that enables the operator to precisely control the manipulator in performing intricate tasks the advanced manipulator may use a spatially correspondent proportioned master-slave control to duplicate movement of the operator's arms or a computer to determine programmed movements.

Figure 8.5
Six Degrees of Freedom Manipulator

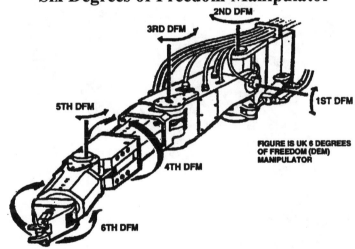

(Slingsby Electronics, Ltd., U.K.)

Robotic systems can conduct work at ocean depths on systems of strategic importance. They are important for military missions that are too dangerous or impractical for manned submersibles or divers. They can be deployed, do their work autonomously or semi-autonomously, and be recovered by a host platform.

Manipulator dexterity, which is expressed in the number of degrees of freedom of movement, determines the usefulness of a manipulator to perform underwater work. The larger the DOF, the more closely the manipulator emulates the human arm. Manipulators with six or more DOF can work inside an object or through or behind a barrier beyond the reach of a submersible. The military utility of this capability is that it permits visually covert tampering with sensors or removal of critical equipment from vessels, aircraft, or missiles on the seafloor. Manipulators are not acoustically covert since their hydraulic operation is noisy.

Figure 8.6
Nine Degrees of Freedom Manipulator

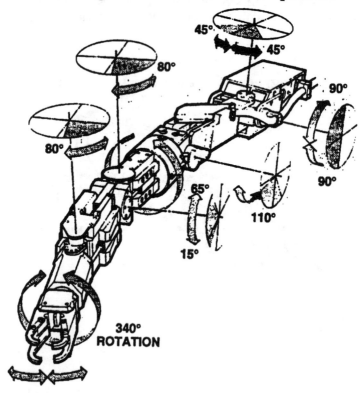

(Slingsby Electronics, Ltd., U.K.)

Like unmanned tethered submersible vehicles, these robots can be used for such covert military missions as ocean salvage and deep sea implant (sensors and mines) in situations where human safety and endurance are concerns. And, as in the case of the submersible vehicles, the robots are virtually undetectable.

Without adequate manipulators, a submersible vehicle equipped with the most advanced power plant, vision system, and electronics would have limited capabilities. Restricting accessibility of adversaries to advanced manipulators makes more difficult their ability to recover, manipulate (tamper with sensors or remove critical equipment), and implant mines and sensors on the ocean floor.

Chapter Nine

UNCLOS Military Commitments?

An issue recently raised in Congress, and particularly in the Senate, revolves around the extent to which U.S. participation in a decision of a U.N. body--in this case the U.N. Security Council and its votes on U.N. peacekeeping--might commit the United States to expend funds and provide personnel for an action not approved by Congress. The immediate impetus for this concern was a U.S. vote in March 1993 in the U.N. Security Council approving the U.N. Operation in Somalia, II (UNOSOM II), with an expanded mandate that included enforcement powers. This operation superseded the U.N.-authorized, U.S.-commanded Unified Task Force in Somalia in May 1993. It was more expensive than the original, very limited first UNOSOM and included U.S. military in administrative/logistic roles and the introduction of U.S. fighting forces as needed. This all occurred without the express permission of Congress. After 18 U.S. troops were killed in early October 1993, Congress began to question the authority for U.S. military participation in such U.N. operations. It enacted into law provisions requiring the executive branch to keep Congress informed on the decisions and possible decisions of the U.N. Security Council in the peace and security area and on the setting up and expanding of peacekeeping operations and possible U.S. participation. (See Section 407, P.L. 103-236, State Department Authorization Act, FY 1994-1995.) Some in Congress might want to have similar consultations and reporting requirements instituted as a way of keeping up with the work of the International Seabed Authority and its organs and bodies. (Browne)

Enforce Maritime Agreements

The development of international maritime law, especially the Third U.N. convention of the Law of the Sea (UNCLOS III), has established a legal environment in which the U.N. could take on a variety of new low-intensity policing functions in support of international agreements. This is especially important in areas of international straits because attempts to police straits could lead to disputes, perhaps even conflicts. For many nations, this mission area could involve coast guards as well as civilian maritime agencies. (Sands)[13]

In a well-timed contribution to the debate on UNCLOS the Center for Naval Analysis (CNA) published a strong analysis on the potential for the International Seabed Authority to take on a blue water police/enforcement role in support of treaty provisions. CNA demonstrated that there is ample precedent and existing regulatory flexibility whereby, if States parties cooperate, the ISA may develop a military arm which may not only radically extend the functions and purposes envisioned for it by the U.S. and its industrialized allies but may one day directly threaten U.S. high seas and economic zone interests as well.

Given the ambiguity embedded in the charter, rules, regulations, and scope of the ISA as well as the highly uncertain ability of the U.S. or its allies to significantly influence events within the new organization the potential of the ISA becoming a runaway train cannot be dismissed. Some of the most likely areas where the ISA may attempt to apply naval power, according to CNA, are summarized below:

1. *Enforcement of fisheries regulation, EEZ arrangements and archpelagic waters.* Under UNCLOS, coastal nations have sovereign rights within 200-n.m. exclusive economic zones (EEZs). In many cases, the added responsibilities of protecting the EEZs may be beyond the capabilities of smaller navies, thus increasing the possibility of disputes. When disputes arise and when adjudication fails, or disputes involving the use or threat of force erupt, naval forces could be called on to establish U.N. maritime peacekeeping operations or to carry out Security Council-mandated Chapter VII enforcement measures.

2. *Measures to protect the marine environment.* Many of the obligations undertaken under UNCLOS concern the protection

of the marine environment.[14] There is a growing understanding that military as well as commercial activities can produce adverse consequences for the maritime environment. Given the dearth of technical and financial resources military environmental issues may be ripe for international cooperation. (Miller 1993) The current laissez-faire approach to enforcement may not work, and naval forces may be asked to do more, including enforcement through the threat of the use of force.[15] Besides enforcement, there may be roles for naval forces in surveillance and in establishing better communication for these purposes between authorities ashore and merchant vessels. Naval forces could also be called on by the United Nations to enforce the Antarctic Treaty provisions, should more be violated.[16]

3. *Protect Sea and Air Traffic.* With the reemergence of piracy in littoral waters, terrorism on the high seas, and the draw-down of national naval forces, multinational naval presence and crisis response for the protection of economic resources and trade may become more important. This is true especially in the world's main navigational straits and passages, which are also its major trade routes. The sovereign immunity of warships is already questioned in some quarters. Moreover, the potential for interfering with customary international law by unilateral threats to close straits is always there. At times, multinational cooperation in this traditional naval mission area may include surveillance, mine sweeping, and convoy and escort operations, even in areas of armed conflict. It may also include greater use of maritime interception operations and the establishing of maritime exclusion zones, or blockades.

4. *Convoy and escort of selected traffic on the high seas.* As a result of increased sensitivity following revelations in Iraq, for example, the United Nations could become involved in protecting the transport of fissile material on the high seas now that Japan is shipping weapons-grade plutonium from Europe to Japan for use in its breeder reactor program. Although the Japanese Maritime Safety Agency is now operating a new escort ship designed specifically for fissile material escort, some have argued that this step alone may be insufficient for adequate protection. Several states have expressed concern about the safety of this shipment as it is transported through the Straits of Malacca, and others have told Japan that shipments will be barred from passing through their territorial waters. (Sands)[17]

5. *ISA protection of offshore assets*, primarily petroleum production platforms and deep-water off-shore port facilities such as pipeheads and ocean mining claims and operations.

Chart 9.1

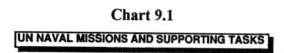

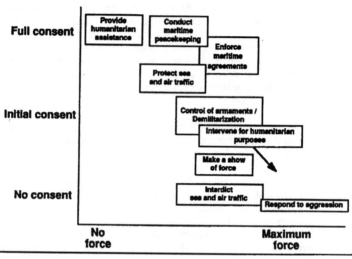

Level of consent and use of force (level of violence)

(Sands)

The level of military force involved can range from zero (as in humanitarian assistance) to moderate (as in humanitarian intervention) to quite considerable (as in responding to aggression). Although most U.N. operations are traditionally thought of as requiring full local consent (conferred or implied), the plausible range of consent can vary considerably, but not without limits. Hence, although a U.N. humanitarian intervention operation is likely to be undertaken with less local consent than humanitarian assistance, interventions with little or no local consent are not likely in a U.N. context.

---

13 For example, the U.S. Coast Guard (USCG) enforces U.S. federal law on the high seas, interdicts smugglers moving drugs and illegal migrants, and enforces fisheries regulations and U S. Law and protects U.S. interests in the exclusive economic zone claimed by the U S Further, the USCG has cutters involved in detection, monitoring interdiction and operational support of third-country drug operations, and conducts joint counter narcotics training and patrols with several countries. The USCG has agreements with Japan and Hong Kong and experience in sea lines of communication

---

(SLOC) through cooperation with the U.S. Navy.

[14]For example, the Convention addresses the dangers of pollution from vessels exercising the right of freedom of navigation, and strengthens the powers of littoral states against polluters.

[15]Sir Brian Urquhart, former Under Secretary-General for Special Political Affairs (the U.N. peacekeeping post), has written that the U.N. needs "a system like this: A convention exists on tankers not being allowed to clean their tanks at sea. So tank cleaning should be monitored, and once you've caught a tanker doing it at sea, and issued a couple of warnings, somebody goes out and drops a very small bomb down a funnel: 'That's it, boys, you've had two warnings to stop it. The third time down you go.' The moment that one tanker, after three warnings, goes to the bottom, I don't think there will be any more tanks cleaned at sea."

[16]The Antarctic Treaty internationalized and demilitarized the Antarctic continent and provided for its cooperative exploration and future use. Several countries have claimed sovereignty over areas of Antarctica, claims the United States and the former Soviet Union did not recognize. Rivalry backed by the threat or use of military force for control of exploitable economic resources is still only a theoretical possibility, and one that still looms small given past scientific cooperation and the continent's isolation. Resource exploitation could in the near term raise environmental protection concerns, about which naval forces operating under a U.N. aegis could be called on to respond because of the Antarctic Treaty and the continent's location and isolation. For a text of the Antarctic Treaty, see United States (1982).

[17]With the approval of the U.S. regarding the security plan (U.S. approval is required for fuel and byproducts of U.S. origin, and U.S. warships, planes, and military intelligence satellites monitored the voyage), the first of 45 shipments over the next seven yrs left France in November 1992. The ship carrying the plutonium casks, *Aka~suki Maru,* was escorted by the Japanese Maritime Safety Agency's new 6,500-ton escort ship, *Slu'kish~'ma* Singapore, Malaysia, and Indonesia have expressed concerns about an unspecified "mishap" involving the shipments, arguing that the fissile material should not be transported through busy waterways or near densely populated areas. To date, Argentina, Brazil, Chile, Hong Kong, Indonesia, Malaysia, the Philippines, Singapore, South Africa, Uruguay, and, in a way that has caught the attention of the Japanese media, the Republic of Nauru has told Japan to keep the shipments out of its territorial waters. The United States has ruled out its passage through the Panama Canal. Others, such as the members of the South Pacific Forum, have urged that the shipments be stopped. See also (Reid; Associated Press; Sanger; Waxman; and Offley).

Chapter Ten

Conclusions

> The U.N. has nothing to do with the interests of the common man; it is an organization for governments. It is the forum where legitimacy is bestowed on the Idi Amin's, the Emperor Bokassa's, the Yasser Arafat's, the Mu'ammar Qadhafi's, and the cannibals, murderers, and other sundry types who rule most of the world's nations. It is, as Mayor Koch so justly observed, a forum of "immorality, hypocrisy, and cowardice." To identify the interests of the U.N., an organization of largely despotic states, or any of its agencies, with the interests of all mankind is tantamount to identifying the interests of a cannibal with the interests of those he had for lunch. (Paul 1983, 25)

> The whole procedure and substance of the "Agreement" appears to have been drafted to be deliberately mysterious. It is a method that as far as we can find is unprecedented in international law to amend a political or legal treaty. We have grave difficulty understanding what status it would have in international law, which countries would be bound by it, how it will be applied in practice, what Congress's role in the process is, what industry's role in the process is, what United States rights and duties are under the "Agreement," [and] how that affects our licenses. (Hoyle)

Dangerous Precedents

The benefits to the United States of UNCLOS participation cannot be denied. They include guidelines on the management of fisheries, the environment, dispute settlement, and marginal improvements in freedom of navigation and overflight. While such issues seem impressive on the surface, their resolution are not a Herculean achievement nor are they critical to the economic health or physical security of the United States. The administration has trumpeted these successes as justification for U.S. accession to UNCLOS, while it has ignored or downplayed serious precedential and strategic issues, engaging in what theologians call adiaphora -- or dwelling on things that are unimportant. A good rhetorician will attempt to sidetrack a discussion away from substantive issues if they do not support his argument and onto adiaphorous issues. The "real" issues presented by accession to UNCLOS have been little discussed since 1982, and they are being sidestepped today in an effort to "sell" the 1994 Agreement.

The stakes for which the United Statesz was playing in UNCLOS extended well beyond the relatively parochial interests of tuna fishermen, peacetime sailors, or future ocean miners. What was being decided was nine-fold.

First, the establishment of a far-reaching precedent regarding control over traditionally "nonterritorial areas." This precedent not only will dictate future oceanic arrangements, but may well encompass such areas as Antarctica and outer space.

Second, the precedent of bestowing on LDCs effective control over corporate activities beyond their national borders, most graphically seen in the deep seabed negotiations, may snowball beyond oceanic areas and provide the procedural avenues and negotiating cohesiveness necessary to allow them to place stricter international controls over the activities of multinational corporations in general.

Third, it is possible that the voting arrangements being adopted for a new International Seabed Authority, based on a one-nation, one-vote principle, which refuses to recognize the institution of an interest group veto as exists in the U.N. Security Council, may eventually create a ground swell within the United Nations itself to revamp the existing voting arrangements and eliminate the Security Council.

Fourth, the momentum generated at UNCLOS by the combination of LDC steamroller-like tactics and U.S. negotiating weakness may effect other alterations in institutional arrangements and global power structures, which can only be estimated now.

Fifth, the ISA, if established in its present form, would be a major disincentive to investment which will effectively shut the United States out from access to future sources of strategic minerals and unnecessarily perpetuate U.S. import dependence.

The metal that will provide the principal income stream from production of manganese nodules is nickel. Over the past decade or so, the nickel market has been weak because supply has simply exceeded demand. The nickel market is once again beginning to grow. Much new growth in the future may result from demand for high-quality, alloy steels in new technologies. Over half of all nickel consumption continues to be in stainless steel. It is interesting to note that several new environmental technologies may become major consumers of stainless steel and others may require nickel in batteries and other "green" equipment. Since the United States produces very little nickel, large additional imports would be necessary if, for example, nickel hydride batteries for electric cars were required or became attractive to the consumer. If the political and legal problems facing ocean mining are resolved satisfactorily, the seabed will be developed when the markets for the metals justify investment. The tragedy would be if the seabed were shut in by a prohibitive seabed mining regime contained in the U.N. Law of the Sea convention and the so-called "Agreement." (Fields 1994, 5)

Sixth, the most curious and potentially most threatening aspect of the U.N. Law of the Sea process is provisional application. The administration does not intend to submit the "Agreement" and the 1982 Convention for advice and consent for some years, possibly not until mid-1998. In the meantime, the United States as a signatory of the "Agreement" may become a "Provisional Member" of the Council, the executive organ of the Seabed Authority. (Hoyle 1994) While provisional application is not a new procedure, it is not commonly used. Article 25 of the 1969 Vienna convention on the Law of Treaties recognizes the procedure. A 1993 Senate study observes,

> In the United States, provisional application of a treaty may be subject to question especially if it gives temporary effect to a treaty prior to its receiving the advice and consent of the Senate. An agreement to apply a treaty provisionally is in essence an executive agreement to undertake temporarily what the treaty may call for permanently. (U.S. Congress 1993, 84) Thus, provisional application of the agreement and U.S. participation in the International Seabed Authority, including the funding for such participation, might be viewed as bypassing or circumventing the role of the Senate in giving its advice and consent to U.S. adherence to a treaty.
>
> Opponents have cited the provisional application process in this instance as one through which the United States has "committed ... to the terms of the Law of the Sea Treaty for up to four years--even if the Senate never ratifies the treaty. This may violate the State Department Basic Authorities Act of 1956 (22 USC 2672)." (Fields 1994, 5) The State Department cites

Section 5 (a) of the same Act, as amended, as authorizing U.S. participation in "international activities ... for which provision has not been made by ... treaty," with the proviso that such authority is not granted for more than one year without approval of Congress. The Department further states that Section 5 (a) "has been construed to allow participation on a provisional basis in succeeding years if the Congress approves a budget submission containing a line item covering the activity in question for each such year." (Browne 1995)

Seventh, the structure, powers, functions, and voting arrangements in the ISA carry the potential for an aggressive enforcement capability developing within UNCLOS. Such a capability may have a military component that may complicate, rather than lend order to, ocean activities. In addition, the United States may find itself facing an unanticipated set of future international political and financial obligations as a result.

Eighth, the compulsory dispute settlement features of the treaty are of concern.

The Senate has historically been reluctant to accept broad compulsory dispute settlement language in treaties pending before it. For example, after nearly 15 years of off-and-on debate, the Senate, in 1935, rejected U.S. adherence to the 1920 Statute of the Permanent Court of International Justice (PCIJ), the judicial arm of the League of Nations. In 1946, when the Senate gave its advice and consent to U.S. ratification of the Statute of the International Court of Justice (ICJ) and acceptance of the compulsory jurisdiction of the Court (under Article 36, paragraph 2 of the Statute), it added the words "as determined by the United States" (the Connally reservation) to indicate the United States would determine whether a question was within its domestic jurisdiction and thus beyond the jurisdiction of the World Court. (This Article 36 declaration was withdrawn, effective April 1986, by the executive branch.) In May 1960, the Senate considered the four 1958 Law of the Sea conventions and an Optional Protocol providing for the compulsory jurisdiction of the ICJ in disputes over the interpretation or application of the conventions. The Senate rejected the Optional Protocol.

This concern that the United States maintain control over what actions might be taken against it, internationally, was reinforced during the last months of 1994, during congressional consideration of the Uruguay Round GATT agreements, the World Trade Organization, and its dispute settlement procedures. As a potential complaining party, the United States wanted a strengthened and expedited process; however, as a potential subject of a complaint, the United States wanted to protect its sovereign control over its own enacted laws and interests. (Browne)

Ninth, UNCLOS provides a plausible cover for foreign navies wishing to build a modern Anit Submarine Warfare or submarine launched ballistic missile firing location capability to acquire the necessary acoustic, bathymetry, and signal processing systems. This may already be happening in the case of the People's Republic of China.

Treaty Status — Overstated Claims

The greatest single accomplishment touted by the administration in seeking Senate ratification of the Treaty and the 1994 Agreement has been a guaranteed seat on the influential Council of the International Seabed Authority. While it may be premature to assess whether the Council will live up to its potential, there is no truth to assertions that the U.S. is guaranteed a seat on that body. The overselling of the Treaty is most evident on this issue.

COUNCIL MEMBERSHIP

After at least twenty weeks of wrangling in the Preparatory Commission and, since November 1994, within the ISA itself an operational formula for the implementation of Council membership has still not been resolved. In fact, the discussions have resurrected many of the North/South issues that so deeply divided UNCLOS in the past and led to President Reagan's rejection of the UNCLOS in 1982. In fact the impasse in constituting the Council has blocked the ISA from electing a Secretary General, a finance committee, judges to the Law of the Sea Tribunal, and the Director of the Enterprise, as well as staffing the other key commission and committee positions that will be so critical in determining the actual course of the UNCLOS organization.

NO GUARANTEED U.S. SEAT

Contradicting administration claims, the minutes of both the ISA and its Preparatory Commission confirm that there is absolutely no guarantee that the United States will have a seat on the Council. In fact, the written rules of the Treaty, the expressed attitudes among many of its dominant Group of 77 members, and the extraordinarily ingratiating behavior of the United States to secure a Council seat any cost in order to sell the Treaty to a dubious Senate virtually ensures that no permanent seat will be possible. The following facts demonstrate why administration claims are false.

1) <u>Treaty and Agreement Rules</u>: The text of both the Treaty and the 1994 Agreement make it very clear that no country may occupy a seat in more than one chamber of the Council at a time. This point was repeated by the president of the ISA's Assembly during its March 1995 meeting.

> Regarding the composition of the 36-member Council, the rules reproduce the five categories of membership outlined in the annex to the Agreement relating to the implementation of Part XI of the Convention. Before electing the members of the Council, the Assembly shall establish lists of countries fulfilling the criteria for membership in each category. States fulfilling criteria in more than one category will be included in all relevant groups, but may only be proposed for election by one group and shall represent only that group in voting. Each group shall nominate only as many candidates as the number of seats. (U.N. Document 1473, 4)

This ironclad limit places the United States in the running for only one seat on the thirty-six-member Council.

2) <u>Principle of Rotation of Council Membership</u>: Embedded in both the Treaty and the Agreement (U.N. Document A/RES/48/263, Annex 3 (10)) is the principle that a policy of rotation must be applied to Council membership to prevent its domination by a single state or group of states.

> The principle of rotation shall apply, as a general rule, when the number of candidates exceeds the number of seats. Each member of the Council shall be elected for four years. At the first election, however, the term of one half of the members of each of the five groups shall be for two years. (U.N. Document 1473, 4)

> . . . the principle of rotation should apply to future elections of candidates. . . and that should be interpreted as meaning that there was a general expectation that members of the group would move on and off the Council. That would not preclude the possibility of individual countries making informal arrangements, such as reciprocal support arrangements; nor would it preclude countries having consecutive terms on the Council, if that was agreed by the group. (U.N. Document 1473)

3) <u>Reemergence of North/South Mistrust</u>: The current discussions within the ISA have seen the surfacing of deep resentment on the part of Group of 77 members toward what they consider to be a

disproportionate role for industrialized states in the new regime. This view, which is supported by many Group of 77 members, needs to be fully understood and seen as a warning sign of the possible direction this infant regime may pursue in the coming years. The president of the Assembly, Hasjim Djalal (Indonesia), summarized much of the debate undertaken during the March 1995 session as cited in the following U.N. document excerpt:

Active and intense consultations had continued on two levels. The first was on the five different groups of members defined in the Agreement. The second level of consultations was on the general distribution of seats in the Council as a whole, which were basically related to the last group of members. Daily consultations had been held, but they had not been conclusive. Among the problems was the question of how to interpret the principle of assuring an equitable geographical distribution for the various regions, he said. There had been some difficulty in defining equitable distribution because several factors had been raised, including past experience in other forums, such as the United Nations. If the model of the United Nations was used, the geographical distribution would be around 11, 10, 7, 5 and 4 for Africa, Asia, Latin America and the Caribbean, Western Europe, and Eastern Europe, respectively. That gave a total of 37, which would necessitate one region conceding a seat in the 36-member Council. There were now 44 African members in the Assembly, 38 from Asia; 23 from Latin America and the Caribbean; 21 Western European and Other States; and 13 European States. If those were divided proportionally by regions alone, the seats would be shared in this manner: 11 for Africa, 10 for Asia, six from Latin America and the Caribbean, five for the Western Europe and Other States Group, and three from the Eastern European States, with one seat left over. In addition to a distribution that was geographically proportional, some members had requested that other criteria be considered, he said. They had requested that the need to seek a proper balance between industrialized countries, on the one hand, and developing countries, on the other, be properly addressed. That would represent the "so-called North-South balance," he said. The aim was that the majority of the South would not be in a position to automatically achieve a decision with a two-thirds majority, only to be vetoed in one of the chambers on the Council. The "North-South" balance would also prevent a minority from constantly blocking decisions. (U.N. Document SEA/1469,4)

Some delegates pointed out that of the 73 ratifications of the Convention only three were from industrialized countries. One delegate suggested that

> The 36 seats in the Council of the International Seabed Authority should be distributed among the regional groups in proportion to their membership in the Assembly of the Authority . . . by dividing the number of members in the Assembly--139--by the 36 Council seats, each Council seat would represent 3.86 Assembly members. By dividing the number of member States in each region by that figure, he calculated the following formula for proportional representation: Africa, which has 44 members, would have 11.39 seats; Asia, with 38 members, should have 9.84 seats; Eastern Europe, with 13 member States, should have 3.36 seats; Latin America and the Caribbean, with 23 members, should get 5.95 seats; and the Western European and Other States, with 21 members, would get 5.44 seats. (U.N. Document SEA/1468, 1)

The Russian representative, recognizing the potential for a serious North/South rift, stated that "the challenge of agreeing on equitable geographical distribution was only part of the problem facing the Assembly. As in the negotiation period for the Convention, a majority had agreed on a position that was not workable. Realization of that fact had led to negotiation of the Agreement on the implementation of Part XI. The Agreement had been hastily drafted, and compromise had been reached only through some sacrifice. The Assembly was now being challenged to put into practice both the Convention and the Agreement. The Assembly should not pit the South against the North, as there were a number of States actively preparing to exploit the resources of the seabed." (U.N. Document SEA/1469, 6)

Unfortunately, the potential for polarization among ISA members is high and will likely be exacerbated by future financing problems, lack of significant achievements, resistance by some member states to back radical initiatives, slow development of seabed resources, and a lack of hoped for revenue sharing. These issues need to be fully explored during the future ratification debate.

4)   <u>U.S. Pattern of Ingratiation and Deception</u>: The Clinton administration, in a desperate attempt to portray the UNCLOS as being in the national interest and worthy of ratification, has compromised away long-term Council representation in exchange for securing a quick seat prior to Senate consideration. This exercise in "political optics"

occurred during the ISA debate over Council representation in the Consumers/Importers Chamber.

> The meeting of Group A--the consumers/importers group--was attended by Belgium, Cape Verde, China, France, Germany, Japan, Marshall Islands, the Republic of Korea, Russian Federation, United States and United Kingdom. (U.N. Document SEA/1494, 1)

> The United States, United Kingdom, Russian Federation, Japan, Germany, Belgium, and Italy expressed their interest in nomination to the Council. Belgium, Italy, and Germany withdrew their requests on the understanding that the principle of rotation would provide opportunities for their election to the Council at a later date. The group agreed to nominate Japan, Russian Federation, United Kingdom, and United States to the Council, with Russian Federation and United States for election for a two-year term and Japan and the United Kingdom for a four-year term.

> The acceptance by the Russian Federation and the United States of two-year terms was on the understanding that the Assembly would affirm that the Council would include the Eastern European State having the largest economy as well as the State having the largest economy on the date of entry into force of the Convention, should those States seek re-election to the Council. The acceptance was also predicated on the understanding that the principle of rotation would apply to Japan and the United Kingdom after four years. (U.N. Document SEA/1473, 6)

Why did the United States and the Russian Federation accept two-year terms instead of vying for the two four-year appointments? The Russians believed they had struck a deal whereby the other group members agreed to re-elect them after the initial two-year term expired and that Japan and the United Kingdom would face a mandatory rotation. The United States, while confirming the Russian view of the two-year term stated that the re-election conditions and mandatory rotation of the United Kingdom and Japan did not apply to U.S. acceptance of a two-year term.

> WESLEY S. SCHOLZ (United States), speaking as coordinator of group A, said that . . . he had assumed that the group had agreed on the nomination of the United States and Russia for two-year terms and the United Kingdom and Japan for four-year terms, assuming that certain conditions had been met.

The United States had agreed to a two-year term, the United Kingdom and Japan had agreed to four year terms, and the Russian Federation had agreed to a two-year term, on the conditions stipulated in the report of the President. (U.N. Document SEA/1473, 10)

It is remarkable that an administration that is strongly promoting U.S. accession to the UNCLOS would be willing to volunteer the United States to a diminished role within its key decision-making body. The failure of the United States to press for re-election guarantees as the Russians have may readily be construed as the act of a desperate delegation attempting to project the appearance of influence at any price in order to deceive the Senate into ratification of the UNCLOS.

RATIFICATIONS

There are now eleven states parties to the Convention which have also accepted the Part XI Agreement. Through the simplified procedure, by the end of July this year, up to 19 more States Parties could be bound by the Agreement. It is also expected that a number of States--particularly Western European States--would follow Australia, Germany, and Italy in accepting both instruments in a relatively short period of time. Other states which are interested in nominating candidates for the election of judges of the International Tribunal for the Law of the Sea would also have further incentive to expedite the process of ratification or accession, in order to be well in time for the election on 1 August 1996.

Thus it may be possible that the 40-States requirement for the entry into force of the Agreement be fulfilled by the end of this year, or at the latest by early 1996.

With regard to the other requirement for its entry into force, i.e., five pioneer investor States from among developed States, plus two more pioneer investor States, I would predict this could be met also without encountering major difficulty, for the following reasons:

First, two out of the five developed States have already been taken by Germany and Italy.

Second, six States whose pioneer investors have been registered, i.e., China, France, India, Japan, the Republic of Korea, and the Russian Federation, have strong incentives to accept the two instruments so as not to lose their exclusive rights over the mining sites allocated to them.

Third, the acceptance of the two instruments by some other pioneer investor countries among EU members are also quite likely. These could be Belgium, the Netherlands and the United Kingdom. Further, I hope we can add the United States to this list as well.

Thus, what is required is the acceptance by five out of France, Japan, Belgium, the Netherlands, the United Kingdom and the United States, all of which have publicly stated their governments intention to do so, or by three out of these plus two plus two out of China, India, and the Republic of Korea.

Finally, I must point out that there are still several States which are not likely to accept the instruments. They are mostly the States which have certain long-standing difficulties with some of the Convention provisions, other than those in Part XI. These countries, however, constitute only a small minority and would in no way pose a major obstacle to the widespread and near-universal acceptance of the Convention and the Agreement. (Hayashi 1995, 5-6)

Options for the U.S. Senate

After a treaty has been signed, the president at a time of his choice submits to the Senate the treaty and any documents that are to be considered an integral part of the treaty and requests its advice and consent to ratification. The president's message is accompanied by a letter of submittal from the secretary of state to the president which contains an analysis of the treaty.

Senate consideration of the treaty is governed by Senate Rule XXX, which was amended in 1986 to simplify the procedure. The treaty is read a first time and the injunction of secrecy is removed by unanimous consent, although normally the text of a treaty has already been made public.

The treaty is then referred to the Senate Committee on Foreign Relations under Senate Rule XXV on jurisdiction. After consideration, the Committee reports the treaty to the Senate with a proposed resolution of ratification that may contain any of the conditions described below. Most treaties are reported without conditions. If the Committee objects to a treaty, or believes the treaty would not receive the necessary majority in the Senate, it usually simply does not report the treaty to the Senate and the treaty remains pending indefinitely on the Committee calendar.

After it is reported from the Committee, a treaty is required to lie over for one calendar day before Senate consideration. The Senate considers the treaty after adoption of a nondebatable motion to go into executive session for that purpose. Rule XXV provides that the treaty may then be read a second time, after which amendments to the treaty may be proposed. The Majority Leader typically asks unanimous consent that the treaty be considered to have passed through all the parliamentary stages up to and including the presentation of the resolution of ratification. After the resolution of ratification is presented, amendments to the treaty itself, which are rare, may not be proposed. The resolution of ratification is then "open to amendment in the form of reservations, declarations, statements, or understandings." Decisions on amendments and conditions are made by a majority vote. Final approval of the resolution of ratification, with any conditions that have been approved, requires a two-thirds majority of those Senators present.

After approving the treaty, the Senate returns it to the President with the resolution of ratification. If he accepts the conditions of the Senate, the President then ratifies the treaty by signing a document referred to as an instrument of ratification. Included in the instrument of ratification are any of the Senate conditions that State Department officials consider require tacit or explicit approval by the other party. The ratification is then complete at the national level and ready for exchange or deposit. When the treaty has entered into force, the President signs a document called a proclamation which publicizes it domestically. (Collier 1991, 2)

If the President objects to any of the Senate conditions, or if the other party to a treaty objects to any of the conditions and further negotiations occur, the President may resubmit the treaty to the Senate for further consideration or simply not ratify it.

The Senate may stipulate various conditions to its approval of a treaty. The Senate rules do not define the scope and nature of the conditions. Practical limits exist to the extent that conditions, although adopted by a majority vote, must be approved by a two-thirds majority of the Senate or the final resolution of ratification will fail. In addition, the president must approve the conditions or he will not sign the instrument of ratification. In the case of conditions having international implications, if the other party does not agree to the conditions, the treaty will not enter into force.

The conditions may be grouped in categories--amendments, reservations, understandings, declarations and other statements. There are some generally recognized distinctions among these conditions, but they are not always used consistently. The important distinction among the various conditions concerns their content or effect. Whatever a condition is named by the Senate, if the president considers that a condition constitutes an amendment or reservation that alters any international obligations, he transmits it to the other party or parties and further negotiations or abandonment of the treaty may result.

Treaty amendments
A proposed amendment to a treaty provides for a change in the language of the treaty itself. Because it alters the obligations of all parties, an amendment must be approved by them.

Reservations
A reservation is a limitation or qualification attached to the resolution of ratification that changes the obligations of one or more of the parties under the treaty. It does not amend the treaty text. A reservation must be communicated to other parties and, in a bilateral treaty, explicitly agreed to by the other party. President Nixon requested a reservation to the Geneva Protocol on the use of poison gases. The reservation stated that the protocol would cease to be binding on the United States in regard to an enemy state if it or any of its allies failed to respect the prohibition.

Understandings
An understanding is an interpretation or elaboration considered consistent with the treaty and ordinarily used to clarify the treaty rather than revise it. The Department of State determines whether an understanding requires transmittal to the other party or parties.

Declarations and Other Statements
Declarations and other statements attached to the resolution of ratification express policy or conditions that are related to the subject of the treaty but do not necessarily affect the provisions of the treaty. Frequently, like some of the understandings mentioned above, declarations and other statements concern internal procedures of the United States rather than international obligations and are intended to assure that Congress or the Senate participate in subsequent policy.

Approval Without Formal Statements or Conditions
Even when it does not place formal conditions in the resolution of ratification, the Senate may leave its imprint on a treaty. The Senate may make its views known or establish requirements on the executive branch in the report of the Foreign Relations

Committee or through other vehicles. Such statements become part of the legislative history but are not formally transmitted to other parties.

Treaty Rejection

A treaty is rejected by the Senate if the resolution of ratification fails to receive the required two-thirds majority. Occasionally a treaty receives the required two-thirds vote but does not enter into force because the reservations or amendments included in the resolution of ratification are not acceptable to the president or to the other parties to the treaty. A reservation that is intended to have this effect is sometimes called a "killer amendment." Rejection of a treaty by Senate vote is relatively rare at the present time. No arms control treaties since World War II have been formally rejected because they failed to receive the two-thirds majority. As an example outside the arms control area, on March 8, 1983, the Senate rejected the Montreal Protocols to the convention for the Unification of Certain Rules Relating to International Carriage by Air and they were returned to the Foreign Relations Committee calendar; the Protocols were reported out again with three conditions February 5, 1991.

Usually treaties that lack adequate support simply sit on the Foreign Relations Committee or Senate calendar and are allowed to die for lack of affirmative Senate action. That is, they are not reported out by the Foreign Relations Committee or are not voted on by the Senate. (Collier 1991, 3-10)

Bottom Line

While UNCLOS has effectively codified many aspects of traditional law and has successfully incorporated several modern issues, such as environment, fisheries, and coastal zone management, these can be regarded as "nice to have" accomplishments but are by no means essential to the political, economic, or military security of the United States. In fact, one of the principal reasons for the establishment of UNCLOS III was to resolve U.S. conflicts with several Latin American states over territorial sea claims in the Pacific Ocean and the repeated seizure of U.S. tuna boats and their crews. After more than ten years of UNCLOS III, ten years of post-UNCLOS III ratification debate, and two more years of negotiation of the Agreement, Nicaragua, Peru, Ecuador, and El Salvador still claim 200-mile territorial seas and refuse to become parties to the Convention.

With regard to Nicaragua and Peru, their abstention could be due to their claim to the 200-mile territorial sea, which is not in conformity with the Convention.

The reasons for the absence or non-participation of these states are not clear. Only Turkey explained that it had some difficulties with certain provisions of the Convention. Ecuador and El Salvador may have chosen not to vote because of their claim to the 200-mile territorial sea. (Hayashi, 5-6)

In fact, the Turkish problems with the UNCLOS may eventually lead to a major shooting war between Turkey and Greece. In July 1995 the Turkish Parliament issued a strong warning to Greece not to extend its territorial sea to twelve nautical miles as allowed in the Convention. The Parliament, concerned that an extension of Greek territorial sea limits to twelve nautical miles would make 70 percent of the Aegean Sea a "Greek lake," empowered the government to take all measures, including military actions if necessary, to protect the vital interests of Turkey. "The balance in the Aegean was established with the Lausanne Peace Treaty of 1923 at which time the territorial waters of both countries were at three miles." (Jane's 1995, 11)

On the other hand, the regulatory, political, technological, economic, and possibly military concessions embedded in the treaty represent a set of potential threats and traps yhat the United States should not walk blithely into.

Treaty supporters within the United States now include a number of former treaty opponents who appear to have resigned themselves to a "this is the best deal we are likely to achieve" philosophy after the Clinton administration's failure to press hard for real change during the 1993-1994 renegotiation. To cite the administration's weak negotiating skill or its failures to argue on behalf of basic U.S. national security interests in international forums makes a poor rationale for ratification of a treaty.

There is a common misperception that existing national security export control mechanisms will act as a safety net to ensure that the treaty will not serve as a conduit for militarily critical technology to be exported to potential adversaries. Unfortunately, the "stovepiped" nature of many government policy actions masks the fact that the Clinton administration has virtually eviscerated the export control process within the U.S. government and has dismantled the international regulatory mechanism as well. (Leitner, 1995) There is no longer a reliable safetynet to prevent foreign military or intelligence services from using the treaty as a cover to acquire highly strategic state-of-the-art technology that may be used to enhance power projection or regional destabilization activities.

Unless the United States is willing to insist on further renegotiation of the treaty to protect these and other vital interests the Senate will have little alternative other than rejection and refusal to ratify. Rejection by the Senate appears to be the only action capable of serving as the catalyst to bring all parties back to the table.

Contracting Out U.S. Foreign Policy

If there is one overarching characterization that can describe U.S. participation in UNCLOS it is taking a giant step forward in the continuing delegation of U.S. foreign policy to the United Nations. Recent milestones along this path include U.S. initiatives to multinationalize peacekeeping operations such as that in Bosnia; "humanitarian relief" operations as in Somalia and Rwanda, and actual belligerent military operations like the Gulf War.

Ironically, this "contracting out" of U.S. foreign policy is quietly taking place against the backdrop of a growing domestic debate on whether to repeal the War Powers Act, which places strict limits on the president's ability to use military force in support of foreign policy objectives. Would the lifting of War Powers restrictions lead the president to commit U.S. forces to ever more complicated and dangerous U.N.-sponsored military operations? Would the potential military commitments hidden in UNCLOS have a greater likelihood of developing? Will the United States eventually find itself in the position of "world policeman," being assigned roles and missions dictated by others?

Many of those in favor of repealing the War Powers Act argue that meddlesome congressional oversight and second-guessing of presidential prerogatives are burdensome constraints. Imagine the second-guessing and interest group politics imposed by 170 nations and their bloated bureaucracy of international civil servants as the "contracting out" of U.S. foreign policy continues.

The International Seabed Authority and UNCLOS represent the surrender, with little or no compensation, of a variety of tangible U.S. security and sovereignty equities over a geographic area encompassing 70 percent of the Earth's surface. The administration is attempting to bind this nation to a treaty and a bureaucratic organization whose basic operating principles are inimical to U.S. interests and that, to date, is officially recognized only by third-world and landlocked states.

The United States has once again approached a negotiation by "giving or offering a concrete, positive, material advantage in exchange for hypothetical concession of a negative activity; a tangible asset is sacrificed for a promise not to make trouble in the future; something measurable and manifest is traded for the promise of something unmeasurable and unverifiable." (Revel 1983, 249)

This negotiating principle is part of a wider technique: *prior concession*. It consists of ceding in advance, even before negotiations begin, what should be the subject of the negotiations and which the West should propose at the end of the talks, not at the start, and then only in exchange for a carefully weighed and at least equivalent counterconcession. (Revel 1983, 249)

It is disturbing to note the extremes to which the Clinton administration may be willing to go, in order to secure ratification of this treaty. A persistent rumor has been circulating among Law of the Sea watchers for the past two years that significant political pressure was applied to the Lockheed Corporation to force it to silence its opposition to the treaty and the 1994 Agreement. As the story goes, at a 1994 interagency meeting where irritation was expressed over vocal treaty opponents, a naval officer volunteered to "take care" of Lockheed. At that time Lockheed was at a very delicate stage of its controversial merger with Martin-Marietta and extremely sensitive to external factors that could raise government objections to the merger. Reportedly, Lockheed personnel summoned by senior management were ordered to cease public criticism of the treaty. Congressional review could uncover the truth behind the rumor and expose the parties involved.

As stated earlier, of the many precedents embodied in the existence of the ISA, the creation of an international bureaucracy with powers to tax, regulate, and enforce its will are perhaps the most dramatic and, in the long term, the most dangerous. The granting of what are essentially sovereign powers is unprecedented and unfortunately fits within a larger pattern of U.N. behavior—that being, to free itself from the political domination of the five permanent members of the Security Council as well as to insulate itself from the uncertainties and political limitations accompanying the traditional state-sponsored financing of U.N. operations.

Secretary-General Boutros-Boutros Ghali recently proposed to establish a "world tax" on airline tickets and currency exchanges as an independent means of financing the U.N.. "Faced with $2.3 billion in arrears from member nations that failed to pay their assessments— including $1.2 billion owed by the United States—U.N. officials and others have long sought an independent means to raise money for the organization's annual budget of roughly $3 billion." (Barber 1996) Disclosure of this plan provoked an immediate negative response in the U.S. Senate when majority leader Bob Dole stated "the United Nations continues its out-of-control pursuit of power" and along with colleagues called for an immediate investigation. (Barber 1996)

Unfortunately, the Law of the Sea Treaty goes far beyond the Ghalli plan and may indeed be viewed as a harbinger of future U.N. efforts to spin-off or reformulate its activities in such a way as to insulate itself from, and possibly become ascendant to, the sovereign character of nation-states.

Let us hope that the U.S. Senate will recognize that the costs to the United States of UNCLOS ratification far outweigh any potential gains and reject this treaty.

Appendix I

UNCLOS Chronology

02/27/95 -- The ISA Assembly is slated to reconvene its first session through March 17 in Jamaica.

11/16/94 -- The first session of the International Seabed Authority (ISA) Assembly convened in Jamaica for three days, Nov. 16-18, 1994 (a ceremonial session).

10/07/94 -- President Clinton sent Convention/Agreement package to the Senate (Treaty Doc. 103-39).

07/29/94 -- The United States signed the 1994 Agreement relating to the Implementation of Part XI of the United Nations Convention on the Law of the Sea.

11/16/93 -- The 60th instrument of ratification was received by the United Nations, thereby activating entry into force one year later.

07/19/90 -- Secretary-General Perez de Cuellar convened the first of 15 meetings of informal consultations held between 1990 and 1994.

12/27/86 -- President Reagan extended the U.S. territorial sea from three to 12 nautical miles.

01/15/85 -- The Minerals Management Service requested comments and information from interested parties to assist in delineating areas for detailed resource, environmental, and economic reviews for possible leasing of sites for recovery of construction materials, placer deposits, phosphorltes, polymetallic sulfides, cobalt-manganese minerals, or other nonenergy minerals within the Exclusive Economic Zone and the Outer Continental Shelf. (See Federal Register v. 50, no. 10, p. 2254).

10/29/84 -- NOAA issued a deep seabed mining exploration license to Kennecott Consortium (Salt Lake City, UT); the site is in the Clarion-Clipperton Fracture Zone of the northeastern equatorial Pacific Ocean and is designated as USA-4. (see Federal Register, v. 49, Nov. 8, 1984, p. 44661)

08/29/84 -- NOAA issued deep seabed mining exploration licenses to three U.S. consortia: Ocean Minerals Co. (Mountain View, Calif.), Ocean Management Inc. (New York, NY.), and Ocean Mining Associates (Gloucester Ponnt,VA); the three sites are in the Clarion-Clipperton Fracture Zone of the northeastern equatorial Pacific Ocean ar.d are designated, respectively, as sites USA-1, USA-2, and USA-3. (See Federal Register, v. 49, Sept. 13, 1984, p. 359,3ff.)

03/10/83 -- President Reagan, by proclamation, established a 200 nautical mile exclusive economic zone in which the United States exercises sovereign rights for the purpose of exploring, exploiting, conserving, and manag ng natural resources, both living and non-living, of the seabed and subsoil and the superjacent waters and with regard to other activities for the economic exploitation and exploration of the zone as well as jurisdiction over the protection and preservation of the marine environment.

12/10/82 -- The U.N. Convention on the Law of the Sea was opened for signature until Dec. 9, 1984, and signed by 119 entities. The United States signed only the Final Act of the Conference.

12/08/82 -- The United States claimed jurisdiction over polymetallic sulfides in the Gorda and Juan de Fuca Ridge areas of the Pacific Ocean, west of the States of Washington and Oregon (Federal Register Dec. 8, 1982, p. 55313).

07/09/82 -- President Reagan announced that the United States would not sign the Law of the Sea Treaty as adopted but would continue to participate at a technical level for the remaining conference negotiating session and sign the Final Act of the Conference.

04/30/82 -- Delegates at the eleventh sessnon of the Law of the Sea Conference adopted a convention by a recorded vote of 130 to 4, with 17 abstentions. The United States,

Venezuela, Turkey, and Israel voted against adoption. Reagan Administration spokesmen announced they would evaluate the pros and cons of rejecting the convention at the final session of the Conference scheduled for December 1982 at Kingston, Jamaica, where a formal signing of the convention will take place. The treaty would come into force 12 months after 60 nations ratify or accede to it.

12/30/82 -- President Reagan announced that the United States would not pay its portion of its 1983 U.N. regular budget assessment estimated to finance the operation of the Preparatory Commission.

12/10/82 -- The United Nations Convention on the Law of the Sea was signed by 119 entities. The United States signed only the Final Act of the Conference.

09/24/82 -- The Law of the Sea Conference ended, after approving the report of the Drafting Committee, deciding to open the Convention for signature in Jamaica, Dec. 6-10, 1982, and approving the Final Act that had been prepared by the Secretariat.

09/22/82 -- The eleventh session of the Third United Nations Conference on the Law of the Sea reconvened in New York for three days.

08/25/82 -- The Drafting Committee of the Law of the Sea Conference ended six and one-half weeks of work, started on July 12, recommending nearly 2,800 technical or drafting changes in six languages, to be considered by the Conference in September.

07/09/82 -- President Reagan announced the United States would not sign the Law of the Sea Convention.

04/30/82 -- The Conference, by a vote of 130 in favor and 4 against (including U.S.), with 17 abstentions, adopted the Convention on the Law of the Sea and the associated resolutions.

04/29/82 -- President Koh proposed additional changes in document A/ CONF.62/L.141/Add.1.

04/28-29/82 -- Debate held in plenary by 53 delegations on document A/Conf.62/L.132 and Add.1.

04/27-28/82 -- Informal consultations were held on the proposals in document A/CONF.62/L.132 and Add.1.

04/26/82 -- The Conference, by vote, rejected three amendments in documents A/CONF.62/L.109 and L.120, dealing with straits transit and reservations to the convention. An amendment enabling Namibia to sign the Convention and participate in the Preparatory Commission (document A/CONF.62/L.137) was revised and accepted by consensus.

04/19/82 -- The Soviet decree on seabed mining was made public.

04/15-17/82 -- Speakers from 87 nations debated the formal amendments.

04/13/82 -- By the 6 p.m. deadline, 31 sets of amendments had been submitted.

04/07/82 -- Conference decided, as of 04/08, that rule 33 on formal amendments would apply. The deadline for submission of formal amendments was 04/13.

04/06/82 -- The Soviet Union indicated it was eligible as a pioneer investor under PIP.

04/05/82 -- U.S. delegation instructions were relaxed.

04/01-02/82 -- Conference documents A/CONF.62/ L.93 and L.94 were issued.

03/30-01/82 -- The Conference debated reports of the Committee chairmen and new proposals. Comments heard from 112 delegations.

03/29/82 -- Committee chairmen presented reports with compromise proposals to plenary meetings.

03/25/82 -- The Group of 11 industrialized nations of the West (G-11) proposal on PIP and the G-11 compromise proposals of 3/19 were issued as informal conference documents with language added on decision-making.

03/23/82 -- The U.S. reportedly rejected G-11 compromise package.

03/22/82 -- France submitted a proposal on PIP.

03/19/82 -- Group of 11 submitted compromise proposals on U.S. seabed concerns.

03/16/82 -- The Group of 77 rejected the U.S. "green book" of amendments to the conference.

03/15/82 -- A PIP proposal is presented by United States, United Kingdom, West Germany, and Japan.

03/12/82 -- The U.S. delegation presented its "green book" of specific amendments.

03/08/82 -- The 11th session of the Law of the Sea Conference convenes in New York for 8 weeks.

03/03-05/82 -- Group of 77 requested complete and specific amendments from the United States.

02/24/82 -- U.S. made available to delegations an informal approaches paper.

01/29/82 -- President Reagan announced that the United States would reenter the U.N. Law of the Sea negotiations (eleventh session), seeking amendments to the draft convention that would give American companies better access to seabed minerals and the U.S. Government a larger role in seabed governing bodies.

10/19/81 -- The American Enterprise Institute held a day-long conference on United States Interests in Law of the Sea: Review and Analysis.

09/15/81 -- National Oceanic and Atmospheric Administration published final rules in the Federal Register (v. 46, no. 178: 45890-45920) setting forth the procedures and substantive requirements governing NOAA's issuance of exploration licenses for deep seabed mining operations.

08/28/81 -- The Law of the Sea Conference closed its 10th session, issuing an official text of the Draft Convention.

08/03/81 -- The 10th session of the Law of the Sea Conference resumed in Geneva for 4 weeks.

04/17-24/81 -- The 10th session of the Law of the Sea Conference adjourned its spring meeting in New York without completing its program of work.

03/07/81 -- The State Department announced that the head of the U.S. delegation to the Law of the Sea Conference, scheduled to convene on March 9, would be replaced.

03/04/81 -- The Reagan Administration decided to seek deferment of final U.N. conference action on the Law of the Sea Treaty, pending a complete review of the draft Convention, and instructed the new U.S. negotiating team to ensure that the negotiations don't end at the Mar. 9 - Apr. 24 New York session of the conference.

03/02/81 -- The State Department announced that the U.S. delegation to the 10th session of the Law of the Sea Conference was under instructions to assure that the informal negotiation stage of the conference was not concluded before the Reagan administration completed its review of the draft convention now before the conference.

08/28/80 -- The 9th session of the Law of the Sea Conference issued a draft convention on the Law of the Sea (Informal Text).

07/14/80 -- The Republican Platform contained the following language relative to the Law of the Sea Conference:"Multilateral negotiations have thus far insufficiently focused attention on U.S. long-term security requirements. A pertinent example of this phenomenon is the Law of the Sea Conference, where negotiations have served to inhibit U.S. exploration of the seabed for its abundant mineral resources. Too much concern has been lavished on nations unable to carry out seabed mining, with insufficient attention paid to gaining early American access to it. A Republican Administration will conduct multilateral negotiations in a manner that reflects America's abilities and long-term interest in access to raw material and energy resources."

09/01/76 -- Secretary of State Kissinger met in New York with delegations to the Law of the Sea Conference. He sought to break negotiation deadlocks over seabed mining issues.

04/08/76 -- Secretary of State Henry A. Kissinger gave a major address on "The Law of the Sea: A Test of International Cooperation" in New York City.

06/20/74 -- The 3rd U.N. Conference on the Law of the Sea opened its first substantive session in Caracas, Venezuela.

12/03/73 -- First session of the Third U.N. Conference on the Law of the Sea convened, starting a process that ended nine years later, on Dec. 10, 1982.

12/03/73 -- The 3rd U.N. Conference on the Law of the Sea opened in New York with a 2-week organizational session.

07/09/73 -- The Senate passed S. Res. 82, in support of the President's ocean policy statement.

04/02/73 -- The House passed H. Res. 330, in support of the President's ocean policy statement.

12/17/70 -- The U.N. General Assembly adopted a 15-point Declaration which, inter alia, recognized that the seabed and ocean floor beyond the limits of national jurisdiction and the resources of that area, are the "common heritage of mankind." The U.N. General Assembly decided to convene a conference on the law of the sea and assigned to the Seabed Committee the task of preparing for the conference.

08/03/70 -- U.S representatives presented to the U.N. Seabed Committee a draft treaty for an international regime and machinery for the international seabed area.

05/23/70 -- President Richard Nixon made a major policy statement setting forth a broad framework for U.S. policy in the oceans.

12/15/69 -- The U.N. General Assembly adopted the "moratorium" resolution that sought to ban all activities of exploitation of the resources on the seabed and ocean floor beyond the limits of national jurisdiction. U.S. spokesmen did not consider the resolution to be binding on the United States.

12/21/68 -- The Ad Hoc Committee created by the U.N. General Assembly was made a permanent U.N. committee, frequently referred to as the Seabed Committee.

12/18/67 -- The U.N. General Assembly established an Ad Hoc Committee to Study the Peaceful Uses of the Seabed and the Ocean Floor Beyond the Limits of National Jurisdiction.

03/00/60 -- The Second U.N. Conference on the Law of the Sea met at Geneva to resolve unsettled issues: breadth of the territorial sea and fishery limits. No solutions were adopted.

02/24/58 -- Delegations from 86 nations met in Geneva to finalize 4 conventions on the law of the sea. The 4 treaties, adopted on Apr. 29, 1958, dealt with territorial sea and the contiguous zone, the high seas, fisheries and the preservation of the living resources of the high seas, and the continental shelf.

Appendix II

UNCLOS and "Agreement" Signatories

Status of the United Nations Law of the Sea Convention
and Part XI Agreement
(As of April 20, 1995)

State or Entity	LOS Convention: Date of Ratification/ Accession(s)/ Succession (s)	Part XI Agreement:		
		Signature	Provisional Application	Consented to be Bound, by: ratification, accession (a)/ definitive signature (s)/ participation (p)
Summary	74	72	115	13
Afghanistan **			Yes	
Albania			Yes	
Algeria		July 29, 1994	Yes	
Andorra **			Yes	
Angola	December 5, 1990			
Antigua and Barbuda	February 2, 1989			
Argentina		July 29, 1994	Yes	
Armenia **			Yes	
Australia	October 5, 1994	July 29, 1994+	Yes	October 5, 1994
Austria **		July 29, 1994+	Yes	
Azerbaijan **				
The Bahamas	July 29, 1983	July 29, 1994	Yes	
Bahrain	May 30, 1985		Yes	
Bangladesh			Yes	
Barbados	October 12, 1993	Nov. 15, 1994	Yes	
Belarus **			Yes	
Belgium		July 29, 1994+	Yes	
Belize	August 13, 1983		Yes	October 21, 1994/s

State or Entity	LOS Convention: Date of Ratification/ Accession(a)/ Succession (s)	Part XI Agreement: Signature	Provisional Application	Consented to be Bound, by: ratification, accession (a)/ definitive signature (s)/ participation (p)
Benin			Yes	
Bhutan **			Yes	
Bolivia **			Yes	
Bosnia-Herzegovina	January 12, 1994/s			
Botswana **	May 2, 1990		Yes	
Brazil	Dec. 22, 1988 *	July 29, 1994+	No	
Brunei			Yes	
Bulgaria			No	
Burkina **		Nov. 30, 1994	Yes	
Burma			Yes	
Burundi **			Yes	
Cambodia			Yes	
Cameroon	November 19, 1985		No	
Canada		July 29, 1994+	Yes	
Cape Verde	August 10, 1987	July 29, 1994+	Yes	
Central African Republic **				
Chad **				
Chile			Yes/1	
China		July 29, 1994+	Yes	
Colombia				
Comoros	June 21, 1994			

State or Entity	LOS Convention: Date of Ratification/ Accession(a)/ Succession (s)	Part XI Agreement:		
		Signature	Provisional Application	Consented to be Bound, by: ratification, accession (a)/ definitive signature (s)/ participation (p)
Congo			Yes	
Cook Islands	Feb. 15, 1995/a		Yes	Feb. 15, 1995 (a)
Costa Rica	September 21, 1992			
Cote d'Ivoire	March 26, 1984	Nov. 25, 1994	Yes	
Croatia	April 5, 1995/a		Yes	April 5, 1996 (s)
Cuba	August 15, 1984 *		Yes/1	
Cyprus	December 12, 1988	Nov. 1, 1994	No	
Czech Republic **		Nov. 16, 1994+	Yes	
Denmark		July 29, 1994+	No	
Djibouti	October 8, 1991			
Dominica	October 24, 1991			
Dominican Republic				
Ecuador				
Egypt	August 26, 1983 *		Yes	
El Salvador				
Equatorial Guinea				
Eritrea			Yes	
Estonia			Yes	
Ethiopia **			Yes	
European Community		July 29, 1994+	Yes/3	

State or Entity	LOS Convention: Date of Ratification/ Accession(a)/ Succession (s)	Part XI Agreement: Signature	Provisional Application	Consented to be Bound, by: ratification, accession (a)/ definitive signature (s)/ participation (p)
Federal Republic of Yugoslavia ****	May 5, 1986 *			
Fiji	December 10, 1982	July 29, 1994	Yes	
Finland		July 29, 1994+	Yes	
France		July 29, 1994+	Yes/3	
Gabon			Yes	
The Gambia	May 22, 1984			
Georgia				
Germany	October 14, 1994/a	July 29, 1994+	Yes	October 14, 1994
Ghana	June 7, 1983		Yes	
Greece		July 29, 1994+	Yes	
Grenada	April 25, 1991	Nov. 14, 1994	Yes	
Guatemala				
Guinea	September 6, 1985	August 26, 1994	Yes	
Guinea-Bissau	August 25, 1986			
Guyana	November 16, 1993		Yes	
Haiti				
Holy See (Vatican City) **				
Honduras	October 5, 1993		Yes ˙	
Hungary **			Yes	
Iceland	June 21, 1985	July 29, 1994	Yes	
India		July 29. 1994+	Yes	

State or Entity	LOS Convention: Date of Ratification/ Accession(a)/ Succession (s)	Part XI Agreement: Signature	Provisional Application	Consented to be Bound, by: ratification, accession (a)/ definitive signature (s)/ participation (p)
Indonesia	February 3, 1986	July 29, 1994	Yes	
Iran			No	
Iraq	July 30, 1985		Yes	
Ireland		July 29, 1994+	No	
Israel				
Italy	January 13, 1995	July 29, 1994+	Yes/3	January 13, 1995
Jamaica	March 21, 1983	July 29, 1994	Yes	
Japan		July 29, 1994+	Yes/3	
Jordan			No	
Kazakhstan **				
Kenya	March 2, 1989		Yes	July 29, 1994/s
Kiribati				
Korea, North				
Korea, South		Nov. 7, 1994	Yes	
Kuwait	May 2, 1986		Yes	
Kyrgystan **				
Laos **		Oct. 27, 1994	Yes	
Latvia				
Lebanon	January 5, 1995			January 5, 1995/p/#
Lesotho **				
Liberia				
Libya			Yes	

State or Entity	LOS Convention: Date of Ratification/ Accession(a)/ Succession (s)	Part XI Agreement: Signature	Provisional Application	Consented to be Bound, by: ratification, accession (a)/ definitive signature (s)/ participation (p)
Liechtenstein **			Yes	
Lithuania				
Luxembourg		July 29, 1994	Yes	
F.Y.R. Macedonia **	August 19, 1994/s			August 19,1994/p/#
Madagascar			Yes	
Malawi **				
Malaysia		August 2, 1994+	Yes	
Maldives		Oct. 10, 1994	Yes	
Mali **	July 16, 1985			
Malta	May 20, 1993*	July 29, 1994	Yes	
Marshall Islands	August 9, 1991/a		Yes	
Mauritania		August 2, 1994+	Yes/2	
Mauritius	Nov. 4, 1994		Yes/1	Nov. 4, 1994/p/#
Mexico	March 18, 1983		No	
Micronesia, Fed. States of	April 29, 1991/a	Aug. 10, 1994+	Yes	
Moldova **			Yes	
Monaco		Nov. 30, 1994+	Yes	
Mongolia **		August 17, 1994	Yes	
Morocco		Oct. 19, 1994	No	
Mozambique			Yes	
Namibia	April 18, 1983***	July 29, 1994	Yes	
Nauru				

State or Entity	LOS Convention: Date of Ratification/ Accession(a)/ Succession (s)	Part XI Agreement:		
		Signature	Provisional Application	Consented to be Bound, by: ratification, accession (a)/ definitive signature (s)/ participation (p)
Nepal **			Yes	
Netherlands		July 29, 1994+	Yes	
New Zealand		July 29, 1994	Yes	
Nicaragua				
Niger **				
Nigeria	August 14, 1986	Oct. 25, 1994/^	Yes	
Niue (N.Z.)				
Norway			Yes	
Oman	August 17, 1989 *		Yes	
Pakistan		August 10, 1994	Yes	
Palau				
Panama				
Papua New Guinea			Yes	
Paraguay **	September 26, 1986	July 29, 1994	Yes	
Peru				
Philippines	May 8, 1984 *	Nov. 15, 1994+	Yes	
Poland		July 29, 1994+	Yes	
Portugal		July 29, 1994+	No	
Qatar			Yes	
Romania			No	
Russia			Yes/3	
Rwanda **				

State or Entity	LOS Convention: Date of Ratification/ Accession(a)/ Succession (s)	Part XI Agreement: Signature	Provisional Application	Consented to be Bound, by: ratification, accession (a)/ definitive signature (s)/ participation (p)
St. Kitts and Nevis	January 7, 1993			
St. Lucia	March 27, 1985			
St. Vincent and the Grenadines	October 1, 1993			
San Marino **				
Sao Tome and Principe	November 3, 1987			
Saudi Arabia			No	
Senegal	October 25, 1984	August 9, 1994+	Yes	
Seychelles	September 16, 1991	July 29, 1994	Yes	December 15, 1994
Sierra Leone	December 12, 1994			Dec. 12, 1994/p/#
Singapore	November 17, 1994		Yes	Nov. 17, 1994/p/#
Slovakia **		November 14, 1994	Yes	
Slovenia		January 19, 1995+	No	
Solomon Islands				
Somalia	July 24, 1989			
South Africa		October 3, 1994	Yes	
Spain		July 29, 1994+	No	
Sri Lanka	July 19, 1994	July 29, 1994/^	Yes	
Sudan	January 23, 1985	July 29, 1994+	Yes	
Suriname			Yes	
Swaziland **		October 12, 1994	Yes	
Sweden		July 29, 1994+	No	

State or Entity	LOS Convention: Date of Ratification/ Accession(a)/ Succession (s)	Part XI Agreement: Signature	Provisional Application	Consented to be Bound, by: ratification, accession (a)/ definitive signature (s)/ participation (p)
Switzerland **		October 26, 1994+	Yes	
Syria				
Tajikistan **				
Tanzania	September 30, 1985	October 7, 1994+	Yes	
Thailand				
Togo	April 16, 1985	August 3, 1994	Yes	
Tonga				
Trinidad and Tobago	April 25, 1986	October 10, 1994	Yes	
Tunisia	April 24, 1985 *		Yes	
Turkey				
Turkmenistan **				
Tuvalu				
Uganda **	November 9, 1990	August 9, 1994	Yes	
Ukraine			Yes	
United Arab Emirates			Yes	
United Kingdom		July 29, 1994+	Yes/2	
United States		July 29, 1994+	Yes/2	
Uruguay	December 10, 1992	July 29, 1994+	No	
Uzbekistan **				
Vanuatu		July 29, 1994+	Yes	
Venezuela				
Vietnam	July 25, 1994		Yes	

State or Entity	LOS Convention: Date of Ratification/ Accession(a)/ Succession (s)	Part XI Agreement: Signature	Provisional Application	Consented to be Bound, by: ratification, accession (a)/ definitive signature (s)/ participation (p)
Western Samoa			Yes	
Yemen	July 21, 1987 *			
Zaire	February 17, 1989			
Zambia **	March 7, 1983	October 13, 1994	Yes/2	
Zimbabwe **	February 24, 1993	October 28, 1994	Yes	

*   With a delaration (s)
**   *Landlocked*
*** UN Council for Namibia
**** Serbia and Montengro have asserted the formation of a joint independent
     state, but this entity has not been recognized as a state by the United States.

+   States or entities which have signed the Agreement, subject to ratification.
#   State bound by the Agreement by having ratified, acceded or succeeded to the
    Convention under Article 4, paragraph 1, of the Agreement.
^   State which has signed the Agreement and selected the application of the
    simplified procedure set out in Article 5 of the Agreement.

1. State applying the Agreement provisionally pursuant to Article 7(1) of the
    Agreement.
2. State applying the Agreement provisionally pursuant to Article 7(1)(b) of the
    Agreement.
3. State applying the Agreement provisionally pursuant to Article 7(1)(c) of the
    Agreement.
4. State applying the Agreement provisionally pursuant to Article 7(1)(d) of the
    Agreement.

Compiled from UN sources by Robert W. Smith, Office of Ocean Affairs, U.S.
Department of State: phone (202) 647-5123; fax (202) 647-9099, to whom changes or
corrections may be sent.

Appendix III

March 3, 1995

OCEAN MANAGEMENT, INC. (U.S. Corp.)

1987 to Present
24.67% - Schlumberger Technology Corp. (U.S.)
25.11% - INCO, Ltd. (Canada)
25.11% - Deep Ocean Mining Co., Ltd. [Consortium of 19
    Japanese Companies] (Japan)
25.11% - AMR [Preussag A.G. & Metallgesellschaft A.G.]
    (Germany)

1982 to 1985
25% - Sedco, Inc. (U.S.)
25% - INCO, Ltd. (Canada)
25% - Deep Ocean Mining Co., Ltd. [Consortium of 19 Japanese
    Companies] (Japan)
25% - AMR [Preussag A.G., Salzgitter A.G., & Metallgesellschaft
    A.G.] (Germany)

OCEAN MINERALS COMPANY

1986 to Present
50% - Cyprus Minerals Co. [Cyprus Mining Co.] (U.S.)

37.528% - Lockheed Missiles & Space Co. [Lockheed Corp.] (U.S.)
12.472% - Lockheed Systems Co., Inc. [Lockheed Corp.] (U.S.)

1982 thru 1985
30.669% - AMOCO Ocean Minerals Co. [Standard Oil Co. of Indiana]
      (U.S.)
6.329% - Lockheed Systems Co., Inc. [Lockheed Corp.] (U.S.)
63.002% - Ocean Minerals, Inc. [U.S. Corp.] *

Ocean Minerals, Inc. **
38.64% - Lockheed Missiles & Space Co. [Lockheed Corp.] (U.S.)
48.68% - Billiton B.V. [Royal Dutch/Shell] (Netherlands)
12.68% - BKW Ocean Minerals [Royal Bos Kallis Westminister
      N.V] (Netherlands)

OCEAN MINING ASSOCIATES

1994 to Present
1/3 - Essex Minerals Co. [USX Corp.] (U.S.)
1/3 - Sun Ocean Ventures, Inc. [Sun Co.] (U.S.)
1/3 - Union Seas, Inc. (U.S. Corp) [Union Miniere S.A.]
   (Belgium)

1989 thru 1993
25% -   Essex Minerals Co. [USX Corp.] (U.S.)
25% -   Sun Ocean Ventures, Inc. [Sun Co.] (U.S.)
25% -   Union Seas, Inc. (U.S. Corp.) [Union Miniere S.A.]
           (Belgium)
25% -   Deep Sea Systems, Inc. (U.S. Corp) [ENI/Italy]
           (Italy) ***

1982 to 1987
25% -   Essex Minerals Co. [U.S. Steel Co.] (U.S.)
25% -   Sun Ocean Ventures, Inc. [Sun Co.] (U.S.)
25% -   Union Seas, Inc. (U.S. Corp.) [Union Miniere S.A.]
           (Belgium)
25% -   Samim Ocean, Inc. (U.S. Corp.) [ENI/Italy] (Italy)

KENNECOTT CONSORTIUM

1989 to 1993****
52% - Kennecott Utah Copper Corp. (U.S. Corp.) [Rio Tinto-
      Zinc, Ltd] (U.K.)
12% - Noranda Exploration, Inc. (U.S. Corp.) [Noranda
      Mines Ltd.] (Canada)
12% - Mitsubishi Corp. (Japan)

12% - R.T.Z. Deep Sea Mining Enterprises, Ltd. [Rio Tinto-Zinc, Ltd.] (U.K.)

12% - Consolidated Gold Fields. P.L.C. (U.K.)

1982 to 1987

40% - Kennecott Corp. (U.S. Corp.) [Sohio/British Petroleum] (U.K.)

12% - Noranda Exploration, Inc. (U.S. Corp.) [Noranda Mines, Ltd.] (Canada)

12% - Mitsubishi Corp. (Japan)

12% - R.T.Z. Deep Sea Mining Enterprises, Ltd. [Rio Tinto-Zinc, Ltd.] (U.K.)

12% - Consolidated Gold Fields, P.L.C. (U.K.)

12% - BP Petroleum Development, Ltd. [British Petroleum] - (U.K.)

* If allocated among the partners, Lockheed Missiles & Space owned 24.344% of the Ocean Minerals Co., Billiton B.V. owned 30.669% and BKW Ocean Minerals owned 7.989%.

** Partnership was dissolved the end of 1985.

*** Sold all rights and interests to remaining partners on December 10, 1993.

**** U.S. license was surrendered on May 21, 1993.

(U.S. NOAA)

Appendix IV

Round-Up of Session   SEA/1502
21 August 1995

ASSEMBLY OF INTERNATIONAL SEABED AUTHORITY CONCLUDES FIRST SESSION,

KINGSTON, 7-17 AUGUST

KINGSTON, 17 August--The Assembly of the International Seabed Authority concluded its first session on Friday, 17 August, after intensive consultations over the past two weeks on the selection of members of the 36 member Council of the Authority. The session was held in three parts, beginning in late 1994 and continuing with two parts in 1995.

The Assembly approved the reports of its open-ended ad hoc working group to study the draft headquarters agreement to be entered into between the Authority and Jamaica as the host country as well as a draft protocol on privileges and immunities of the Authority and its staff.

It also decided to recommend to the General Assembly that it be allowed to hold its second session in two parts, the first starting on 11 March 1996 and lasting three weeks, if necessary. The second part would be held for two weeks, beginning on 5 August 1996.

The session, which began its final part on 7 August, ended without agreement on the composition of the Council of the Authority which is to be based on criteria laid down in the 1982 United Nations Convention on the Law of the Sea and the 1994 Agreement on the Implementation of Part XI of the Convention. In all, there are five groups to be represented on the Council, with members representing groups of States with a common economic or other special interest, or a regional grouping. Overall, the Council is to have an equitable geographical distribution and a balance between developed and developing states.

Reporting on progress made on the Council's membership, Assembly President Hasjim Djalal (Indonesia), noted that some groups had agreed on their candidates, while others still faced difficulties and needed additional time to arrive at a consensus. The Assembly,therefore, decided to hold informal inter-sessional consultations in New York from 6 to 8 December, in an attempt to resolve the question of membership of the Council and other related issues.

The Council is the executive organ of the Authority, with vast powers to oversee the operation of the institution, powers that include recommending candidates for Secretary-General of the Authority and overall financial, administrative and budgetary control over the Authority. The Agreement on the Implementation of Part XI of the Law of the Sea Convention gives the Council additional powers through revised decision-making procedure that make it difficult for the Assembly to take any decision that is not supported by the Council.

In the absence of a Council and a Secretary-General of the Authority, the Assembly requested that the Kingston Office for the Law of the Sea continue as the interim secretariat of the Authority as of 1 October.

On the budgetary arrangements for the Authority, the President noted that provision had been made for the expenses of the Authority, amounting to $776,000, only until the end of this year. The budget of the Authority for 1996 was to be prepared by the Secretary-General of the Authority. Since he is yet to be elected, the Secretariat of the United Nations, solely as a stopgap measure, had proposed retaining the same appropriations allotted for the Authority in 1995 during the biennium 1995-1996.

During the session, the final report of the Preparatory Commission for the International Seabed Authority and for the International Tribunal for the Law of the Sea was introduced by the Rapporteur of the Commission, Kenneth Rattray (Jamaica). The submission of the report concludes the work and mandate of the Commission which was to stay in existence until the conclusion of the first session of the Assembly.

The Assembly approved the report of its Credentials Committee without a vote, thus accepting the credentials of 72 States and the European Community which participated in this session.   Members of the

Committee are Austria (Chairman), China, Japan, Nigeria, Cameroon, Costa Rica, Uruguay, Poland and the United States.

At an earlier meeting, the Assembly had decided that the Federal Republic of Yugoslavia (Serbia and Montenegro) should not participate in its first session. The President noted that some delegations did not wish to participate in that decision.

Interim Arrangements

The General Assembly (resolution 48/263) decided to fund the administrative expenses of the Authority on a temporary basis in accordance with the recommendations contained in the Agreement Relating to the Implementation of Part XI of the Convention. The Agreement specified that the budget of the Authority should be funded from the regular budget of the United Nations until one year after the entry into force of the Agreement. In any case, this temporary arrangement, irrespective of whether the Agreement has come into force by then, will end on 16 November 1998 when the provisional application of the Agreement comes to an end.

The failure to select a Council has prevented the composition and election of a Finance Committee, one of whose functions is to review the administrative budget of the Authority and to make appropriate recommendations to the Council and the Assembly. In his report to the Assembly, the President noted that the budget of the Authority for 1996 was to have been prepared by the Secretary-General of the Authority, who is yet to be elected. To bridge this gap, and purely as a stop-gap measure, the Secretariat of the United Nations has proposed keeping the same basic budget resources allotted to the Authority in 1995 during the biennium 1996-1997. That would be a temporary measure, pending submission of the budget of the Authority, as agreed by its Assembly, to the fiftieth session of the General Assembly.

The President went on to note that it was unlikely to elect a Secretary General of the Authority, one of whose tasks would be to prepare the draft budget for review by the Finance Committee, before March 1996. That would be too late for the General Assembly to consider it at its fiftieth session. Therefore, he suggested that the Secretary-General of the United Nations be entrusted with the task of preparing the budget of the Authority for 1996.

Linked to the budgetary measures, the President suggested that the Assembly use the facilities and staff of the Kingston Office for the Law of the Sea from 1 October until the time the Secretary-General of the Authority took office. He explained that decision was urgent in view of the fact that the Kingston Office, under present arrangements, and which has been providing secretariat service to the Authority, was to be abolished as of 30 November.

Council of Seabed Authority

The Convention on the Law of the Sea set up the International Seabed Authority to administer the resources of the deep seabed beyond the limits of national jurisdiction. The two main organs of the Authority are the Assembly, whose membership consists of all parties to the Convention, as well as all those States who have agreed to the provisional application of the 1994 Agreement. The other main organ is the Council, which will consist of 36 members elected by the Assembly. According to the Agreement, the membership of the Council is to reflect four main elements: States with a special interest in deep seabed mining, such as the largest consumers or largest producers of the same minerals to be mined from the seabed; States that have pioneered large investments and activity in the Area; developing countries with special interests, such as land-locked or populous States; and an equitable geographical representation, as well as a balance between developed and developing states.

Membership in the Council is of particular relevance in view of the powers assigned to that body. Although the Assembly of the Authority is designated by the Convention as the supreme organ of the Authority, the Council is given wide-ranging powers as the executive organ. Among the matters over which the Council will have direct control are the financial and budgetary arrangements of the Authority and the review and approval of contracts for the exploration and exploitation of areas of the international seabed. The Council has become even more important in light of the decisionmaking procedures contained in the 1994 Agreement. In essence, the Agreement prohibits the Assembly from taking any decision on a matter of substance that contradicts a decision taken by the Council.

Most significantly, the Agreement specifies: "Decisions of the Assembly on any matter for which the Council also has competence or any administrative, budgetary or financial matter shall be based on the recommendations of the Council. If the Assembly does not accept the recommendation of the Council on any matter, it shall return the matter to the Council for further consideration. The Council shall reconsider the matter in the light of views expressed by the Assembly."

The Agreement has also significantly revised the decision-making procedures in the Council by emphasizing that all efforts should be made to reach a consensus on any matter before the Council. Should efforts to reach consensus fail, matters of substance are to be decided by a two-thirds majority of the members of the Council present and voting, with the proviso that any decision must not be opposed by a majority in any of the interest groups represented in the Council.

The Agreement and the Convention provide that the Council shall consist of 36 members elected by the Assembly in the following order:

-- Group A, consisting of four members from among those States parties that, during the last five years for which statistics are available, have either consumed more than 2 per cent of the total world consumption or have imported more than 2 per cent of the total world imports of the commodities produced from the categories of minerals to be derived from the Area;

-- Group B, consisting of four members from the among the eight parties that have made the largest investment, either directly or through their nationals, in seabed mining activities;

-- Group C, consisting of four members from among parties that, on the basis of production in areas under their national jurisdiction, are major net exporters of the categories of minerals to be derived from the Area, including at least two developing states whose exports of such mineral shave a substantial bearing on their economies;

-- Group D, which will have six members from among developing states parties representing special interests, including States with large populations, States which are land-locked or geographically disadvantaged, island States, States which are major importers of the categories of minerals to be derived from the Area, States which are potential producers of such minerals and least developed States; and

-- Group E, consisting of 18 members elected according to the principle of equitable geographical distribution of seats in the Council as a whole, provided that each geographical region shall have at least one member elected under this criteria.

The composition of the Council is of a particularly delicate nature since many of the States eligible for membership in one group could also put forward their candidacies for other groups where their interests will be represented. For example, the United States, now a candidate for the group of largest consumers, can also be a candidate for the group of States with the largest investment in seabed mining (Group B).

In his report, the President reported on a certain degree of progress achieved; Group A had agreed on the candidates for its four seats -- Japan, the Russian Federation, the United Kingdom and the United States. However, some members of Group A felt that the final arrangements for the selection of those candidates would depend on progress achieved in Group B, where more time was needed to resolve the arrangements. Group C had made promising progress, and successfully reached an understanding on the allocation of seats. On the other hand, Group D was still to identify the six candidates for the seat available to it. As regards Group E, he said he was satisfied that the

Group had taken a somewhat flexible position on the distribution of seats among the respective regional groups.

Report of Preparatory Commission

Kenneth Rattray (Jamaica), Rapporteur of the Preparatory Commission, for the International Seabed Authority and the International Tribunal for the Law of the Sea, introduced the report of the Commission (LOS/PCN/153,Vols.113). He recalled that the Commission had first addressed and established the rules for the registration of pioneer investors. In particular, it was able to resolve the difficult issue of overlapping claims which were found to exist in the north-east Pacific, between France, Japan and the Soviet Union.

The resolution of that issue paved the way for the registration of the first group of applicants as pioneer investors. Altogether, seven pioneer investors were registered by the Commission. He noted that the report on the Status on the Implementation of the Obligation of the Registered Pioneer Investors under Resolution II and the related Understandings, prepared by the Secretariat, is contained in document LOS/PCN/145 of 15 December 1994 and is to be found in pages 203 to 221 of Volume I of the report.

In light of the Agreement adopted by the General Assembly on 28 July 1994, the Preparatory Commission decided to recommend to the Authority that the recommendations contained in its report should be adjusted so as to be in conformity with the Agreement.

The Preparatory Commission's report comprises 13 volumes. It covers reports and other relevant documents of its plenary, including the General Committee and the Training Panel (vols. I-V); Special Commission 1 (vols.VIIX), Special Commission 2 (vols. X-XI) and Special Commission 3 (vols. XIIXIII). There is a separate document, LOS/PCN/152 (vols. I-IV) on the work of Special Commission 4, which dealt with the International Tribunal for the Law of the Sea.

The plenary's responsibilities within the framework of the Preparatory Commission included preparing draft rules of procedure for the organs of the Authority and also draft agreements concerning the relationship of the Authority with the United Nations, the host country and the parties to the Convention on the Law of the Sea. The plenary had submitted recommendations concerning administrative arrangements of the Authority, its initial financial and secretariat requirements, as well as staff and financial regulations of the Authority.

Special Commission 1 was charged with undertaking studies on the problems which would be encountered by developing land-based producer States likely to be most seriously affected by the production of minerals derived from the international seabed area, to minimize their difficulties and help them make necessary economic adjustments. Special Commission 2 was mandated to adopt measures necessary for the early entry into effective operation of the Enterprise, the mining arm of the Authority. Special Commission 3 was given the task of preparing rules, regulations and procedures for the exploration and exploitation of the Area, the seabed mining code.

The report was submitted in accordance with paragraph 11 of resolution I of the Third United Nations Conference on the Law of the Sea which mandated the Commission with presenting to the Authority a final report on all matters within its mandate, with the exception of its report on practical arrangements for the International Tribunal for the Law of the Sea.

Headquarters Agreement

The ad hoc working group that dealt with the final draft agreement between the International Seabed Authority and the Government of Jamaica, regarding the headquarters of the Authority (LOS/PCN/153,Vol.V),considered among other things, the nature, duties and obligations of the Authority and Jamaica as the designated seat of the Authority. Among the areas addressed in the draft are the legal capacity of the Authority, law and authority in the headquarters, protection of the headquarters' communication facilities, freedom of the Authority to publish and broadcast, ministries of the Authority, and its exemption from taxes and customs duties.

The draft covers undertakings to be assumed by Jamaica, as the host country, for example, to employ its best endeavours to enable the Authority to obtain the most favourable conditions as regards exchange rates, banking commission in exchange transactions, and the like. As another example, the Jamaican authorities, if so requested by the Secretary-General of the Authority, would provide a sufficient number of police for the preservation of law and order in the headquarters of the Authority.

The Authority, for its part, would have the power to adopt regulations, operative within its headquarters, for the purpose of establishing the necessary conditions for the final and independent exercise of its functions. The Authority, however, must inform the Jamaican Government of any regulations adopted in this respect.

The Authority would also make suitable decisions for the settlement of disputes arising out of contracts of a private law nature to which the Authority is party. As to disputes between the Authority and the Government of Jamaica, the agreement calls for binding arbitration, should efforts fail to settle the dispute through consultations, negotiations or other agreed methods of settlement.

The working group also examined the draft of the privileges and immunities of the Authority. Notably, the Agreement provides that in case of a contradiction between the draft and the protocol, the terms of the headquarters agreement should prevail.

Appendix V

UNCLOS History

History of Conference

The present Conference is the third in a series that has already produced conventions which, for many States, have become a part of international law. The first United Nations Conference on the Law of the Sea met at Geneva in 1958, with 86 States participating, and drew up four international conventions which are still in force; the number of parties ranges from 35 to 55. These treaties deal with the territorial sea and contiguous zone, the high seas, fishing and conservation of the living resources of the high seas, and the continental shelf.

A second Conference, convened by the General Assembly in Geneva in 1960 to resolve disagreements over the breadth of the territorial sea and fishery limits, was unable to adopt any substantive proposal on these matters.

Steps leading to the convening of the Third Conference began 15 years ago, in 1967, when the Assembly, following an initiative by Malta, established a 35-member Ad Hoc Committee to Study the Peaceful Uses of the Sea-Bed and the Ocean Floor beyond the Limits of National Jurisdiction. This was replaced the following year by a 42-member Committee on the Peaceful Uses of the Sea-Bed and the Ocean Floor beyond the Limits of National Jurisdiction, twice enlarged until it became a 91-member body in 1971.

On the basis of work done in the Sea-Bed Committee, the Assembly, in 1970, adopted the Declaration of Principles Governing the Sea-Bed and the Ocean Floor, and the Subsoil Thereof, beyond the Limits of National Jurisdiction (resolution 2749 (XXV)). This document, the first internationally agreed set of principles covering the area, begins with the concept that the zone and its resources "are the common heritage of mankind" and "shall not be subject to appropriation by any means by States or persons".

The decision to convene the Third Conference in 1973 was taken by the Assembly in 1970. The objectives specified for the Conference in resolution 2750 C (XXV) of 1970 were to "deal with the establishment of an equitable international regime — including an international machinery — for the area and the resources of the sea-bed and the ocean floor, and the subsoil thereof, beyond the limits of national jurisdiction, a precise definition of the area, and a broad range of related issues including those concerning the regimes of the high seas, the continental shelf, the territorial sea (including the question of its breadth and the question of international straits) and contiguous zone, fishing and conservation of the living resources of the high seas (including the question of the preferential rights of coastal States), the preservation of the marine environment (including, *inter alia*, the prevention of pollution) and scientific research".

Between 1971 and 1973, the Sea-Bed Committee worked as the preparatory body for the Conference, sifting through hundreds of treaty articles submitted by many States. It produced a six-volume report setting out attempts to consolidate these proposals into draft articles, mostly in alternative versions.

In 1973 the Assembly decided that the task of the Conference should be "to adopt a convention dealing with all matters relating to the law of the sea" (resolution 3067 (XXVIII)). It asked the Conference to bear in mind "that the problems of ocean space are closely interrelated and need to be considered as a whole".

The Conference has held 10 sessions since 1973, as follows:

First session, New York, December 1973: Officers are elected, work begins on rules of procedure.

Second session, Caracas, June/August 1974: Rules of procedure are adopted; 115 countries express views in general debate; an attempt is made to reduce to manageable proportions the alternative texts submitted by the Sea-Bed Committee.

Third session, Geneva, March/May 1975: A "single negotiating text" is produced by the Committee Chairmen, setting out in treaty language provisions to be used as a basis for negotiations on most of the points considered for inclusion in a final convention.

Fourth session, New York, March/May 1976: The results of negotiations are set out in a "revised single negotiating text" prepared by the officers of the Conference.

Fifth session, New York, August/September 1976: Further progress is made in several areas on the basis of the revised text, but an impasse is reported on the question of how deep-sea mining should be organized and regulated.

Sixth session, New York, May/July 1977: An "informal composite negotiating text" results from further deliberations on sea-bed and other outstanding issues.

Seventh session, Geneva, March/May 1978; New York, August/September 1978: Seven negotiating groups are set up to tackle the "hard-core" issues standing in the way of agreement.

Eighth session, Geneva, March/April 1979; New York, July/August 1979:
First revision of the 1977 negotiating text emerges; a decision is taken to
complete work on the convention in 1980.

Ninth session, New York, March/April 1980; Geneva, July/August 1980:
"Draft convention on the law of the sea (informal text)" produced; Conference
decides to hold its final session in 1981.

Tenth session, New York, March/April 1981; Geneva, August 1981: "Draft
convention on the law of the sea" issued as the first official text, replacing
earlier informal ones; compromise formula on delimitation of overlapping
maritime boundaries emerges; Jamaica and the Federal Republic of Germany are
chosen as seats for the International Sea-Bed Authority and the International
Tribunal for the Law of the Sea, respectively; United States cites
difficulties with sea-bed provisions; "final decision-making session" is set
for 1982.

The Conference has now been in session for a total of 85 weeks over the
past nine years, making it by far the longest special conference ever held by
the United Nations.

Structure of Conference

The Conference has three main committees, each composed of all States
participating in the Conference. Established at the first (organizational)
session in 1973, they have held both formal and informal (private) meetings.
The Conference is to decide what role they will play, if any, in the
decision-making phase of the forthcoming session. (For the subjects and
Chairmen of the main committees, see page 2 of this release.)

In addition, informal plenary meetings of the Conference function as a
main Committee presided over by President Koh. They are to continue dealing
with final clauses (including participation in the convention) and the
recommendations of the Drafting Committee.

Informal negotiations on sea-bed matters were carried out during the past
three years in the Working Group of 21 on First Committee Matters. It was
composed of roughly equal numbers of representatives from developing and
industrialized (including socialist) countries, with the participants from
each group changing according to the issues being discussed.

Matters pertaining to the proposed Preparatory Commission have been
discussed in both the First Committee and the Working Group of 21, under the
joint chairmanship of President Koh and Chairman Engo, reflecting the fact
that this matter falls within the province of both the informal plenary and
the Committee.

There are three standing committees of restricted membership, as follows:

General Committee -- composed of the 31 States which are Vice-Presidents
of the Conference, the 15 States whose representatives hold an office in
one of the main committees, the President and the Rapporteur-General of
the Conference. The 45 States on the Committee are:

Algeria (Vice-President)
Australia (First Committee Rapporteur)
Bolivia (Vice-President)
Brazil (First Committee
    Vice-Chairman)
Bulgaria (Third Committee Chairman)
Chile (Vice-President)
China (Vice-President)
Colombia (Third Committee
    Vice-Chairman)
Cyprus (Third Committee
    Vice-Chairman)
Czechoslovakia (Second Committee
    Vice-Chairman)
Dominican Republic (Vice-President)
Egypt (Vice-President)
Fiji (Second Committee Rapporteur)
France (Vice-President)
German Democratic Republic (First
    Committee Vice-Chairman)
Federal Republic of Germany (Third
    Committee Vice-Chairman)
Iceland (Vice-President)
Indonesia (Vice-President)
Iran (Vice-President)
Iraq (Vice-President)
Ireland (Vice-President)
Japan (First Committee Vice-Chairman)

Kenya (Second Committee Vice-Chairman)
Kuwait (Vice-President)
Liberia (Vice-President)
Madagascar (Vice-President)
Nepal (Vice-President)
Nigeria (Vice-President)
Norway (Vice-President)
Pakistan (Vice-President)
Peru (Vice-President)
Poland (Vice-President)
Sri Lanka (Vice-President)
Sudan (Third Committee Rapporteur)
Trinidad and Tobago (Vice-President)
Tunisia (Vice-President)
Turkey (Second Committee
    Vice-Chairman)
USSR (Vice-President)
United Kingdom (Vice-President)
Venezuela (Second Committee
    Chairman)
Uganda (Vice-President)
United Republic of Cameroon (First
    Committee Chairman)
United States (Vice-President)
Yugoslavia (Vice-President)
Zaire (Vice-President)
Zambia (Vice-President)

Drafting Committee -- composed of 23 members: Chairman, J. Alan Beesley (Canada), and representatives of Afghanistan, Argentina, Austria, Ecuador, El Salvador, Ghana, India, Italy, Lesotho, Malaysia, Mauritania, Mauritius, Mexico, Philippines, Romania, Sierra Leone, Spain, Syria, Thailand, Soviet Union, United Republic of Tanzania and United States. Reporting to the Committee are Language Groups for each of the six official languages of the convention and a body called Co-ordinators of the Language Groups.

Credentials Committee -- composed of nine members: Chairman, Karl Wolf (Austria), and representatives of Chad, China, Costa Rica, Hungary, Ireland, Ivory Coast, Japan and Uruguay.

Bernardo Zuleta is Special Representative of the Secretary-General to the Conference and heads the Conference secretariat. The Executive Secretary is David L.D. Hall.

(U.N. Doc. SEA/460)

Appendix VI

The Views of the United States Ocean Mining Licensees
on Trends in the Negotiations to make the United
Nations convention on the Law of the Sea of 1982
Universally Acceptable

March 15, 1994

SUMMARY

Congress and the Administration have requested the views of the
United States ocean mining licensees on current efforts to "reform" the
United Nations convention on the Law of the Sea of 1982. The Law of the
Sea (LOS) convention has received the requisite 60 ratification's and will
enter into force on November 16, 1994. None of these ratification's is by a
major industrialized country. No country in which a private or government
business entity with an ocean mining program is located has ratified the
convention. All countries with an interest in seabed mining insist that Part
IX of the convention must be significantly changed if a workable seabed
mining regime is to be established. The seabed mining industry worldwide
has stated that the regime set out in Part XI is prohibitive to private or
government investment. When this paper was prepared, industry had just
received a revision of the negotiating text, commonly called the .... Draft
Agreement" dated 14 February 1994, taking into account the latest round
of negotiations. The "Agreement" text does nothing to change industry's
assessment that the trend in the negotiations will fail to produce a regime
that can attract private investment in ocean mining.

The licensees now operate under United States domestic law, which
establishes protection for ocean mining investment internationally
through an arrangement called the "reciprocating states" regime. The
domestic statute in the United States is the Deep Seabed Hard Mineral

Resources Act of 1980. With the "reciprocating states" regime, this law and similar laws patterned after it in other countries provide a sound basis for investment. The efficiency and minimalist system of regulation of the current ocean mining regime form a sound approach against which any "reformed" Law of the Sea convention regime must be compared.

From an investor's standpoint, the "Draft Agreement on Matters Relating to Implementation of United Nations convention on the Law of the Sea's" proposed "fixes" to the problems of the convention are far too limited in scope. While the fixes attack a number of important problems, they leave the fundamental ideology, shape and policies of Part XI intact. The convention, even if the provisions of the "Draft Agreement" were controlling, would:

fail to provide assured access to qualified applicants because of ambiguities;

create a privileged class of investor for pioneers and discourage new entrants;

impose up-front training obligations on United States licensees;

create the risk that unreasonable fees may be imposed on private investors;

establish the International Seabed Authority, a novel, untested international organization possessing very broad discretionary powers. The Seabed Authority will be the first international organization with control and regulatory powers over a resource and with taxing powers over private persons.

It will be partially controlled by countries whose interest is to make seabed mining impossible;

establish an unnecessarily large and unwieldy bureaucracy, which is not subject to checks and balances;

rely on decision making mechanisms that will promote gridlock;

fail to provide investors with judicial and administrative due process;

maintain the ideologically bankrupt concepts and policies of the so-called New International Economic Order;

encourage discrimination in favor of developing countries, which presumably includes joint ventures among and with developing countries;

provide for the creation of an "in-house" competitor, the "Enterprise," which would be the mining company operating arm of the Seabed Authority,

impose political and economic burdens on industry to assist in the establishment of competitors through the so-called "banking system" under which a miner must give half of its mine site to the Seabed Authority to be given to the Enterprise and developing countries;

provide advantages such as technology transfer to the Enterprise and developing country competitors, which could give them cost advantages over private investors; and

commit the United States to participation in the implementation of the convention regime and possibly major changes in the United States seabed mining law and program some years before the United States has decided to ratify or reject the convention.

It must be emphasized that this list is meant to be illustrative, not exhaustive, nor does the list attempt to rank the issues in order of importance. These are major features that will convince boards of directors and other senior corporate decision makers that the political/legal risk of seabed mining is totally unacceptable.

Except in those cases in which the "Draft Agreement" expressly supersedes the provisions of Part XI of the 1982 convention, Part XI continues to govern ocean mining as provided in the 1982 text. Industry's detailed views on Part XI are set out in the 1980 American Mining Congress analysis of what was then the Draft convention, which was adopted with only minor changes as the United Nations convention on the Law of the Sea in April 1982. The reader should keep in mind that the 1980 AMC text was meant to be a list of surgery needed to each provision in the Draft convention to make it minimally acceptable to investors as a basis for investment, not to create an ideal regime. Because of the overwhelming number of fixes that would be required, the licensees recommended in 1992 that the United States seek complete overhaul of Part XI. This approach was rejected by United States negotiators and by the U.N. process. The result is that the Secretary General's process is hurrying to adopt an approach that is at best ambiguous in form and substance. It is the view of the United States licensees that, if the present course is maintained, there will be no private investment in ocean mining exploration or production under the convention.

Perspective Of The United States Ocean Mining Licensees On Ocean Mining Investment

The "Ocean Mining Industry" Is Part of the Mining Industry.
There are currently three United States ocean mining licensees. A year ago there were four. Because the licensees have not yet entered into the

commercial recovery phase, some in Washington have challenged the existence of the ocean mining industry. Some suggest that the industry has died. This is the wrong way of looking at the matter. There never was and never will be an "ocean mining industry." There is a mining industry, a part of which intends to develop mineral resources of the deep seabed. Metals produced from the seabed will be fungible, that is, interchangeable, with metals produced on land. The resources of the deep seabed must be seen as a reserve to be developed commercially when the cost of doing so is competitive with or more economically and environmentally advantageous than land based mining and not before then.

Mining Investors Employ Risk Analysis In Evaluating Investment Opportunities.
    In evaluating the United Nations convention on the Law of the Sea, government and industry take very different approaches. Because this is not well understood, dialogue between the two is fraught with the danger of miscommunication. Government tends to assess the convention from the standpoint of principles, precedents, value of written rules, policy goals, and strategic objectives. Industry, on the other hand, while not immune to issues of principle, is primarily concerned with how the convention would affect their investment. Issues of primary concern to industry are assured access, security of tenure, and stability of economic conditions controlled by regulations and procedures. In deciding whether to proceed into commercial recovery, miners use a technique called risk analysis. The primary kinds of risk evaluated in the decision to invest in commercial recovery are:

> technology risk;
> market risk; and
> political/legal risk.

The decision to enter commercial recovery will not be made until the risk analysis demonstrates the potential for a return on investment competitive with, or better than, alternative corporate investment opportunities available to the parent companies of the consortia.

Technology risk arises from the question of whether the technology developed to mine and process a mineral resource will indeed work.

The United States licensees are satisfied that the at-sea and on-shore engineering systems they have developed will do the job. Mining is basically a materials movement exercise. The technology of how to remove ocean minerals from the sea floor and get them to the surface is proven. Refinements in that technology will no doubt be developed in the future, but the basic approach and systems have been developed and tested. One might draw an analogy between a 1909 Ford Model T and a 1994 Ford Mustang. Both have four wheels, an internal combustion engine, a drive shaft, and a steering wheel. The concepts remain the same. The significant difference is that evolutionary improvements in the basic system enable the new car to go faster and carry more.

Market risk arises from the question of whether the market will buy the metals produced by the venture at a price that will enable the venture to achieve its financial goals.

If the venture is to be successful in the marketplace, the market price of the metals must exceed the cost of production of the metals to a degree that will return the investment and yield a profit commensurate with the level of technical, market, and political/legal risks. Since the metals produced from the seabed are fungible with metals produced on land, the market price of metals from the seabed is determined by the price that consumers are willing to pay for all metals. Until the relationship between cost of production and selling price justifies the development of new sources of metals, no new mines will be brought on stream, whether on land or at sea.

Over the past decade, the world has suffered, from the perspective of the mining industry, from a glut of metals, a large percentage of which have been sold at prices below production costs by government mining enterprises. Production has exceeded the ability of the market to absorb all the metals produced. Even low cost producers are not producing at capacity. Seabed mining is, at best, anticipated to be a middle cost producer. Therefore, at the present time, no room exists in the market for the new mines contemplated for the oceans.

Political/legal risk arises from the danger that the law and policies of the host country (or in the case of the LOS convention, an international organization) will interfere with the successful completion of the project.

Mining projects are generally anticipated to twenty or thirty years, that is, long enough to enable a venture to recover its capital costs and earn a profit stream. The perception that the governing body has the capability, regardless of current intent, to interfere capriciously with successful completion of the project as planned will discourage investment. That is why the United States has such a strong system of laws and judicial review with built in checks and balances.

What is necessary to create a satisfactory legal/political environment? In order to provide a basis for prudent investment the legal/political regime of the host government must be stable and predictable with clear and reasonable laws, rules, regulations, terms, conditions and restrictions. Miners and bankers routinely evaluate the administrative, legislative, and judicial organs for reasonableness, stability, predictability and accountability.

The trend in the current U.N. negotiations suggests that the resulting convention will fail to establish a satisfactory legal/political environment for investment. Indeed, since the negotiations began, one United States licensee has already abandoned its license. At the time of abandonment of its license in May 1993, the Kennecott Consortium stated that the lack of any foreseeable satisfactory resolution of the legal regime because of the continuing conflict over Law of the Sea seabed regime was the main cause of the decision to abandon. The remaining three licensees see no prospect for private seabed mining investment if the United States and other seabed mining countries adopt a regime based on the current approach.

Part XI Must Be Entirely Replaced.

In the view of the United States ocean mining licensees, only radical surgery or an entirely new approach to Part)a could establish in the convention a regime and machinery that could attract private investment in ocean mining. As the United States licensees stated to the Secretaries of State, Defense, Commerce, and Treasury in 1992, nothing less than a complete and thorough renegotiation of Part XI could produce legal/political conditions under which an investor could commit funds prudently, without fear of being accused of wasting corporate assets. Unfortunately, the process under the auspices of the Secretary General of the United Nations has by its terms of reference rejected a thorough renegotiation of Part XI.

In writing to the four Secretaries in 1992, the four licensees stated: "We feel that the United States Government needs very much to:

(a) clarify its position on where it stands on the contents and form of acceptable major changes to Part XI and whether it wants to become a participant in the Secretary General's consultations or remain an observer,

(b) reject ambiguous "fixes" or general principles that merely substitute uncertainty for unacceptable provisions of Part XI;

(c) state unambiguously in advance of any multilateral decisions tore-negotiate Part XI the minimum acceptable changes necessary to remove the obstacles to ocean mining contained in Part XI;

(d) establish effective procedures for industry input to the deliberations; and

(e) clarify and recognize that there are many issues beyond those on the Secretary General's agenda that must be resolved satisfactorily for the regime to attract private investment. We would call your attention to the letter of December 5, 1980, from the American Mining Congress to Ambassador George Aldrich with an extensive critique of the Draft Law of the Sea convention. In addition, several very important problems arise for private industry from the work of the Preparatory Commission relating to access to exploration. These must be resolved for any "fixed" Law of the Sea convention would put the American licensees' programs in peril."

Current Trends Indicate The U.N. Negotiations Will Produce Another Regime Prohibitive To Private Investment.

Industry has grave concerns about the direction of the current negotiations. The United States has never articulated its objectives with regard to the specific provisions of Part M that must be changed to make the 1982 convention acceptable to the United States. Likewise, as the Secretary General's process has evolved, the Administration has failed to clarify its views on what procedure to change the convention is necessary to satisfy the United States. The participants in the Secretary General's process have made a conscious effort to avoid the normal methods of amending a treaty. How the substantive provisions of the "Draft Agreement" would relate to and affect the 1982 convention is a deliberate mystery. From an investor's standpoint, while the "Draft Agreement" would make some beneficial changes to very important problems in the convention, it would, more importantly, leave some of the greatest obstacles to investment unchanged.

The "Draft Agreement" would resolve many of the "government issues," that is, the issues of concern primarily to governments, relating to control, governance, and precedent. These include financing of the Seabed Authority and decision-making in that organization, and production controls and government assistance, and amendment of the regime, but it leaves untouched the fundamental problem for the prospective investor, that is: the convention seabed mining regime continues to be a system of government ownership and political control over economic activity at a time when the world is turning away from centrally managed economics toward privatization and market oriented policies. Thus, the convention regime remains the victim of "old think," which by its very nature would put privately financed seabed mining at a disadvantage in competition with both its regulator and land based mining.

The LTN process now intends to adopt a "protocol on provisional application of the United Nations convention on the Law of the Sea. We are told that the Secretary General's group intends to complete negotiations this summer in order to bring into force the protocol, or whatever this document is, before entry into force of the convention in November. The procedure by which this protocol will enter into force and its status as a legal instrument amending the convention remain uncertain. These uncertainties are significant disincentives to investment.

We are told that the procedure of amending the convention will be a form of tacit consent." The tacit amendment approach is used often for the fairly non-controversial technical standards set out in technical annexes of treaties, such as the convention on Prevention of Pollution of the Sea by Ships, but, to our knowledge, this procedure has never been used for highly contentious political and contractual provisions of a major political convention. We wonder what will be the relationship between the protocol and the 1982 convention when it enters into force this November in its 1982 form as ratified by sixty countries. Which will control? The Protocol purports to control the interpretation of the convention, but does not amend it. Is there precedent for such an approach for a major political treaty? How has this approach worked in the past?

The Boat Paper Approach Fails To Cure Many Fundamental Problems In Part XI and Creates A Few New Obstacles To Private Investment.

From the standpoint of the private investor, the boat/paper in combination with the 1982 convention fails to create a regime that can attract private investment in ocean mining. Even if the approach worked exactly as its proponents argue it will, the convention would fail to provide assured access to qualified privately financed applicants because of ambiguities;

The "Draft Agreement" attempts to provide greater specificity to the access system through decision-making in the Council and the Technical Commission. This is an improvement over Part XI alone, but fails to take into account that assured access is determined by the totality of the requirements and hurdles that an investor must go through to obtain and maintain mining rights.

create a privileged class of investor for pioneers and discourage new entrants;

The "Draft Agreement" like the 1982 convention, Resolution II, creates a privileged class for pioneer explorers. This goes beyond grandfather rights and would discriminate against new entrants;

permit the Seabed Authority to impose unreasonable financial obligations on private investors;

The fees that could be imposed on seabed mining investors are arbitrary and bear no real relation to the requirements of the Authority or due diligence. They may be imposed up-front and in addition to the high costs resulting from the banking, compulsory exploration, and mandatory training systems. The convention provides for a $250,000 application fee on an application for exploration rights by a pioneer explorer. This bears no relation to the cost of processing an application fee. NOAA's experience under the domestic United States program demonstrates that this fee is excessive and redundant in light of the evaluations and other work already accomplished by NOAA with previously paid, much smaller, United States license fees. In addition, the convention in Annex II provides for a $1,000,000 annual fee to be paid by pioneer explorers. The "Draft Agreement" postpones the fee during the exploration phase, but permits the Authority to demand $1,000,000 per annum for the exploration period when the miner enters into commercial production. The financial terms of contracts could result in double taxation on miners by the Seabed Authority and by the miner's sponsoring government.

impose training obligations on pioneer explorers at an unreasonable stage in their projects.

These training obligations are being met by Japan, France, and Russia through government training programs for training personnel from developing countries in marine sciences. How would American industry be expected to deal with these obligations? We have no indication that the United States government is willing to assume these obligations. A pioneer explorer will only be entering the learning curve in its own operations. To expect it to bear the cost and time of providing training in a program during start-up is unreasonable.

establish the International Seabed Authority, an untried international organization with very broad discretionary powers, the first with regulatory powers over a resource and taxing power over private persons, which will be partially controlled by States whose interest is to make seabed mining impossible;

The International Seabed Authority would be the first international organization with regulatory and taxing powers over private investors and their operations. Through its regulatory powers, it will have broad discretion to interfere with and even shut down the mining operations of investors. The Council, the executive organ of the Seabed Authority, will have members whose interests are hostile to seabed mining. At the same time, no due process exists to provide a means for a miner to directly bring a judicial or administrative action to challenge a discretionary act of the Seabed Authority.

The approach sought by the United States and other industrialized countries relies heavily on the ability of governments to protect their interests by blocking action in the Council. This may be adequate for governments, but to a private investor facing operating and regulatory uncertainties during a pioneer period, the risk of gridlock when decisions are needed from the Council constitutes a risk that, without opportunity for a hearing, the Seabed Authority may be shut down or delay its operation for a period during which its revenue will be impaired.

provide for the creation of the "Enterprise," which would be the State mining company operating arm of the Seabed Authority;

The Enterprise is to be the mining company of the Seabed Authority. It is a relic from the time when developing countries were enamored of the notion of State ownership of the means of production. An opportunity existed in the summer of 1992 for the industrialized countries to get rid of the Enterprise by making its removal from the convention a key issue. They did not. Negotiators now say it is politically impossible to remove the Enterprise from the convention. Accordingly, the industrialized countries negotiated a provision that the Enterprise will only be brought into operation by affirmative vote of the Council. Experience cautions that while in theory the United States could block the Enterprise from start up, such will be politically impossible. Even if the United States blocked start-up of the Enterprise, this would invite retaliation against United States mining operators. The provisions relating to the Enterprise have been mitigated somewhat by making it subject to the same regulatory and financial burdens as the private operator, but its advantages inherent in the "banking system," mandatory training obligations, and technology transfer continue to provide it with significant cost advantages.

maintain the political and economic burdens on industry to assist in the establishment of competitors through the so-called "banking system" under which a miner must give a mine site equal to its own or half of its mine site to the Seabed Authority to be mined by the Enterprise or developing countries;

The 1982 convention imposes several burdens cited above on private investors to subsidize and assist in the establishment and operations of their primary competitor, the Enterprise. As noted, the "Draft Agreement" goes some distance to put the private investor and the Enterprise on an equal footing, but private applicants are still required to give for the cost-free use of the Enterprise a fully explored site equal in value to the applicant's mine site. The miner must offer two fully explored sites. The Authority may choose either one at its discretion for the benefit of the Enterprise or developing countries. The "Draft Agreement" appears to try to mitigate the long term effect of this, but its approach may force the private operator into a joint venture if it wishes to develop the other site it has explored.

The policies that the Authority is to implement, set out in Article 150 and elsewhere in Part XI, articulate the bankrupt, anti-private enterprise principles of the New International Economic Order. They are based on the model of a centrally planned economy and lay the foundation for (1) discrimination in favor of developing countries and (2) protection of land-based producer interests. By itself, this might not be a serious problem, but in combination with the broad discretion given the Authority in the convention, it increases the risk that the Authority would act to impair the miner's investment and deprive investors of judicial and administrative due process;

Due process, both administrative and judicial, are vital to any invest or mineral development. The miner needs to be able to protect its investment against arbitrary decisions of the regulator. One need only look at United States regulatory practice to see the importance of administrative and judicial remedies to the investor. Regulators by their nature and in diligent pursuance of their mandates tend to lean toward the side of heavy regulation. Most United States regulatory law has developed through judicial decision. In civil law countries, national systems of administrative courts exist to resolve disputes between citizens and the national government. Nothing similar exists in the Law of the Sea convention. The dispute settlement provisions of the convention are modeled after those customary in international law, which governs the relations between nations. The Law of the Sea convention presents a situation novel in international law, under which a private investor would be regulated directly by an international organization. At the same time, the miner would have no direct access to dispute settlement on regulatory matters.

Mining investors need a dispute settlement mechanism in which they may participate directly. Under the LOS convention, a miner must request its government bring a dispute settlement case on the miner's behalf

Experience indicates that the United States government will find times when, for sound reasons of policy, it does not wish to do so. In such cases, the miner will be without redress. Only with the right to bring an action directly on its own behalf can the miner be assured of due process. We note as an important postscript that the convention prohibits even member governments from challenging discretionary acts of the Seabed Authority.

commit the United States to participation and implementation of the convention regime and possibly major changes in the United States seabed mining law and program some years before the United States has decided to ratify the convention.

The procedure contemplated currently in the United Nations is that the document that implements the changes in the convention will be a Protocol for Provisional Application of the 1982 convention, incorporating the "interpretation" provisions set out in the "Draft Agreement". States that indicate the intent of becoming Parties to the 1982 convention will be permitted to participate in the Council and presumably the other organs of the Seabed Authority. The details of how this participation would work have not yet been spelled out. Nevertheless, we have been told that the United States would participate in the Authority some years before it must decide whether to ratify of reject the convention. This would provide the benefit of enabling the United States to assess the reasonableness of the Council and Authority in implementing the regime. But it would also have the effect of severely and adversely intertwining the United States ocean mining program and the international regime some years before the Administration presents the treaty to the Senate for advice and consent.

What effect would this procedure have on the present position of the United States concerning the legal status of the seabed and its resources? After several years of participation, how would the United States protect its interests in ocean mining in the event that it decided not to become a Contracting Party? How will the vast number of ambiguities be resolved. Even after reading the "Draft Agreement" thoroughly and be briefed on it, we are left wondering how the system would work. For example, we remain mystified about how the revised Review Conference would work. These and the voluminous ambiguities and unknowns in the convention force the United States licensees to believe that the current approach leads to a dead end.

Appendix VII

UNCLOS III--Part XI

SECTION 1. GENERAL PROVISIONS

Article 133
Use of terms

For the purposes of this Part:

(a) "resources" means all solid, liquid or gaseous mineral resources in situ in the Area at or beneath the sea-bed, including polymetallic nodules;
(b) resources, when recovered from the Area, are referred to as"minerals".

Article 134
Scope of this Part

1. This Part applies to the Area.

2. Activities in the Area shall be governed by the provisions of this Part.

3. The requirements concerning deposit of, and publicity to be given to, the charts or lists of geographical coordinates showing the limits referred to in article 1, paragraph 1 (1), are set forth in Part VI.

4. Nothing in this article affects the establishment of the outer limits of the continental shelf in accordance with Part VI or the validity of agreements relating to delimitation between States with opposite or adjacent coasts.

Article 135
Legal status of the superjacent waters and air space

Neither this Part nor any rights granted or exercised pursuant thereto shall affect the legal status of the waters superjacent to the Area or that of the air space above those waters.

SECTION 2. PRINCIPLES GOVERNING THE AREA

Article 136
Common heritage of mankind

The Area and its resources are the common heritage of mankind.

Article 137
Legal status of the Area and its resources

1. No State shall claim or exercise sovereignty or sovereign rights over any part of the Area or its resources, nor shall any State or natural or juridical person appropriate any part thereof. No such claim or exercise of sovereignty or sovereign rights nor such appropriation shall be recognized.

2. All rights in the resources of the Area are vested in mankind as a whole on whose behalf the Authority shall act. These resources are not subject to alienation. The minerals recovered from the Area, however, may only be alienated in accordance with this Part and the rules, regulations and procedures of the Authority.

3. No State or natural or juridical person shall claim, acquire or exercise rights with respect to the minerals recovered from the Area except in accordance with this Part. Otherwise, no such claim, acquisition or exercise of such rights shall be recognized.

Article 138
General conduct of States in relation to the Area

The general conduct of States in relation to the Area shall be in accordance with the provisions of this Part, the principles embodied in the Charter of the United Nations and other rules of international law in the interests of maintaining peace and security and promoting international cooperation and mutual understanding .

Article 139
Responsibility to ensure compliance and liability for damage

1. States Parties shall have the responsibility to ensure that activities in the Area, whether carried out by States Parties, or state enterprises or natural or juridical persons which possess the nationality of States Parties or are effectively controlled by them or their nationals, shall be carried out in conformity with this Part. The same responsibility

applies to international organizations for activities in the Area carried out by such organizations.

2. Without prejudice to the rules of international law and Annex III, article 22, damage caused by the failure of a state party or international organization to carry out its responsibilities under this Part shall entail liability, States Parties or international organizations acting together shall bear joint and several liability. A state party shall not however be liable for damage caused by any failure to comply with this Part by a person whom it has sponsored under article 153, paragraph 2(b), if the state party has taken all necessary and appropriate measures to secure effective compliance under article 153, paragraph 4, and Annex III, article 4, paragraph 4.

3. States Parties that are members of international organizations shall take appropriate measures to ensure the implementation of this article with respect to such organizations.

Article 140
Benefit of mankind

1. Activities in the Area shall, as specifically provided for in this Part, be carried out for the benefit of mankind as a whole, irrespective of the geographical location of States, whether coastal or land-locked, and taking into particular consideration the interests and needs of developing states and of peoples who have not attained full independence or other self-governing status recognized by the United Nations in accordance with General Assembly resolution 1514 (XV) and other relevant General Assembly resolutions.

2. The Authority shall provide for the equitable sharing of financial and other economic benefits derived from activities in the Area through any appropriate mechanism on a non-discriminatory basis, in accordance with article 160, paragraph 2 (f) (i).

Article 141
Use of the Area exclusively for peaceful purposes

The Area shall be open to use exclusively for peaceful purposes by all States, whether coastal or land-locked, without discrimination and without prejudice to the other provisions of this Part.

Article 142
Rights and legitimate interests of coastal States

1. Activities in the Area, with respect to resource deposits in the Area which lie across limits of national jurisdiction, shall be conducted with due regard to the rights and legitimate interests of any coastal State across whose jurisdiction such deposits lie.

2. Consultations, including a system of prior notification, shall be maintained with the State concerned, with a view to avoiding infringement of such rights and interests. In cases where activities in the Area may result in the exploitation of resources lying within national jurisdiction, the prior consent of the coastal State concerned shall be required.

3. Neither this Part nor any rights granted or exercised pursuant thereto shall affect the rights of coastal States to take such measures consistent with the relevant provisions of Part XII as may be necessary to prevent, mitigate or eliminate grave and imminent danger to their coastline, or related interests from pollution or threat thereof or from other hazardous occurrences resulting from or caused by any activities in the Area.

Article 143
Marine scientific research

1. Marine scientific research in the Area shall be carried out exclusively for peaceful purposes and for the benefit of mankind as a whole in accordance with Part XIII.

2. The Authority may carry out marine scientific research concerning the Area and its resources, and may enter into contracts for that purpose. The Authority shall promote and encourage the conduct of marine scientific research in the Area, and shall co-ordinate and disseminate the results of such research and analysis when available.

3. States Parties may carry out marine scientific research in the Area. States Parties shall promote international co-operation in marine scientific research in the Area by:

(a) participating in international programmes and encouraging co-operation in marine scientific research by personnel of different countries and of the Authority;

(b) ensuring that programmes are developed through the Authority or other international organizations as appropriate for the benefit of developing states and technologically less developed States with a view to:

(i) strengthening their research capabilities;

(ii) training their personnel and the personnel of the Authority in the techniques and applications of research;

(iii) fostering the employment of their qualified personnel in research in the Area;

(c) effectively disseminating the results of research and analysis when available, through the Authority or other international channels when appropriate.

Article 144
Transfer of technology

1. The Authority shall take measures in accordance with this Convention:

(a) to acquire technology and scientific knowledge relating to activities in the Area; and

(b) to promote and encourage the transfer to developing States of such technology and scientific knowledge so that all States Parties benefit therefrom.

2. To this end the Authority and States Parties shall co.operate in promoting the transfer of technology and scientific knowledge relating to activities in the Area so that the Enterprise and all States Parties may benefit therefrom. In particular they shall initiate and promote:

(a) programmes for the transfer of technology to the Enterprise and to developing States with regard to activities in the Area, including, inter alia, facilitating the access of the Enterprise and of developing States to the relevant technology, under fair and reasonable terms and conditions;

(b) measures directed towards the advancement of the technology of the Enterprise and the domestic technology of developing States, particularly by providing opportunities to personnel from the Enterprise and from developing States for training in marine science and technology and for their full participation in activities in the Area.

Article 145
Protection of the marine environment

Necessary measures shall be taken in accordance with this Convention with respect to activities in the Area to ensure effective protection for the marine environment from harmful effects which may arise from such activities. To this end the Authority shall adopt appropriate rules, regulations and procedures for inter alia:

(a) the prevention, reduction and control of pollution and other hazards to the marine environment, including the coastline, and of interference with the ecological balance of the marine environment, particular attention being paid to the need for protection from harmful effects of such activities as drilling, dredging, excavation, disposal of waste, construction and operation or maintenance of installations, pipelines and other devices related to such activities;

(b) the protection and conservation of the natural resources of the Area and the prevention of damage to the flora and fauna of the marine environment.

Article 146
Protection of human life

With respect to activities in the Area, necessary measures shall be taken to ensure effective protection of human life. To this end the Authority shall adopt appropriate rules, regulations and procedures to supplement existing international law as embodied in relevant treaties.

Article 147
Accommodation of activities in the Area and in the marine environment

1. Activities in the Area shall be carried out with reasonable regard for other activities in the marine environment.

2. Installations used for carrying out activities in the Area shall be subject to the following conditions:

(a) such installations shall be erected, emplaced and removed solely in accordance with this Part and subject to the rules, regulations and procedures of the Authority. Due notice must be given of the erection, emplacement and removal of such installations, and permanent means for giving warning of their presence must be maintained;

(b) such installations may not be established where interference may be caused to the use of recognized sea lanes essential to international navigation or in areas of intense fishing activity;

(c) safety zones shall be established around such installations with appropriate markings to ensure the safety of both navigation and the installations. The configuration and location of such safety zones shall not be such as to form a belt impeding the lawful access of shipping to particular maritime zones or navigation along international sea lanes;

(d) such installations shall be used exclusively for peaceful purposes;

(e) such installations do not possess the status of islands. They have no territorial sea of their own, and their presence does not affect the delimitation of the territorial sea, the exclusive economic zone or the continental shelf.

3. Other activities in the marine environment shall be conducted with reasonable regard for activities in the Area.

Article 148
Participation of developing States in activities in the Area

The effective participation of developing States in activities in the Area shall be promoted as specifically provided for in this Part, having due regard to their special interests and needs, and in particular to the special need of the landlocked and geographically disadvantaged among them to overcome obstacles arising from their disadvantaged location, including remoteness from the Area and difficulty of access to and from it.

Article 149
Archaeological and historical objects

All objects of an archaeological and historical nature found in the Area shall be preserved or disposed of for the benefit of mankind as a whole, particular regard being paid to the preferential rights of the State or country of origin, or the State of cultural origin, or the State of historical and archaeological origin.

SECTION 3. DEVELOPMENT OF RESOURCES
OF THE AREA

Article 150
Policies relating to activities in the Area

Activities in the Area shall, as specifically provided for in this Part, be carried out in such a manner as to foster healthy development of the world economy and balanced growth of international trade, and to promote international cooperation for the over-all development of all countries, especially developing States, and with a view to ensuring:

(a) the development of the resources of the Area;
(b) orderly, safe and rational management of the resources of the Area, including the efficient conduct of activities in the Area and, in accordance with sound principles of conservation, the avoidance of unnecessary waste;
(c) the expansion of opportunities for participation in such activities consistent in particular with articles 144 and 148;
(d) participation in revenues by the Authority and the transfer of technology to the Enterprise and developing States as provided for in this Convention;
(e) increased availability of the minerals derived from the Area as needed in conjunction with minerals derived from other sources, to ensure supplies to consumers of such minerals;
(f) the promotion of just and stable prices remunerative to producers and fair to consumers for minerals derived both from the Area and from other sources, and the promotion of long-term equilibrium between supply and demand;
(g) the enhancement of opportunities for all States Parties, irrespective of their social and economic systems or geographical location, to participate in the development of the resources of the Area and the prevention of monopolization of activities in the Area;
(h) the protection of developing countries from adverse effects on their economies or on their export earnings resulting from a reduction in the price of an affected mineral, or in the volume of exports of that mineral, to the extent that such reduction is caused by activities in the Area, as provided in article 151;
(i) the development of the common heritage for the benefit of mankind as a whole; and
(j) conditions of access to markets for the imports of minerals produced from the resources of the Area and for imports of commodities produced from such minerals shall not be more

favourable than the most favourable applied to imports from other sources.

Article 151
Production policies

1. (a) Without prejudice to the objectives set forth in article 150 and for the purpose of implementing subparagraph (h) of that article, the Authority, acting through existing forums or such new arrangements or agreements as may be appropriate, in which all interested parties, including both producers and consumers, participate, shall take measures necessary to promote the growth, efficiency and stability of markets for those commodities produced from the minerals derived from the Area, at prices remunerative to producers and fair to consumers. All States Parties shall co-operate to this end.

   (b) The Authority shall have the right to participate in any commodity interested parties including both producers and consumers participate. The Authority shall have the right to become a party to any arrangement or agreement resulting from such conferences. Participation of the Authority in any organs established under those arrangements or agreements shall be in respect of production in the Area and in accordance with the relevant rules of those organs.

   (c) The Authority shall carry out its obligations under the arrangements or agreements referred to in this paragraph in a manner which assures a uniform and non-discriminatory implementation in respect of all production in the Area of the minerals concerned. In doing so, the Authority shall act in a manner consistent with the terms of existing contracts and approved plans of work of the Enterprise.

2. (a) During the interim period specified in paragraph 3, commercial production shall not be undertaken pursuant to an approved plan of work until the operator has applied for and has been issued a production authorization by the Authority. Such production authorizations may not be applied for or issued more than five years prior to the planned commencement of commercial production under the plan of work unless, having regard to the nature and timing of project development, the rules, regulations and procedures of the Authority prescribe another period.

   (b) In the application for the production authorization, the operator shall specify the annual quantity of nickel expected to be recovered under the approved plan of work. The application shall include a schedule of expenditures to be made by the operator after he has received the authorization which are reasonably calculated to allow him to begin commercial production on the date planned.

(c) For the purposes of subparagraphs (a) and (b), the Authority shall establish appropriate performance requirements in accordance with Annex III, article 17.

(d) The Authority shall issue a production authorization for the level of production applied for unless the sum of that level and the levels already authorized exceeds the nickel production ceiling, as calculated pursuant to paragraph 4 in the year of issuance of the authorization, during any year of planned production falling within the interim period.

(e) When issued, the production authorization and approved application shall become a part of the approved plan of work.

(f) If the operator's application for a production authorization is denied pursuant to subparagraph (d), the operator may apply again to the Authority at any time.

3. The interim period shall begin five years prior to 1 January of the year in which the earliest commercial production is planned to commence under an approved plan of work. If the earliest commercial production is delayed beyond the year originally planned, the beginning of the interim period and the production ceiling originally calculated shall be adjusted accordingly. The interim period shall last 25 years or until the end of the Review Conference referred to in article 155 or until the day when such new arrangements or agreements as are referred to in paragraph 1 enter into force, whichever is earliest. The Authority shall resume the power provided in this article for the remainder of the interim period if the said arrangements or agreements should lapse or become ineffective for any reason whatsoever.

4. (a) The production ceiling for any year of the interim period shall be the sum of:

(i) the difference between the trend line values for nickel consumption as calculated pursuant to subparagraph (b), for the year immediately prior to the year of the earliest commercial production and the year immediately prior to the commencement of the interim period; and

(ii) sixty per cent of the difference between the trend line values for nickel consumption, as calculated pursuant to subparagraph (b), for the year for which the production authorization is being applied for and the year immediately prior to the year of the earliest commercial production.

(b) For the purposes of subparagraph (a):

(i) trend line values used for computing the nickel production ceiling shall be those annual nickel consumption values on a trend line computed during the year in which a production authorization is issued. The trend line shall be derived from a linear regression of the logarithms of actual nickel consumption for the most recent 15-year period for which such data are available, time being the independent variable. This trend line shall be referred to as the original trend line;

(ii) if the annual rate of increase of the original trend line is less than 3 per cent, then the trend line used to determine the quantities referred to in subparagraph (a) shall instead be one passing through the original trend line at the value for the first year of the relevant 15-year period, and increasing at 3 per cent annually; provided however that the production ceiling established for any year of the interim period may not in any case exceed the difference between the original trend line value for that year and the original trend line value for the year immediately prior to the commencement of the interim period.

5. The Authority shall reserve to the Enterprise for its initial production a quantity of 38,000 metric tonnes of nickel from the available production ceiling calculated pursuant to paragraph 4.

6. (a) An operator may in any year produce less than or up to 8 per cent more than the level of annual production of minerals from polymetallic nodules specified in his production authorization, provided that the over-all amount of production shall not exceed that specified in the authorization. Any excess over 8 per cent and up to 20 per cent in any year, or any excess in the first and subsequent years following two consecutive years in which excesses occur, shall be negotiated with the Authority, which may require the operator to obtain a supplementary production authorization to cover additional production.

(b) Applications for such supplementary production authorizations shall be considered by the Authority only after all pending applications by operators who have not yet received production authorizations have been acted on and due account has been taken of other likely applicants. The Authority shall be guided by the principle of not exceeding the total production allowed under the production ceiling in any year of the interim period. It shall not authorize the production under any plan of work of a quantity in excess of 46,500 metric tonnes of nickel per year.

7. The levels of production of other metals such as copper, cobalt and manganese extracted from the polymetallic nodules that are recovered pursuant to a production authorization should not be higher than those which would have been produced had the operator produced the maximum level of nickel from those nodules pursuant to this article. The Authority shall establish rules, regulations and procedures pursuant to Annex III, article 17, to implement this paragraph.

8. Rights and obligations relating to unfair economic practices under relevant multilateral trade agreements shall apply to the exploration for and exploitation of minerals from the Area. In the settlement of disputes arising under this provision, States Parties which are Parties to such multilateral trade agreements shall have recourse to the dispute settlement procedures of such agreements.

9. The Authority shall have the power to limit the level of production of minerals from the Area, other than minerals from polymetallic nodules, under such conditions and applying such methods as may be appropriate by adopting regulations in accordance with article 161, paragraph 8.

10. On the recommendation of the Council on the basis of advice from the Economic Planning Commission, the Assembly shall establish a system of compensation or take other measures of economic adjustment assistance including co-operation with specialized agencies and other international organizations to assist developing countries which suffer serious adverse effects on their export earnings or economies resulting from a reduction in the price of an affected mineral or in the volume of exports of that mineral, to the extent that such reduction is caused by activities in the Area. The Authority on request shall initiate studies on the problems of those States which are likely to be most seriously affected with a view to minimizing their difficulties and assisting them in their economic adjustment.

Article 152
Exercise of powers and functions by the Authority

1. The Authority shall avoid discrimination in the exercise of its powers and functions, including the granting of opportunities for activities in the Area.

2. Nevertheless, special consideration for developing States, including particular consideration for the land-locked and geographically

disadvantaged among them, specifically provided for in this Part shall be permitted.

Article 153
System of exploration and exploitation

1. Activities in the Area shall be organized, carried out and controlled by the Authority on behalf of mankind as a whole in accordance with this article as well as other relevant provisions of this Part and the relevant Annexes, and the rules, regulations and procedures of the Authority.

2. Activities in the Area shall be carried out as prescribed in paragraph 3:
(a) by the Enterprise, and
(b) in association with the Authority by States Parties, or state enterprises or natural or juridical persons which possess the nationality of States Parties or are effectively controlled by them or their nationals, when sponsored by such States, or any group of the foregoing which meets the requirements provided in this Part and in Annex III.

3. Activities in the Area shall be carried out in accordance with a formal written plan of work drawn up in accordance with Annex III and approved by the Council after review by the Legal and Technical Commission. In the case of activities in the Area carried out as authorized by the Authority by the entities specified in paragraph 2(b), the plan of work shall, in accordance with Annex III, article 3, be in the form of a contract. Such contracts may provide for joint arrangements in accordance with Annex III, article 11.

4. The Authority shall exercise such control over activities in the Area as is necessary for the purpose of securing compliance with the relevant provisions of this Part and the Annexes relating thereto, and the rules, regulations and procedures of the Authority, and the plans of work approved in accordance with paragraph 3. States Parties shall assist the Authority by taking all measures necessary to ensure such compliance in accordance with article 139.

5. The Authority shall have the right to take at any time any measures provided for under this Part to ensure compliance with its provisions and the exercise of the functions of control and regulation assigned to it thereunder or under any contract. The Authority shall have the right to

inspect all installations in the Area used in connection with activities in the Area.

6. A contract under paragraph 3 shall provide for security of tenure. Accordingly, the contract shall not be revised, suspended or terminated except in accordance with Annex III, articles 18 and 19.

Article 154
Periodic review

Every five years from the entry into force of this Convention, the Assembly shall undertake a general and systematic review of the manner in which the international regime of the Area established in this Convention has operated in practice. In the light of this review the Assembly may take, or ecommend that other organs take, measures in accordance with the provisions and procedures of this Part and the Annexes relating thereto which will lead to the improvement of the operation of the regime.

Article 155
The Review Conference

1. Fifteen years from 1 January of the year in which the earliest commercial production commences under an approved plan of work, the Assembly shall convene a conference for the review of those provisions of this Part and the relevant Annexes which govern the system of exploration and exploitation of the resources of the Area. The Review Conference shall consider in detail, in the light of the experience acquired during that period:

(a) whether the provisions of this Part which govern the system of exploration and exploitation of the resources of the Area have achieved their aims in all respects, including whether they have benefited mankind as a whole;

(b) whether, during the 15-year period, reserved areas have been exploited in an effective and balanced manner in comparison with non-reserved areas;

(c) whether the development and use of the Area and its resources have been undertaken in such a manner as to foster healthy development of the world economy and balanced growth of international trade;

(d) whether monopolization of activities in the Area has been prevented;

(e) whether the policies set forth in articles 150 and 151 have been fulfilled; and

(f) whether the system has resulted in the equitable sharing of benefits derived from activities in the Area, taking into particular consideration the interests and needs of the developing States.

2. The Review Conference shall ensure the maintenance of the principle of the common heritage of mankind, the international regime designed to ensure equitable exploitation of the resources of the Area for the benefit of all countries, especially the developing States, and an Authority to organize, conduct and control activities in the Area. It shall also ensure the maintenance of the principles laid down in this Part with regard to the exclusion of claims or exercise of sovereignty over any part of the Area, the rights of States and their general conduct in relation to the Area, and their participation in activities in the Area in conformity with this Convention, the prevention of monopolization of activities in the Area, the use of the Area exclusively for peaceful purposes, economic aspects of activities in the Area, marine scientific research, transfer of technology, protection of the marine environment, protection of human life, rights of coastal States, the legal status of the waters superjacent to the Area and that of the air space above those waters and accommodation between activities in the Area and other activities in the marine environment.

3. The decision-making procedure applicable at the Review Conference shall be the same as that applicable at the Third United Nations Conference on the Law of the Sea. The Conference shall make every effort to reach agreement on any amendments by way of consensus and there should be no voting on such matters until all efforts at achieving consensus have been exhausted.

4. If, five years after its commencement, the Review Conference has not reached agreement on the system of exploration and exploitation of the resources of the Area, it may decide during the ensuing 12 months, by a three-fourths majority of the States Parties, to adopt and submit to the States Parties for ratification or accession such amendments changing or modifying the system as it determines necessary and appropriate. Such amendments shall enter into force for all States Parties 12 months after the deposit of instruments of ratification or accession by three fourths of the States Parties.

5. Amendments adopted by the Review Conference pursuant to this article shall not affect rights acquired under existing contracts.

SECTION 4. THE AUTHORITY
SUBSECTION A. GENERAL PROVISIONS

Article 156
Establishment of the Authority

1. There is hereby established the International Sea-Bed Authority, which shall function in accordance with this Part.

2. All States Parties are ipso facto members of the Authority.

3. Observers at the Third United Nations Conference on the Law of the Sea who have signed the Final Act and who are not referred to in article 305, paragraph 1 (c), (d), (e) or (f), shall have the right to participate in the Authority as observers, in accordance with its rules, regulations and procedures.

4. The seat of the Authority shall be in Jamaica.

5. The Authority may establish such regional centres or offices as it deems necessary for the exercise of its functions.

Article 157
Nature and fundamental principles of the Authority

1. The Authority is the organization through which States Parties shall, in accordance with this Part, organize and control activities in the Area, particularly with a view to administering the resources of the Area.

2. The powers and functions of the Authority shall be those expressly conferred on it by this Convention. The Authority shall have such incidental powers, consistent with this Convention, as are implicit in and necessary for the exercise of those powers and functions with respect to activities in the Area.

3. The Authority is based on the principle of the sovereign equality of all its members.

4. All members of the Authority shall fulfil in good faith the obligations assumed by them in accordance with this Part in order to ensure to all of them the rights and benefits resulting from membership.

Article 158
Organs of the Authority

1. There are hereby established, as the principal organs of the Authority, an Assembly, a Council and a Secretariat.

2. There is hereby established the Enterprise, the organ through which the Authority shall carry out the functions referred to in article 170, paragraph 1.

3. Such subsidiary organs as may be found necessary may be established in accordance with this Part.

4. Each principal organ of the Authority and the Enterprise shall be responsible for exercising those powers and functions which are conferred on it. In exercising such powers and functions each organ shall avoid taking any action which may derogate from or impede the exercise of specific powers and functions conferred on another organ.

SUBSECTION B. THE ASSEMBLY

Article 159
Composition, procedure and voting

1. The Assembly shall consist of all the members of the Authority. Each member shall have one representative in the Assembly, who may be accompanied by alternates and advisers.

2. The Assembly shall meet in regular annual sessions and in such special sessions as may be decided by the Assembly, or convened by the Secretary- General at the request of the Council or of a majority of the members of the Authority.

3. Sessions shall take place at the seat of the Authority unless otherwise decided by the Assembly.

4. The Assembly shall adopt its rules of procedure. At the beginning of each regular session, it shall elect its President and such other officers as may be required. They shall hold office until a new President and other officers are elected at the next regular session.

5. A majority of the members of the Assembly shall constitute a quorum.

6. Each member of the Assembly shall have one vote.

7. Decisions on questions of procedure, including decisions to convene special sessions of the Assembly, shall be taken by a majority of the members present and voting.

8. Decisions on questions of substance shall be taken by a two-thirds majority of the members present and voting, provided that such majority includes a majority of the members participating in the session. When the issue arises as to whether a question is one of substance or not, that question shall be treated as one of substance unless otherwise decided by the Assembly by the majority required for decisions on questions of substance.

9. When a question of substance comes up for voting for the first time, the President may, and shall, if requested by at least one fifth of the members of the Assembly, defer the issue of taking a vote on that question for a period not exceeding five calendar days. This rule may

be applied only once to any question, and shall not be applied so as to defer the question beyond the end of the session.

10. On a written request addressed to the President and sponsored by at least one fourth of the members of the Authority for an advisory opinion on the conformity with this Convention of a proposal before the Assembly on any matter, the Assembly shall request the Sea-Bed Disputes Chamber of the International Tribunal for the Law of the Sea to give an advisory opinion thereon and shall defer voting on that proposal pending receipt of the advisory opinion by the Chamber. If the advisory opinion is not received before the final week of the session in which it is requested, the Assembly shall decide when it will meet to vote on the deferred proposal.

Article 160
Powers and functions

1. The Assembly, as the sole organ of the Authority consisting of all the members, shall be considered the supreme organ of the Authority to which the other principal organs shall be accountable as specifically provided for in this Convention. The Assembly shall have the power to establish general policies in conformity with the relevant provisions of this Convention on any question or matter within the competence of the Authority.

2. In addition, the powers and functions of the Assembly shall be:

(a) to elect the members of the Council in accordance with article 161;

(b) to elect the Secretary-General from among the candidates proposed by the Council;

(c) to elect, on the recommendation of the Council, the members of the Governing Board of the Enterprise and the Director-General of the Enterprise;

(d) to establish such subsidiary organs as it finds necessary for the exercise of its functions in accordance with this Part. In the composition of these subsidiary organs due account shall be taken of the principle of equitable geographical distribution and of special interests and the need for members qualified and competent in the relevant technical questions dealt with by such organs;

(e) to assess the contributions of members to the administrative budget of the Authority in accordance with an agreed scale of assessment based on the scale used for the regular budget of the United Nations until the Authority shall have sufficient income from other sources to meet its administrative expenses;

(f) (i) to consider and approve, on the recommendation of the Council the rules, regulations and procedures on the equitable sharing of financial and other economic benefits derived from activities in the Area and the payments and contributions made pursuant to article 82, taking into particular consideration the interests and needs of developing States and peoples who have not attained full independence or other self-governing status. If the Assembly does not approve the recommendations of the Council, the Assembly shall return them to the Council for reconsideration in the light of the views expressed by the Assembly; (ii) to consider and approve the rules, regulations and procedures of the Authority, and any amendments thereto, provisionally adopted by the Council pursuant to article 162, paragraph 2 (o)(ii). These rules, regulations and procedures shall relate to prospecting, exploration and exploitation in the Area, the financial management and internal administration of the Authority, and, on the recommendation of the Governing Board of the Enterprise, to the transfer of funds from the Enterprise to the Authority;

(g) to decide on the equitable sharing of financial and other economic benefits derived from activities in the Area, consistent with this Convention and the rules, regulations and procedures of the Authority;

(h) to consider and approve the proposed annual budget of the Authority submitted by the Council;

(i) to examine periodic reports from the Council and from the Enterprise and special reports requested from the Council or any other organ of the Authority;

(j) to initiate studies and make recommendations for the purpose of promoting international co-operation concerning activities in the Area and encouraging the progressive development of international law relating thereto and its codification;

(k) to consider problems of a general nature in connection with activities in the Area arising in particular for developing States, as well as those problems for States in connection with activities in the Area that are due to their geographical location, particularly for land-locked and geographically disadvantaged States;

(l) to establish, on the recommendation of the Council, on the basis of advice from the Economic Planning Commission, a system of compensation or other measures of economic adjustment assistance as provided in article 151, paragraph 10;

(m) to suspend the exercise of rights and privileges of membership pursuant to article 185;

(n) to discuss any question or matter within the competence of the Authority and to decide as to which organ of the Authority shall deal with any such question or matter not specifically entrusted to a particular organ, consistent with the distribution of powers and functions among the organs of the Authority.

SUBSECTION C. THE COUNCIL

Article 161
Composition, procedure and voting

1. The Council shall consist of 36 members of the Authority elected by the Assembly in the following order:

(a) four members from among those States Parties which, during the last five years for which statistics are available, have either consumed more than 2 per cent of total world consumption or have had net imports of more than 2 per cent of total world imports of the commodities produced from the categories of minerals to be derived from the Area, and in any case one State from the Eastern European (Socialist) region, as well as the largest consumer;

(b) four members from among the eight States Parties which have the largest investments in preparation for and in the conduct of activities in the Area, either directly or through their nationals, including at least one State from the Eastern European (Socialist) region;

(c) four members from among States Parties which on the basis of production in areas under their jurisdiction are major net exporters of the categories of minerals to be derived from the Area, including at least two developing States whose exports of such minerals have a substantial bearing on their economies;

(d) six members from among developing States Parties, representing special interests. The special interests to be represented shall include those of States with large populations, States which are land-locked or geographically disadvantaged, States which are major importers of the categories of minerals to be derived from the Area, States which are potential producers of such minerals, and least developed States;

(e) eighteen members elected according to the principle of ensuring an equitable geographical distribution of seats in the Council as a whole, provided that each geographical region shall have at least one member elected under this subparagraph. For this purpose, the geographical regions shall be Africa, Asia, Eastern European (Socialist), Latin America and Western European and Others.

2. In electing the members of the Council in accordance with paragraph 1, the Assembly shall ensure that:

(a) land-locked and geographically disadvantaged States are represented to a degree which is reasonably proportionate to their representation in the Assembly;

(b) coastal States, especially developing States, which do not qualify under paragraph 1 (a), (b), (c) or (d) are represented to a degree which is reasonably proportionate to their representation in the Assembly;

(c) each group of States Parties to be represented on the Council is represented by those members, if any, which are nominated by that group.

3. Elections shall take place at regular sessions of the Assembly. Each member of the Council shall be elected for four years. At the first election, however, the term of one half of the members of each group referred to in paragraph 1 shall be two years.

4. Members of the Council shall be eligible for re-election, but due regard should be paid to the desirability of rotation of membership.

5. The Council shall function at the seat of the Authority, and shall meet as often as the business of the Authority may require, but not less than three times a year.

6. A majority of the members of the Council shall constitute a quorum.

7. Each member of the Council shall have one vote.

8. (a) Decisions on questions of procedure shall be taken by a majority of the members present and voting.

(b) Decisions on questions of substance arising under the following provisions shall be taken by a two-thirds majority of the members present and voting, provided that such majority includes a majority of the members of the Council: article 162, paragraph 2, subparagraphs (f); (g); (h); (i); (n); (p); (v); article 191.

(c) Decisions on questions of substance arising under the following provisions shall be taken by a three-fourths majority of the members present and voting, provided that such majority includes a majority of the members of the Council: article 162, paragraph 1; article 162, paragraph 2, subparagraphs (a); (b); (c); (d); (e); (l); (q); (r); (s); (t); (u) in cases of non-compliance by a contractor or a sponsor; (w) provided that orders issued thereunder may be binding for not more than 30 days unless confirmed by a decision taken in accordance with subparagraph (d); article 162, paragraph 2, subparagraphs (x); (y); (z); article 163, paragraph 2; article 174, paragraph 3; Annex IV, article 11.

(d) Decisions on questions of substance arising under the following provisions shall be taken by consensus: article 162, paragraph 2(m) and (o); adoption of amendments to Part XI.

(e) For the purposes of subparagraphs (d), (f) and (g), "consensus" means the absence of any formal objection. Within 14 days of the submission of a proposal to the Council, the President of the Council shall determine whether there would be a formal objection to the adoption of the proposal. If the President determines that there would be such an objection, the President shall establish and convene, within three days following such determination, a conciliation committee consisting of not more than nine members of the Council, with the President as chairman, for the purpose of reconciling the differences and producing a proposal which can be adopted by consensus. The committee shall work expeditiously and report to the Council within 14 days following its establishment. If the committee is unable to recommend a proposal which can be adopted by consensus, it shall set out in its report the grounds on which the proposal is being opposed.

(f) Decisions on questions not listed above which the Council is authorized to take by the rules, regulations and procedures of the Authority or otherwise shall be taken pursuant to the subparagraphs of this paragraph specified in the rules, regulations and procedures or, if not specified therein, then pursuant to the subparagraph determined by the Council if possible in advance, by consensus.

(g) When the issue arises as to whether a question is within subparagraph (a), (b), (c) or (d), the question shall be treated as being within the subparagraph requiring the higher or highest majority or consensus as the case may be, unless otherwise decided by the Council by the said majority or by consensus.

9. The Council shall establish a procedure whereby a member of the Authority not represented on the Council may send a representative to attend a meeting of the Council when a request is made by such member, or a matter particularly affecting it is under consideration. Such a representative shall be entitled to participate in the deliberations butnot to vote.

Article 162
Powers and functions

1. The Council is the executive organ of the Authority. The Council shall have the power to establish, in conformity with this Convention

and the general policies established by the Assembly, the specific policies to be pursued by the Authority on any question or matter within the competence of the Authority.

2. In addition, the Council shall:

(a) supervise and co-ordinate the implementation of the provisions of this Part on all questions and matters within the competence of theAuthority and invite the attention of the Assembly to cases ofnon-compliance;

(b) propose to the Assembly a list of candidates for the election of the Secretary-General;

(c) recommend to the Assembly candidates for the election of the members of the Governing Board of the Enterprise and the Director-General of the Enterprise;

(d) establish, as appropriate, and with due regard to economy and efficiency, such subsidiary organs as it finds necessary for the exercise of its functions in accordance with this Part. In the composition of subsidiary organs, emphasis shall be placed on the need for members qualified and competent in relevant technical matters dealt with by those organs provided that due account shall be taken of the principle of equitable geographical distribution and of special interests;

(e) adopt its rules of procedure including the method of selecting its president;

(f) enter into agreements with the United Nations or other international organizations on behalf of the Authority and within its competence, subject to approval by the Assembly;

(g) consider the reports of the Enterprise and transmit them to the Assembly with its recommendations;

(h) present to the Assembly annual reports and such special reports as the Assembly may request;

(i) issue directives to the Enterprise in accordance with article 170;

(j) approve plans of work in accordance with Annex III, article 6. The Council shall act on each plan of work within 60 days of its submission by the Legal and Technical Commission at a session of the Council in accordance with the following procedures:

(i) if the Commission recommends the approval of a plan of work, it shall be deemed to have been approved by the Council if no member of the Council submits in writing to the President within 14 days a specific objection alleging non-compliance with the requirements of Annex III, article 6. If there is an objection, the conciliation procedure set forth in article 161, paragraph 8(e), shall apply. If, at the end of the conciliation procedure, the objection is still maintained, the plan of work shall be deemed to have been approved by the Council unless the Council disapproves it by consensus among itsmembers excluding any State or States making the application or sponsoring the applicant;

(ii) if the Commission recommends the disapproval of a plan of work or does not make a recommendation, the Council may approve the plan of work by a three-fourths majority of the members present and voting, provided that such majority includes a majority of the members participating in the session;

(k) approve plans of work submitted by the Enterprise in accordance with Annex IV, article 12, applying, mutatis mutandis, the procedures set forth in subparagraph (j);

(l) exercise control over activities in the Area in accordance with article 153, paragraph 4, and the rules, regulations and procedures of the Authority;

(m) take, on the recommendation of the Economic Planning Commission, necessary and appropriate measures in accordance with article 150, subparagraph (h), to provide protection from the adverse economic effects specified therein;

(n) make recommendations to the Assembly, on the basis of advice from the Economic Planning Commission, for a system of compensation or other measures of economic adjustment assistance as provided in article 151, paragraph 10;

(o) (i) recommend to the Assembly rules, regulations and procedures on the equitable sharing of financial and other economic benefits derived from activities in the Area and the payments and contributions made pursuant to article 82, taking into particular consideration the interests and needs of the developing States and peoples who have not attained full independence or other self-governing status;

(ii) adopt and apply provisionally, pending approval by the Assembly, the rules, regulations and procedures of the Authority, and any amendments thereto, taking into account the recommendations of the Legal and Technical Commission or other subordinate organ concerned. These rules, regulations and procedures shall relate to prospecting, exploration and exploitation in the Area and the financial management and internal administration of the Authority. Priority shall be given to the adoption of rules, regulations and procedures for the exploration for and exploitation of polymetallic nodules. Rules, regulations and procedures for the exploration for and exploitation of any resource other than polymetallic nodules shall be adopted within three years from the date of a request to the Authority by any of its members to adopt such rules, regulations and procedures in respect of such resource. All rules, regulations and procedures shall remain in effect on a provisional basis until approved by the Assembly or until amended by the Council in the light of any views expressed by the Assembly;

(p) review the collection of all payments to be made by or to the Authority in connection with operations pursuant to this Part;

(q) make the selection from among applicants for production authorizations pursuant to Annex III, article 7, where such selection is required by that provision;

(r) submit the proposed annual budget of the Authority to the Assembly for its approval;

(s) make recommendations to the Assembly concerning policies on any question or matter within the competence of the Authority;

(t) make recommendations to the Assembly concerning suspension of the exercise of the rights and privileges of membership pursuant to article 185;

(u) institute proceedings on behalf of the Authority before the Sea-Bed Disputes Chamber in cases of non-compliance;

(v) notify the Assembly on a decision by the Sea-Bed Disputes Chamber in proceedings instituted under subparagraph (u), and make any recommendations which it may find appropriate with respect to measures to be taken;

(w) issue emergency orders, which may include orders for the suspension or adjustment of operations, to prevent serious harm to the marine environment arising out of activities in the Area;

(x) disapprove areas for exploitation by contractors or the Enterprise in cases where substantial evidence indicates the risk of serious harm to the marine environment;

(y) establish a subsidiary organ for the elaboration of draft financial rules, regulations and procedures relating to: (i) financial management in accordance with articles 171 to 175; and (ii) financial arrangements in accordance with Annex III, article 13 and article 17, paragraph 1 (c);

(z) establish appropriate mechanisms for directing and supervising a staff of inspectors who shall inspect activities in the Area to determine whether this Part, the rules, regulations and procedures of the Authority, and the terms and conditions of any contract with the Authority are being complied with.

Article 163
Organs of the Council

1. There are hereby established the following organs of the Council:

(a) an Economic Planning Commission;
(b) a Legal and Technical Commission.

2. Each Commission shall be composed of 15 members, elected by the Council from among the candidates nominated by the States Parties. However, if necessary, the Council may decide to increase the size of either Commission having due regard to economy and efficiency.

3. Members of a Commission shall have appropriate qualifications in the area of competence of that Commission. States Parties shall nominate candidates of the highest standards of competence and integrity with qualifications in relevant fields so as to ensure the effective exercise of the functions of the Commissions.

4. In the election of members of the Commissions, due account shall be taken of the need for equitable geographical distribution and the representation of special interests.

5. No state party may nominate more than one candidate for the same Commission. No person shall be elected to serve on more than one Commission.

6. Members of the Commissions shall hold office for a term of five years. They shall be eligible for re-election for a further term.

7. In the event of the death, incapacity or resignation of a member of a Commission prior to the expiration of the term of office, the Council shall elect for the remainder of the term, a member from the same geographical region or area of interest.

8. Members of Commissions shall have no financial interest in any activity relating to exploration and exploitation in the Area. Subject to their responsibilities to the Commissions on which they serve, they shall not disclose, even after the termination of their functions, any industrial secret, proprietary data which are transferred to the Authority in accordance with Annex III, article 14, or any other confidential information coming to their knowledge by reason of their duties for the Authority.

9. Each Commission shall exercise its functions in accordance with such guidelines and directives as the Council may adopt.

10. Each Commission shall formulate and submit to the Council for approval such rules and regulations as may be necessary for the efficient conduct of the Commission's functions.

11. The decision-making procedures of the Commissions shall be established by the rules, regulations and procedures of the Authority. Recommendations to the Council shall, where necessary, be accompanied by a summary on the divergencies of opinion in the Commission.

12. Each Commission shall normally function at the seat of the Authority and shall meet as often as is required for the efficient exercise of its functions.

13. In the exercise of its functions, each Commission may, where appropriate, consult another commission, any competent organ of the United Nations or of its specialized agencies or any international organizations with competence in the subject-matter of such consultation.

Article 164
The Economic Planning Commission

1. Members of the Economic Planning Commission shall have appropriate qualifications such as those relevant to mining, management of mineral resource activities, international trade or international economics. The Council shall endeavour to ensure that the membership of the Commission reflects all appropriate qualifications. The Commission shall include at least two members from developing States whose exports of the categories of minerals to be derived from the Area have a substantial bearing on their economies.

2. The Commission shall:

(a) propose, on the request of the Council, measures to implement decisions relating to activities in the Area taken in accordance with this Convention;
(b) review the trends of and the factors affecting supply, demand and prices of materials which may be derived from the Area, bearing in mind the interests of both importing and exporting countries, and in particular of the developing States among them;
(c) examine any situation likely to lead to the adverse effects referred to in article 150, subparagraph (h), brought to its attention by the state party or States Parties concerned, and make appropriate recommendations to the Council;
(d) propose to the Council for submission to the Assembly, as provided in article 151, paragraph 10, a system of compensation or other measures of economic adjustment assistance for developing States

which suffer adverse effects caused by activities in the Area. The Commission shall make the recommendations to the Council that are necessary for the application of the system or other measures adopted by the Assembly in specific cases.

Article 165
The Legal and Technical Commission

1. Members of the Legal and Technical Commission shall have appropriate qualifications such as those relevant to exploration for and exploitation and processing of mineral resources, oceanology, protection of the marine environment, or economic or legal matters relating to ocean mining and related fields of expertise. The Council shall endeavour to ensure that the membership of the Commission reflects all appropriate qualifications.

2. The Commission shall:

(a) make recommendations with regard to the exercise of the Authority's functions on the request of the Council;
(b) review formal written plans of work for activities in the Area in accordance with article 153, paragraph 3, and submit appropriate recommendations to the Council. The Commission shall base its recommendations solely on the grounds stated in Annex III and shall report fully thereon to the Council;
(c) supervise, on the request of the Council, activities in the Area, where appropriate, in consultation and collaboration with any entity carrying out such activities or State or States concerned and report to the Council;
(d) prepare assessments of the environmental implications of activities in the Area;
(e) make recommendations to the Council on the protection of the marine environment, taking into account the views of recognized experts in that field;
(f) formulate and submit to the Council the rules regulations and procedures referred to in article 162, paragraph 2(o) taking into account all relevant factors including assessments of the environmental implications of activities in the Area;
(g) keep such rules, regulations and procedures under review and recommend to the Council from time to time such amendments thereto as it may deem necessary or desirable;
(h) make recommendations to the Council regarding the establishment of a monitoring programme to observe, measure evaluate and analyse by recognized scientific methods, on a regular basis, the risks or

effects of pollution of the marine environment resulting from activities in the Area, ensure that existing regulations are adequate and are complied with and co-ordinate the implementation of the monitoring programme approved by the Council;

(i) recommend to the Council that proceedings be instituted on behalf of the Authority before the Sea-Bed Disputes Chamber, in accordance with this Part and the relevant Annexes taking into account particularly article 187;

(j) make recommendations to the Council with respect to measures to be taken, on a decision by the Sea-Bed Disputes Chamber in proceedings instituted in accordance with subparagraph (i);

(k) make recommendations to the Council to issue emergency orders, which may include orders for the suspension or adjustment of operations, to prevent serious harm to the marine environment arising out of activities in the Area. Such recommendations shall be taken up by the Council on a priority basis;

(l) make recommendations to the Council to disapprove areas for exploitation by contractors or the Enterprise in cases where substantial evidence indicates the risk of serious harm to the marine environment;

(m) make recommendations to the Council regarding the direction and supervision of a staff of inspectors who shall inspect activities in the Area to determine whether the provisions of this Part, the rules, regulations and procedures of the Authority and the terms and conditions of any contract with the Authority are being complied with;

(n) calculate the production ceiling and issue production authorizations on behalf of the Authority pursuant to article 151, paragraphs 2 to 7, following any necessary selection among applicants for production authorizations by the Council in accordance with Annex III, article 7.

3. The members of the Commission shall, on request by any state party or other party concerned, be accompanied by a representative of such State or other party concerned when carrying out their function of supervision and inspection.

SUBSECTION D. THE SECRETARIAT

Article 166
The Secretariat

1. The Secretariat of the Authority shall comprise a Secretary-General and such staff as the Authority may require.

2. The Secretary-General shall be elected for four years by the Assembly from among the candidates proposed by the Council and may be re-elected.

3. The Secretary-General shall be the chief administrative officer of the Authority, and shall act in that capacity in all meetings of the Assembly, of the Council and of any subsidiary organ, and shall perform such other administrative functions as are entrusted to the Secretary-General by these organs.

4. The Secretary-General shall make an annual report to the Assembly on the work of the Authority.

Article 167
The staff of the Authority

1. The staff of the Authority shall consist of such qualified scientific and technical and other personnel as may be required to fulfil the administrative functions of the Authority.

2. The paramount consideration in the recruitment and employment of the staff and in the determination of their conditions of service shall be the necessity of securing the highest standards of efficiency, competence and integrity. Subject to this consideration, due regard shall be paid to the importance of recruiting the staff on as wide a geographical basis as possible.

3. The staff shall be appointed by the Secretary-General. The terms and conditions on which they shall be appointed, remunerated and dismissed shall be in accordance with the rules, regulations and procedures of the Authority.

Article 168
International character of the Secretariat

1. In the performance of their duties the Secretary-General and the staff shall not seek or receive instructions from any government or from any other source external to the Authority. They shall refrain from any action which might reflect on their position as international officials responsible only to the Authority. Each state party undertakes to respect the exclusively international character of the responsibilities of the Secretary-General and the staff and not to seek to influence them in the discharge of their responsibilities. Any violation of responsibilities by a staff member shall be submitted to the appropriate administrative tribunal as provided in the rules, regulations and procedures of the Authority.

2. The Secretary-General and the staff shall have no financial interest in any activity relating to exploration and exploitation in the Area. Subject to their responsibilities to the Authority, they shall not disclose, even after the termination of their functions, any industrial secret, proprietary data which are transferred to the Authority in accordance with Annex III, article 14, or any other confidential information coming to their knowledge by reason of their employment with the Authority.

3. Violations of the obligations of a staff member of the Authority set forth in paragraph 2 shall, on the request of a state party affected by such violation, or a natural or juridical person, sponsored by a state party as provided in article 153, paragraph 2(b), and affected by such violation, be submitted by the Authority against the staff member concerned to a tribunal designated by the rules, regulations and procedures of the Authority. The Party affected shall have the right to take part in the proceedings. If the tribunal so recommends, the Secretary-General shall dismiss the staff member concerned.

4. The rules, regulations and procedures of the Authority shall contain such provisions as are necessary to implement this article.

Article 169
Consultation and co-operation with international and non-governmental organizations

1. The Secretary-General shall, on matters within the competence of the Authority, make suitable arrangements, with the approval of the Council, for consultation and co-operation with international and non-

governmental organizations recognized by the Economic and Social Council of the United Nations.

2. Any organization with which the Secretary-General has entered into an arrangement under paragraph 1 may designate representatives to attend meetings of the organs of the Authority as observers in accordance with the rules of procedure of these organs. Procedures shall be established for obtaining the views of such organizations in appropriate cases.

3. The Secretary-General may distribute to States Parties written reports submitted by the non-governmental organizations referred to in paragraph 1 on subjects in which they have special competence and which are related to.

SUBSECTION E. THE ENTERPRISE

Article 170
The Enterprise

1. The Enterprise shall be the organ of the Authority which shall carry out activities in the Area directly, pursuant to article 153, paragraph 2(a), as well as the transporting, processing and marketing of minerals recovered from the Area.

2. The Enterprise shall, within the framework of the international legal personality of the Authority, have such legal capacity as is provided for in the Statute set forth in Annex IV. The Enterprise shall act in accordance with this Convention and the rules, regulations and procedures of the Authority, as well as the general policies established by the Assembly, and shall be subject to the directives and control of the Council.

3. The Enterprise shall have its principal place of business at the seat of the Authority.

4. The Enterprise shall, in accordance with article 173, paragraph 2, and Annex IV, article 11, be provided with such funds as it may require to carry out its functions, and shall receive technology as provided in article 144 and other relevant provisions of this Convention.

SUBSECTION F. FINANCIAL ARRANGEMENTS
OF THE AUTHORITY

Article 171
Funds of the Authority

The funds of the Authority shall include:

(a) assessed contributions made by members of the Authority in accordance with article 160, paragraph 2(e);
(b) funds received by the Authority pursuant to Annex III, article 13, in connection with activities in the Area;
(c) funds transferred from the Enterprise in accordance with Annex IV, article 10;
(d) funds borrowed pursuant to article 174;
(e) voluntary contributions made by members or other entities; and
(f) payments to a compensation fund, in accordance with article 151, paragraph 10, whose sources are to be recommended by the Economic Planning Commission.

Article 172
Annual budget of the Authority

The Secretary-General shall draft the proposed annual budget of the Authority and submit it to the Council. The Council shall consider the proposed annual budget and submit it to the Assembly, together with any recommendations thereon. The Assembly shall consider and approve the proposed annual budget in accordance with article 160, paragraph 2(h).

Article 173
Expenses of the Authority

1. The contributions referred to in article 171, subparagraph (a), shall be paid into a special account to meet the administrative expenses of the Authority until the Authority has sufficient funds from other sources to meet those expenses.

2. The administrative expenses of the Authority shall be a first call on the funds of the Authority. Except for the assessed contributions referred to in article 171, subparagraph (a), the funds which remain after payment of administrative expenses may, inter alia:

(a) be shared in accordance with article 140 and article 160, paragraph 2(g);
(b) be used to provide the Enterprise with funds in accordance with article 170, paragraph 4; (c) be used to compensate developing States in accordance with article 151, paragraph 10, and article 160, paragraph 2(1).

Article 174
Borrowing power of the Authority

1. The Authority shall have the power to borrow funds.

2. The Assembly shall prescribe the limits on the borrowing power of the Authority in the financial regulations adopted pursuant to article 160, paragraph 2(f).

3. The Council shall exercise the borrowing power of the Authority.

4. States Parties shall not be liable for the debts of the Authority.

Article 175
Annual audit

The records, books and accounts of the Authority, including its annual financial statements, shall be audited annually by an independent auditor appointed by the Assembly.

SUBSECTION G. LEGAL STATUS, PRIVILEGES AND IMMUNITIES

Article 176
Legal status

The Authority shall have international legal personality and such legal capacity as may be necessary for the exercise of its functions and the fulfilment of its purposes.

Article 177
Privileges and immunities

To enable the Authority to exercise its functions, it shall enjoy in the territory of each state party the privileges and immunities set forth in this subsection. The privileges and immunities relating to the Enterprise shall be those set forth in Annex IV, article 13.

Article 178
Immunity from legal process

The Authority, its property and assets, shall enjoy immunity from legal process except to the extent that the Authority expressly waives this immunity in a particular case.

Article 179
Immunity from search and any form of seizure

The property and assets of the Authority, wherever located and by whomsoever held, shall be immune from search, requisition, confiscation, expropriation or any other form of seizure by executive or legislative action.

Article 180
Exemption from restrictions, regulations, controls and moratoria

The property and assets of the Authority shall be exempt from restrictions, regulations, controls and moratoria of any nature.

Article 181
Archives and official communications of the Authority

1. The archives of the Authority, wherever located, shall be inviolable.

2. Proprietary data, industrial secrets or similar information and personnel records shall not be placed in archives which are open to public inspection.

3. With regard to its official communications, the Authority shall be accorded by each state party treatment no less favourable than that accorded by that State to other international organizations.

Article 182
Privileges and immunities of certain persons connected with the Authority

Representatives of States Parties attending meetings of the Assembly, the Council or organs of the Assembly or the Council, and the

Secretary-General and staff of the Authority, shall enjoy in the territory of each state party:

(a) immunity from legal process with respect to acts performed by them in the exercise of their functions, except to the extent that the State which they represent or the Authority, as appropriate, expressly waives this immunity in a particular case;

(b) if they are not nationals of that state party, the same exemptions from immigration restrictions, alien registration requirements and national service obligations, the same facilities as regards exchange restrictions and the same treatment in respect of travelling facilities as are accorded by that State to the representatives, officials and employees of comparable rank of other States Parties.

Article 183
Exemption from taxes and customs duties

1. Within the scope of its official activities, the Authority, its assets and property, its income, and its operations and transactions, authorized by this Convention, shall be exempt from all direct taxation and goods imported or exported for its official use shall be exempt from all customs duties. The Authority shall not claim exemption from taxes which are no more than charges for services rendered.

2. When purchases of goods or services of substantial value necessary for the official activities of the Authority are made by or on behalf of the Authority, and when the price of such goods or services includes taxes or duties, appropriate measures shall, to the extent practicable, be taken by States Parties to grant exemption from such taxes or duties or provide for their reimbursement. Goods imported or purchased under an exemption provided for in this article shall not be sold or otherwise disposed of in the territory of the state party which granted the exemption, except under conditions agreed with that state party.

3. No tax shall be levied by States Parties on or in respect of salaries and emoluments paid or any other form of payment made by the Authority to the Secretary-General and staff of the Authority, as well as experts performing missions for the Authority, who are not their nationals.

SUBSECTION H. SUSPENSION OF THE EXERCISE OF RIGHTSAND PRIVILEGES OF MEMBERS

Article 184
Suspension of the exercise of voting rights

A state party which is in arrears in the payment of its financial contributions to the Authority shall have no vote if the amount of its arrears equals or exceeds the amount of the contributions due from it for the preceding two full years. The Assembly may, nevertheless, permit such a member to vote if it is satisfied that the failure to pay is due to conditions beyond the control of the member.

Article 185
Suspension of exercise of rights
and privileges of membership

1. A state party which has grossly and persistently violated the provisions of this Part may be suspended from the exercise of the rights and privileges of membership by the Assembly on the recommendation of the Council.

2. No action may be taken under paragraph 1 until the Sea-Bed Disputes Chamber has found that a state party has grossly and persistently violated the provisions of this Part.

SECTION 5. SETTLEMENT OF DISPUTES AND ADVISORY OPINIONS

Article 186
Sea-Bed Disputes Chamber of the
International Tribunal for the Law of the Sea

The establishment of the Sea-Bed Disputes Chamber and the manner in which it shall exercise its jurisdiction shall be governed by the provisions of this section, of Part XV and of Annex VI.

Article 187
Jurisdiction of the Sea-Bed Disputes Chamber

The Sea-Bed Disputes Chamber shall have jurisdiction under this Part and the Annexes relating thereto in disputes with respect to activities in the Area falling within the following categories:

(a) disputes between States Parties concerning the interpretation or application of this Part and the Annexes relating thereto;

(b) disputes between a state party and the Authority concerning:
   (i) acts or omissions of the Authority or of a state party alleged to be in violation of this Part or the Annexes relating thereto or of rules, regulations and procedures of the Authority adopted in accordance therewith; or
   (ii) acts of the Authority alleged to be in excess of jurisdiction or a misuse of power;

(c) disputes between parties to a contract, being States Parties, the Authority or the Enterprise, state enterprises and natural or juridical persons referred to in article 153, paragraph 2 (b), concerning:
   (i) the interpretation or application of a relevant contract or a plan of work; or
   (ii) acts or omissions of a party to the contract relating to activities in the Area and directed to the other party or directly affecting its legitimate interests;

(d) disputes between the Authority and a prospective contractor who has been sponsored by a State as provided in article 153, paragraph 2 (b), and has duly fulfilled the conditions referred to in Annex III, article 4, paragraph 6, and article 13, paragraph 2, concerning the refusal of a contract or a legal issue arising in the negotiation of the contract;

(e) disputes between the Authority and a state party, a state enterprise or a natural or juridical person sponsored by a state party as provided for in article 153, paragraph 2(b), where it is alleged that the Authority has incurred liability as provided in Annex III, article 22;

(f) any other disputes for which the jurisdiction of the Chamber is specifically provided in this Convention.

Article 188
Submission of disputes to a special chamber of the International Tribunal for the Law of the Sea or an ad hoc chamber of the Sea-Bed Disputes Chamber or to binding commercial arbitration

1. Disputes between States Parties referred to in article 187, subparagraph (a), may be submitted:

(a) at the request of the parties to the dispute, to a special chamber of the International Tribunal for the Law of the Sea to be formed in accordance with Annex VI, articles 15 and 17; or

(b) at the request of any party to the dispute, to an ad hoc chamber of the Sea-Bed Disputes Chamber to be formed in accordance with Annex VI, article 36.

2. (a) Disputes concerning the interpretation or application of a contract referred to in article 187, subparagraph (c) (i), shall be submitted, at the request of any party to the dispute, to binding commercial arbitration, unless the parties otherwise agree. A commercial arbitral tribunal to which the dispute is submitted shall have no jurisdiction to decide any question of interpretation of this Convention. When the dispute also involves a question of the interpretation of Part XI and the Annexes relating thereto, with respect to activities in the Area, that question shall be referred to the Sea-Bed Disputes Chamber for a ruling.

(b) If, at the commencement of or in the course of such arbitration, the arbitral tribunal determines, either at the request of any party to the dispute or proprio motu, that its decision depends on a ruling of the Sea-Bed Disputes Chamber, the arbitral tribunal shall refer such question to the Sea-Bed Disputes Chamber for such ruling. The arbitral tribunal shall then proceed to render its award in conformity with the ruling of the SeaBed Disputes Chamber.

(c) In the absence of a provision in the contract on the arbitration procedure to be applied in the dispute, the arbitration shall be conducted in accordance with the UNCITRAL Arbitration Rules or such other arbitration rules as may be prescribed in the rules, regulations and procedures of the Authority, unless the parties to the dispute otherwise agree.

Article 189
Limitation on jurisdiction with regard to decisions of the Authority

The Sea-Bed Disputes Chamber shall have no jurisdiction with regard to the exercise by the Authority of its discretionary powers in accordance with this Part; in no case shall it substitute its discretion for that of the Authority. Without prejudice to article 191, in exercising its jurisdiction pursuant to article 187, the Sea-Bed Disputes Chamber shall not pronounce itself on the question of whether any rules, regulations and procedures of the Authority are in conformity with this Convention, nor declare invalid any such rules, regulations and procedures. Its jurisdiction in this regard shall be confined to deciding claims that the application of any rules, regulations and procedures of the Authority in individual cases would be in conflict with the contractual obligations of the parties to the dispute or their obligations under this Convention, claims concerning excess of jurisdiction or misuse of power, and to claims for damages to be paid or other remedy to be given to the party concerned for the failure of the other party to comply with its contractual obligations or its obligations under this Convention.

Article 190
Participation and appearance of sponsoring States Parties in proceedings

1. If a natural or juridical person is a party to a dispute referred to in article 187, the sponsoring State shall be given notice thereof and shall have the right to participate in the proceedings by submitting written or oral statements.

2. If an action is brought against a state party by a natural or juridical person sponsored by another state party in a dispute referred to in article 187, subparagraph (c), the respondent State may request the State sponsoring that person to appear in the proceedings on behalf of that person. Failing such appearance, the respondent State may arrange to be represented by a juridical person of its nationality.

Article 191
Advisory opinions

The Sea-Bed Disputes Chamber shall give advisory opinions at the request of the Assembly or the Council on legal questions arising within the scope of their activities. Such opinions shall be given as a matter of urgency.

Appendix VIII

1994 "Agreement"

A/RES/48/263 (33 ILM 1309)

AGREEMENT RELATING TO THE IMPLEMENTATION OF PART XI OF THE UNITED NATIONS CONVENTION ON THE LAW OF THE SEA OF 10 DECEMBER 1982 (28 Jul 1994)

The General Assembly,

Prompted by the desire to achieve universal participation in the United Nations Convention on the Law of the Sea of 10 December 1982 hereinafter referred to as the "Convention") and to promote appropriate representation in the institutions established by it,

Reaffirming that the seabed and ocean floor and subsoil thereof, beyond the limits of national Jurisdiction (hereinafter referred to as the "Area"), as well as the resources of the Area, are the common heritage of mankind,

Recalling that the Convention in its Part XI and related provisions (hereinafter referred to as "Part XI") established a regime for the Area and its resources,

Taking note of the consolidated provisional final report of the Preparatory Commission for the International Seabed Authority and for the International Tribunal for the Law of the Sea,

Recalling its resolution 48/28 of 9 December 1993 on the law of the sea,

Recognizing that political and economic changes, including in particular a growing reliance on market principles, have necessitated the re-evaluation of some aspects of the regime for the Area and its resources,

Noting the initiative of the Secretary-General which began in 1990 to promote dialogue aimed at achieving universal participation in the Convention,

Welcoming the report of the Secretary-General on the outcome of his informal consultations, including the draft of an agreement relating to the implementation of Part XI,

Considering that the objective of universal participation in the Convention may best be achieved by the adoption of an agreement relating to the implementation of Part XI,

Recognizing the need to provide for the provisional application of such an agreement from the date of entry into force of the Convention on 16 November 1994,

1. Expresses its appreciation to the Secretary-General for his report on the informal consultations;

2. Reaffirms the unified character of the United Nations Convention on the Law of the Sea of 10 December 1982;

3. Adopts the Agreement relating to the implementation of Part XI of the United Nations Convention on the Law of the Sea of 10 December 1982 (hereinafter referred to as the "Agreement"), the text of which is annexed to the present resolution;

4. Affirms that the Agreement shall be interpreted and applied together with Part XI as a single instrument;

5. Considers that future ratifications or formal confirmations of or accessions to the Convention shall represent also consent to be bound by the Agreement and that no State or entity may establish its consent to be bound by the Agreement unless it has previously established or establishes at the same time its consent to be bound by the Convention;

6. Calls on States which consent to the adoption of the Agreement to refrain from any act which would defeat its object and purpose;

7. Expresses its satisfaction at the entry into force of the Convention on 16 November 1994;

8. Decides to fund the administrative expenses of the International Seabed Authority in accordance with section 1, paragraph 14, of the Annex to the Agreement;

9. Requests the Secretary-General to transmit immediately certified copies of the Agreement to the States and entities referred to in article 3 thereof, with a view to facilitating universal participation in the Convention and the Agreement, and to draw attention to articles 4 and 5 of the Agreement;

10. Also requests the Secretary-General immediately to open the Agreement for signature in accordance with article 3 thereof;

11. Urges all States and entities referred to in article 3 of the Agreement to consent to its provisional application as from 16 November 1994 and to establish their consent to be bound by the Agreement at the earliest possible date;

12. Also urges all such States and entities that have not already done so to take all appropriate steps to ratify, formally confirm or accede to the Convention at the earliest possible date in order to ensure universal participation in the Convention;

13. Calls on the Preparatory Commission for the International Seabed Authority and for the International Tribunal for the Law of the Sea to take into account the terms of the Agreement when drawing up its final report.

ANNEX

AGREEMENT RELATING TO THE IMPLEMENTATION OF PART XI OF THE UNITED NATIONS CONVENTION ON THE LAW OF THE SEA OF 10 DECEMBER 1982

The States Parties to this Agreement,

Recognizing the important contribution of the United Nations Convention on the Law of the Sea of 10 December 1982 nl (hereinafter referred to as "the Convention") to the maintenance of peace, justice and progress for all peoples of the world,

Reaffirming that the seabed and ocean floor and subsoil thereof, beyond the limits of national jurisdiction (hereinafter referred to as "the Area"), as well as the resources of the Area, are the common heritage of mankind,

Mindful of the importance of the Convention for the protection and preservation of the marine environment and of the growing concern for the global environment,

Having considered the report of the Secretary-General of the United Nations on the results of the informal consultations among States held from 1990 to 1994 on outstanding issues relating to Part XI and related provisions of the Convention (hereinafter referred to as "Part XI"),

Noting the political and economic changes, including market oriented approaches, affecting the implementation of Part XI,

Wishing to facilitate universal participation in the Convention,

Considering that an agreement relating to the implementation of Part XI would best meet that objective,

Have agreed as follows:

Article 1
Implementation of Part XI

1. The States Parties to this Agreement undertake to implement Part XI in accordance with this Agreement.

2. The Annex forms an integral part of this Agreement.

Article 2
Relationship between this Agreement and Part XI

1. The provisions of this Agreement and Part XI shall be interpreted and applied together as a single instrument. In the event of any inconsistency between this Agreement and Part XI, the provisions of this Agreement shall prevail.

2. Articles 309 to 319 of the Convention shall apply to this Agreement as they apply to the Convention.

Article 3
Signature

This Agreement shall remain open for signature at United Nations Headquarters by the States and entities referred to in article 305, paragraph 1 (a), (c), (d), (e) and (f), of the Convention for 12 months from the date of its adoption.

Article 4
Consent to be bound

1. After the adoption of this Agreement, any instrument of ratification or formal confirmation of or accession to the Convention shall also represent consent to be bound by this Agreement.

2. No State or entity may establish its consent to be bound by this Agreement unless it has previously established or establishes at the same time its consent to be bound by the Convention.

3. A State or entity referred to in article 3 may express its consent to be bound by this Agreement by:

(a) Signature not subject to ratification, formal confirmation or the procedure set out in article 5;

(b) Signature subject to ratification or formal confirmation, followed by ratification or formal confirmation;

(c) Signature subject to the procedure set out in article 5; or

(d) Accession.

4. Formal confirmation by the entities referred to in article 305, paragraph 1 (f), of the Convention shall be in accordance with Annex IX of the Convention.

5. The instruments of ratification, formal confirmation or accession shall be deposited with the Secretary-General of the United Nations.

Article 5
Simplified procedure

1. A State or entity which has deposited before the date of the adoption of this Agreement an instrument of ratification or formal confirmation of or accession to the Convention and which has signed this Agreement in accordance with article 4, paragraph 3 (c), shall be considered to have established its consent to be bound by this Agreement 12 months after the date of its adoption, unless that State or entity notifies the depositary in writing before that date that it is not availing itself of the simplified procedure set out in this article.

2. In the event of such notification, consent to be bound by this Agreement shall be established in accordance with article 4, paragraph 3 (b).

Article 6
Entry into force

1. This Agreement shall enter into force 30 days after the date on which 40 States have established their consent to be bound in accordance with articles 4 and 5, provided that such States include at least seven of the States referred to in paragraph 1 (a) of resolution II of the Third United Nations Conference on the Law of the Sea (hereinafter referred to as "resolution II") and that at least five of those States are developed States. If these conditions for entry into force are fulfilled before 16 November 1994, this Agreement shall enter into force on 16 November 1994.

2. For each State or entity establishing its consent to be bound by this Agreement after the requirements set out in paragraph 1 have been fulfilled, this Agreement shall enter into force on the thirtieth day following the date of establishment of its consent to be bound.

Article 7
Provisional application

1. If on 16 November 1994 this Agreement has not entered into force, it shall be applied provisionally pending its entry into force by:

(a) States which have consented to its adoption in the General Assembly of the United Nations, except any such State which before 16 November 1994 notifies the depositary in writing either that it will not so apply this Agreement or that it will consent to such application only on subsequent signature or notification in writing;

(b) States and entities which sign this Agreement, except any such State or entity which notifies the depositary in writing at the time of signature that it will not so apply this Agreement;

(c) States and entities which consent to its provisional application by so notifying the depositary in writing;

(d) States which accede to this Agreement.

2. All such States and entities shall apply this Agreement provisionally in accordance with their national or internal laws and regulations, with effect from 16 November 1994 or the date of signature, notification of consent or accession, if later.

3. Provisional application shall terminate on the date of entry into force of this Agreement. In any event, provisional application shall terminate on 16 November 1998 if at that date the requirement in article 6, paragraph 1, of consent to be bound by this Agreement by at least seven of the States (of which at least five must be developed States) referred to in paragraph 1 (a) of resolution II has not been fulfilled.

Article 8
States Parties

1. For the purposes of this Agreement, "States Parties" means States which have consented to be bound by this Agreement and for which this Agreement is in force.

2. This Agreement applies mutatis mutandis to the entities referred to in article 305, paragraph 1 (c), (d), (e) and (f), of the Convention which become Parties to this Agreement in accordance with the conditions relevant to each, and to that extent "States Parties" refers to those entities.

Article 9
Depositary

The Secretary-General of the United Nations shall be the depositary of this Agreement.

Article 10
Authentic texts

The original of this Agreement, of which the Arabic, Chinese, English, French, Russian and Spanish texts are equally authentic, shall be deposited with the Secretary-General of the United Nations.

IN WITNESS WHEREOF, the undersigned Plenipotentiaries, being duly authorized thereto, have signed this Agreement.

DONE AT NEW YORK, this day of July, one thousand nine hundred and ninety-four.

Annex

SECTION 1. COSTS TO STATES PARTIES AND INSTITUTIONAL ARRANGEMENTS

1. The International Seabed Authority (hereinafter referred to as "the Authority") is the organization through which States Parties to the Convention shall, in accordance with the regime for the Area established in Part XI and this Agreement, organize and control activities in the Area, particularly with a view to administering the resources of the Area. The powers and functions of the Authority shall be those expressly conferred on it by the Convention. The Authority shall have such incidental powers, consistent with the Convention, as are implicit in, and necessary for, the exercise of those powers and functions with respect to activities in the Area.

2. In order to minimize costs to States Parties, all organs and subsidiary bodies to be established under the Convention and this Agreement shall be cost-effective. This principle shall also apply to the frequency, duration and scheduling of meetings.

3. The setting up and the functioning of the organs and subsidiary bodies of the Authority shall be based on an evolutionary approach, taking into account the functional needs of the organs and subsidiary bodies concerned in order that they may discharge effectively their respective responsibilities at various stages of the development of activities in the Area.

4. The early functions of the Authority on entry into force of the Convention shall be carried out by the Assembly, the Council, the Secretariat, the Legal and Technical Commission and the Finance Committee. The functions of the Economic Planning Commission shall be performed by the Legal and Technical Commission until such time as the Council decides otherwise or until the approval of the first plan of work for exploitation.

5. Between the entry into force of the Convention and the approval of the first plan of work for exploitation, the Authority shall concentrate on:

(a) Processing of applications for approval of plans of work for exploration in accordance with Part XI and this Agreement;

(b) Implementation of decisions of the Preparatory Commission for the International Seabed Authority and for the International Tribunal for the Law of the Sea (hereinafter referred to as "the Preparatory Commission") relating to the registered pioneer investors and their certifying States, including their rights and obligations, in accordance with article 308, paragraph 5, of the Convention and resolution II, paragraph 13;

(c) Monitoring of compliance with plans of work for exploration approved in the form of contracts;

(d) Monitoring and review of trends and developments relating to deep seabed mining activities, including regular analysis of world metal market conditions and metal prices, trends and prospects;

(e) Study of the potential impact of mineral production from the Area on the economies of developing land-based producers of those minerals which are likely to be most seriously affected, with a view to minimizing their difficulties and assisting them in their economic adjustment, taking into account the work done in this regard by the Preparatory Commission;

(f) Adoption of rules, regulations and procedures necessary for the conduct of activities in the Area as they progress. Notwithstanding the provisions of Annex III, article 17, paragraph 2 (b) and (c), of the Convention, such rules, regulations and procedures shall take into account the terms of this Agreement, the prolonged delay in commercial deep seabed mining and the likely pace of activities in the Area;

(g) Adoption of rules, regulations and procedures incorporating applicable standards for the protection and preservation of the marine environment;

(h) Promotion and encouragement of the conduct of marine scientific research with respect to activities in the Area and the collection and dissemination of the results of such research and analysis, when available, with particular emphasis on research related to the environmental impact of activities in the Area;

(i) Acquisition of scientific knowledge and monitoring of the development of marine technology relevant to activities in the Area, in particular technology relating to the protection and preservation of the marine environment;

(j) Assessment of available data relating to prospecting and exploration;

(k) Timely elaboration of rules, regulations and procedures for exploitation, including those relating to the protection and preservation of the marine environment.

6. (a) An application for approval of a plan of work for exploration shall be considered by the Council following the receipt of a recommendation on the application from the Legal and Technical Commission. The processing of an application for approval of a plan of work for exploration shall be in accordance with the provisions of the Convention, including Annex III thereof, and this Agreement, and subject to the following:

(i) A plan of work for exploration submitted on behalf of a State or entity, or any component of such entity, referred to in resolution II, paragraph 1 (a) (ii) or (iii), other than a registered pioneer investor, which had already undertaken substantial activities in the Area prior to the entry into force of the Convention, or its successor in interest, shall be considered to have met the financial and technical qualifications necessary for approval of a plan of work if the sponsoring State or States certify that the applicant has expended an amount equivalent to at least U.S. $ 30 million in research and exploration activities and has expended no less than 10 per cent of that amount in the location, survey and evaluation of the area referred to in the plan of work. If the plan of work otherwise satisfies the requirements of the Convention and any rules, regulations and procedures adopted pursuant thereto, it shall be approved by the Council in the form of a contract. The provisions of section 3, paragraph 11, of this Annex shall be interpreted and applied accordingly;

(ii) Notwithstanding the provisions of resolution II, paragraph 8(a), a registered pioneer investor may request approval of a plan of work for exploration within 36 months of the entry into force of the Convention. The plan of work for exploration shall consist of documents, reports and other data submitted to the Preparatory Commission both before and after registration and shall be accompanied by a certificate of compliance, consisting of a factual report describing the status of fulfilment of obligations under the pioneer investor regime, issued by the Preparatory Commission in accordance with resolution II, paragraph 11 (a). Such a plan of work shall be considered to be approved. Such an approved plan of work shall be in the form of a contract concluded between the Authority and the registered pioneer investor in accordance with Part XI and this Agreement. The fee of U.S. $ 250,000 paid pursuant to resolution II, paragraph 7(a), shall be deemed to be the fee relating to the exploration phase pursuant to section 8, paragraph 3, of this Annex. Section 3, paragraph 11, of this Annex shall be interpreted and applied accordingly;

(iii) In accordance with the principle of non-discrimination, a contract with a State or entity or any component of such entity referred to in subparagraph (a) (i) shall include arrangements which shall be similar to and no less favourable than those agreed with any registered pioneer investor referred to in subparagraph (a) (ii). If any of the States or entities or any components of such entities referred to in subparagraph (a) (i) are granted more favourable arrangements, the Council shall make similar and no less favourable arrangements with regard to the rights and obligations assumed by the registered pioneer investors referred to in subparagraph (a) (ii), provided that such arrangements do not affect or prejudice the interests of the Authority;

(iv) A State sponsoring an application for a plan of work pursuant to the provisions of subparagraph (a) (i) or (ii) may be a state party or a State which is applying this Agreement provisionally in accordance with article 7, or a State which is a member of the Authority on a provisional basis in accordance with paragraph 12;

(v) Resolution II, paragraph 8 (c), shall be interpreted and applied in accordance with subparagraph (a) (iv).

(b) The approval of a plan of work for exploration shall be in accordance with article 153, paragraph 3, of the Convention.

7. An application for approval of a plan of work shall be accompanied by an assessment of the potential environmental impacts of the proposed activities and by a description of a programme for oceanographic and baseline environmental studies in accordance with the rules, regulations and procedures adopted by the Authority.

8. An application for approval of a plan of work for exploration, subject to paragraph 6 (a) (i) or (ii), shall be processed in accordance with the procedures set out in section 3, paragraph 11, of this Annex.

9. A plan of work for exploration shall be approved for a period of 15 years. On the expiration of a plan of work for exploration, the contractor shall apply for a plan of work for exploitation unless the contractor has already done so or has obtained an extension for the plan of work for exploration. Contractors may apply for such extensions for periods of not more than five years each. Such extensions shall be approved if the contractor has made efforts in good faith to comply with the requirements of the plan of work but for reasons beyond the contractor's control has been unable to complete the necessary preparatory work for proceeding to the exploitation stage or if the prevailing economic circumstances do not justify proceeding to the exploitation stage.

10. Designation of a reserved area for the Authority in accordance with Annex III, article 8, of the Convention shall take place in connection with approval of an application for a plan of work for exploration or approval of an application for a plan of work for exploration and exploitation.

11. Notwithstanding the provisions of paragraph 9, an approved plan of work for exploration which is sponsored by at least one State provisionally applying this Agreement shall terminate if such a State ceases to apply this Agreement provisionally and has not become a member on a provisional basis in accordance with paragraph 12 or has not become a state party.

12. On the entry into force of this Agreement, States and entities referred to in article 3 of this Agreement which have been applying it provisionally in accordance with article 7 and for which it is not in force may continue to be members of the Authority on a provisional basis pending its entry into force for such States and entities, in accordance with the following subparagraphs:

(a) If this Agreement enters into force before 16 November 1996, such States and entities shall be entitled to continue to participate as members of the Authority on a provisional basis on notification to the depositary of the Agreement by such a State or entity of its intention to participate as a member on a provisional basis. Such membership shall terminate either on 16 November 1996 or on the entry into force of this Agreement and the Convention for such member, whichever is earlier. The Council may, on the request of the State or entity concerned, extend such membership beyond 16 November 1996 for a further period or periods not exceeding a total of two years provided that the Council is satisfied that the State or entity concerned has been making efforts in good faith to become a party to the Agreement and the Convention;

(b) If this Agreement enters into force after 15 November 1996, such States and entities may request the Council to grant continued membership in the Authority on a provisional basis for a period or periods not extending beyond 16 November 1998. The Council shall grant such membership with effect from the date of the request if it is satisfied that the State or entity has been making efforts in good faith to become a party to the Agreement and the Convention;

(c) States and entities which are members of the Authority on a provisional basis in accordance with subparagraph (a) or (b) shall apply the terms of Part XI and this Agreement in accordance with their national or internal laws, regulations and annual budgetary appropriations and shall have the same rights and obligations as other members, including:

(i) The obligation to contribute to the administrative budget of the Authority in accordance with the scale of assessed contributions;

(ii) The right to sponsor an application for approval of a plan of work for exploration. In the case of entities whose components are natural or juridical persons possessing the nationality of more than one State, a plan of work for exploration shall not be approved unless all the States whose natural or juridical persons comprise those entities are States Parties or members on a provisional basis;

(d) Notwithstanding the provisions of paragraph 9, an approved plan of work in the form of a contract for exploration which was sponsored pursuant to subparagraph (c) (ii) by a State which was a member on a provisional basis shall terminate if such membership ceases and the State or entity has not become a state party;

(e) If such a member has failed to make its assessed contributions or otherwise failed to comply with its obligations in accordance with this paragraph, its membership on a provisional basis shall be terminated.

13. The reference in Annex III, article 10, of the Convention to performance which has not been satisfactory shall be interpreted to mean that the contractor has failed to comply with the requirements of an approved plan of work in spite of a written warning or warnings from the Authority to the contractor to comply therewith.

14. The Authority shall have its own budget. Until the end of the year following the year during which this Agreement enters into force, the administrative expenses of the Authority shall be met through the budget of the United Nations. Thereafter, the administrative expenses of the Authority shall be met by assessed contributions of its members, including any members on a provisional basis, in accordance with articles 171, subparagraph (a), and 173 of the Convention and this Agreement, until the Authority has sufficient funds from other sources to meet those expenses. The Authority shall not exercise the power referred to in article 174, paragraph 1, of the Convention to borrow funds to finance its administrative budget.

15. The Authority shall elaborate and adopt, in accordance with article 162, paragraph 2 (o) (ii), of the Convention, rules, regulations and procedures based on the principles contained in sections 2, 5, 6, 7 and 8 of this Annex, as well as any additional rules, regulations and procedures necessary to facilitate the approval of plans of work for exploration or exploitation, in accordance with the following subparagraphs:

(a) The Council may undertake such elaboration any time it deems that all or any of such rules, regulations or procedures are required for the conduct of activities in the Area, or when it determines that commercial exploitation is imminent, or at the request of a State whose national intends to apply for approval of a plan of work for exploitation;

(b) If a request is made by a State referred to in subparagraph (a) the Council shall, in accordance with article 162, paragraph 2 (o), of the Convention, complete the adoption of such rules, regulations and procedures within two years of the request;

(c) If the Council has not completed the elaboration of the rules, regulations and procedures relating to exploitation within the prescribed time and an application for approval of a plan of work for exploitation is pending, it shall none the less consider and provisionally approve such plan of work based on the provisions of the Convention and any rules, regulations and procedures that the Council may have adopted provisionally, or on the basis of the norms contained in the Convention and the terms and principles contained in this Annex as well as the principle of non-discrimination among contractors.

16. The draft rules, regulations and procedures and any recommendations relating to the provisions of Part XI, as contained in

the reports and recommendations of the Preparatory Commission, shall be taken into account by the Authority in the adoption of rules, regulations and procedures in accordance with Part XI and this Agreement.

17. The relevant provisions of Part XI, section 4, of the Convention shall be interpreted and applied in accordance with this Agreement.

SECTION 2. THE ENTERPRISE

1. The Secretariat of the Authority shall perform the functions of the Enterprise until it begins to operate independently of the Secretariat. The Secretary-General of the Authority shall appoint from within the staff of the Authority an interim Director-General to oversee the performance of these functions by the Secretariat.

These functions shall be:

(a) Monitoring and review of trends and developments relating to deep seabed mining activities, including regular analysis of world metal market conditions and metal prices, trends and prospects;

(b) Assessment of the results of the conduct of marine scientific research with respect to activities in the Area, with particular emphasis on research related to the environmental impact of activities in the Area;

(c) Assessment of available data relating to prospecting and exploration, including the criteria for such activities;

(d) Assessment of technological developments relevant to activities in the Area, in particular technology relating to the protection and preservation of the marine environment;

(e) Evaluation of information and data relating to areas reserved for the Authority;

(f) Assessment of approaches to joint-venture operations;

(g) Collection of information on the availability of trained manpower;

(h) Study of managerial policy options for the administration of the Enterprise at different stages of its operations.

2. The Enterprise shall conduct its initial deep seabed mining operations through joint ventures. On the approval of a plan of work for exploitation for an entity other than the Enterprise, or on receipt by the Council of an application for a joint-venture operation with the Enterprise, the Council shall take up the issue of the functioning of the Enterprise independently of the Secretariat of the Authority. If joint-venture operations with the Enterprise accord with sound commercial principles, the Council shall issue a directive pursuant to article 170, paragraph 2, of the Convention providing for such independent functioning.

3. The obligation of States Parties to fund one mine site of the Enterprise as provided for in Annex IV, article 11, paragraph 3, of the Convention shall not apply and States Parties shall be under no obligation to finance any of the operations in any mine site of the Enterprise or under its joint-venture arrangements.

4. The obligations applicable to contractors shall apply to the Enterprise. Notwithstanding the provisions of article 153, paragraph 3, and Annex III, article 3, paragraph 5, of the Convention, a plan of work for the Enterprise on its approval shall be in the form of a contract concluded between the Authority and the Enterprise.

5. A contractor which has contributed a particular area to the Authority as a reserved area has the right of first refusal to enter into a joint-venture arrangement with the Enterprise for exploration and exploitation of that area. If the Enterprise does not submit an application for a plan of work for activities in respect of such a reserved area within 15 years of the commencement of its functions independent of the Secretariat of the Authority or within 15 years of the date on which that area is reserved for the Authority, whichever is the later, the contractor which contributed the area shall be entitled to apply for a plan of work for that area provided it offers in good faith to include the Enterprise as a joint-venture partner.

6. Article 170, paragraph 4, Annex IV and other provisions of the Convention relating to the Enterprise shall be interpreted and applied in accordance with this section.

SECTION 3. DECISION-MAKING

1. The general policies of the Authority shall be established by the Assembly in collaboration with the Council.

2. As a general rule, decision-making in the organs of the Authority should be by consensus.

3. If all efforts to reach a decision by consensus have been exhausted, decisions by voting in the Assembly on questions of procedure shall be taken by a majority of members present and voting, and decisions on questions of substance shall be taken by a two-thirds majority of members present and voting, as provided for in article 159, paragraph 8, of the Convention.

4. Decisions of the Assembly on any matter for which the Council also has competence or on any administrative, budgetary or financial matter shall be based on the recommendations of the Council. If the Assembly does not accept the recommendation of the Council on any matter, it shall return the matter to the Council for further consideration. The Council shall reconsider the matter in the light of the views expressed by the Assembly.

5. If all efforts to reach a decision by consensus have been exhausted, decisions by voting in the Council on questions of procedure shall be taken by a majority of members present and voting, and decisions on questions of substance, except where the Convention provides for decisions by consensus in the Council, shall be taken by a two-thirds majority of members present and voting, provided that such decisions are not opposed by a majority in any one of the chambers referred to in paragraph 9. In taking decisions the Council shall seek to promote the interests of all the members of the Authority.

6. The Council may defer the taking of a decision in order to facilitate further negotiation whenever it appears that all efforts at achieving consensus on a question have not been exhausted.

7. Decisions by the Assembly or the Council having financial or budgetary implications shall be based on the recommendations of the Finance Committee.

8. The provisions of article 161, paragraph 8 (b) and (c), of the Convention shall not apply.

9. (a) Each group of States elected under paragraph 15 (a) to (c) shall be treated as a chamber for the purposes of voting in the Council. The developing States elected under paragraph 15 (d) and (e) shall be treated as a single chamber for the purposes of voting in the Council.

(b) Before electing the members of the Council, the Assembly shall establish lists of countries fulfilling the criteria for membership in the groups of States in paragraph 15 (a) to (d). If a State fulfils the criteria for membership in more than one group, it may only be proposed by one group for election to the Council and it shall represent only that group in voting in the Council.

10. Each group of States in paragraph 15 (a) to (d) shall be represented in the Council by those members nominated by that group. Each group shall nominate only as many candidates as the number of seats required to be filled by that group. When the number of potential candidates in each of the groups referred to in paragraph 15 (a) to (e) exceeds the number of seats available in each of those respective groups, as a general rule, the principle of rotation shall apply. States members of each of those groups shall determine how this principle shall apply in those groups.

11. (a) The Council shall approve a recommendation by the Legal and Technical Commission for approval of a plan of work unless by a two-thirds majority of its members present and voting, including a majority of members present and voting in each of the chambers of the Council, the Council decides to disapprove a plan of work. If the Council does not take a decision on a recommendation for approval of a plan of work within a prescribed period, the recommendation shall be deemed to have been approved by the Council at the end of that period. The prescribed period shall normally be 60 days unless the Council decides to provide for a longer period. If the Commission recommends the disapproval of a plan of work or does not make a recommendation, the Council may nevertheless approve the plan of work in accordance with its rules of procedure for decision-making on questions of substance.

(b) The provisions of article 162, paragraph 2 (j), of the Convention shall not apply.

12. Where a dispute arises relating to the disapproval of a plan of work, such dispute shall be submitted to the dispute settlement procedures set out in the Convention.

13. Decisions by voting in the Legal and Technical Commission shall be by a majority of members present and voting.

14. Part XI, section 4, subsections B and C, of the Convention shall be interpreted and applied in accordance with this section.

15. The Council shall consist of 36 members of the Authority elected by the Assembly in the following order:

(a) Four members from among those States Parties which, during the last five years for which statistics are available, have either consumed more than 2 per cent in value terms of total world consumption or have had net imports of more than 2 per cent in value terms of total world imports of the commodities produced from the categories of minerals to be derived from the Area, provided that the four members shall include one State from the Eastern European region having the largest economy in that region in terms of gross domestic product and the State, on the date of entry into force of the Convention, having the largest economy in terms of gross domestic product, if such States wish to be represented in this group;

(b) Four members from among the eight States Parties which have made the largest investments in preparation for and in the conduct of activities in the Area, either directly or through their nationals;

(c) Four members from among States Parties which, on the basis of production in areas under their jurisdiction, are major net exporters of the categories of minerals to be derived from the Area, including at least two developing States whose exports of such minerals have a substantial bearing on their economies;

(d) Six members from among developing States Parties, representing special interests. The special interests to be represented shall include those of States with large populations, States which are land-locked or geographically disadvantaged, island States, States which are major importers of the categories of minerals to be derived from the Area, States which are potential producers of such minerals and least developed States;

(e) Eighteen members elected according to the principle of ensuring an equitable geographical distribution of seats in the Council as a whole, provided that each geographical region shall have at least one member elected under this subparagraph. For this purpose, the geographical regions shall be Africa, Asia, Eastern Europe, Latin America and the Caribbean and Western Europe and Others.

16. The provisions of article 161, paragraph 1, of the Convention shall not apply.

SECTION 4. REVIEW CONFERENCE

The provisions relating to the Review Conference in article 155, paragraphs 1, 3 and 4, of the Convention shall not apply. Notwithstanding the provisions of article 314, paragraph 2, of the Convention, the Assembly, on the recommendation of the Council, may undertake at any time a review of the matters referred to in article 155, paragraph 1, of the Convention. Amendments relating to this Agreement and Part XI shall be subject to the procedures contained in articles 314, 315 and 316 of the Convention, provided that the principles, regime and other terms referred to in article 155, paragraph 2, of the Convention shall be maintained and the rights referred to in paragraph 5 of that article shall not be affected.

SECTION 5. TRANSFER OF TECHNOLOGY

1. In addition to the provisions of article 144 of the Convention, transfer of technology for the purposes of Part XI shall be governed by the following principles:

(a) The Enterprise, and developing States wishing to obtain deep seabed mining technology, shall seek to obtain such technology on fair and reasonable commercial terms and conditions on the open market, or through joint-venture arrangements;

(b) If the Enterprise or developing States are unable to obtain deep seabed mining technology, the Authority may request all or any of the contractors and their respective sponsoring State or States to cooperate with it in facilitating the acquisition of deep seabed mining technology by the Enterprise or its joint venture, or by a developing State or States seeking to acquire such technology on fair and reasonable commercial terms and conditions, consistent with the effective protection of intellectual property rights. States Parties undertake to cooperate fully and effectively with the Authority for this purpose and to ensure that contractors sponsored by them also cooperate fully with the Authority;

(c) As a general rule, States Parties shall promote international technical and scientific cooperation with regard to activities in the Area either between the parties concerned or by developing training, technical assistance and scientific cooperation programmes in marine science and technology and the protection and preservation of the marine environment.

2. The provisions of Annex III, article 5, of the Convention shall not apply.

SECTION 6. PRODUCTION POLICY

1. The production policy of the Authority shall be based on the following principles:

(a) Development of the resources of the Area shall take place in accordance with sound commercial principles;

(b) The provisions of the General Agreement on Tariffs and Trade, its relevant codes and successor or superseding agreements shall apply with respect to activities in the Area;

(c) In particular, there shall be no subsidization of activities in the Area except as may be permitted under the agreements referred to in subparagraph (b). Subsidization for the purpose of these principles shall be defined in terms of the agreements referred to in subparagraph (b);

(d) There shall be no discrimination between minerals derived from the Area and from other sources. There shall be no preferential access to markets for such minerals or for imports of commodities produced from such minerals, in particular:

(i)   By the use of tariff or non-tariff barriers; and

(ii)   Given by States Parties to such minerals or commodities produced by their state enterprises or by natural or juridical persons which possess their nationality or are controlled by them or their nationals;

(e) The plan of work for exploitation approved by the Authority in respect of each mining area shall indicate an anticipated production schedule which shall include the estimated maximum amounts of minerals that would be produced per year under the plan of work;

(f) The following shall apply to the settlement of disputes concerning the provisions of the agreements referred to in subparagraph (b):

(i) Where the States Parties concerned are parties to such agreements, they shall have recourse to the dispute settlement procedures of those agreements;

(ii) Where one or more of the States Parties concerned are not parties to such agreements, they shall have recourse to the dispute settlement procedures set out in the Convention;

(g) In circumstances where a determination is made under the agreements referred to in subparagraph (b) that a State party has engaged in subsidization which is prohibited or has resulted in adverse effects on the interests of another state party and appropriate steps have not been taken by the relevant state party or States Parties, a state party may request the Council to take appropriate measures.

2. The principles contained in paragraph 1 shall not affect the rights and obligations under any provision of the agreements referred to in paragraph 1 (b), as well as the relevant free trade and customs union agreements, in relations between States Parties which are parties to such agreements.

3. The acceptance by a contractor of subsidies other than those which may be permitted under the agreements referred to in paragraph 1 (b) shall constitute a violation of the fundamental terms of the contract forming a plan of work for the carrying out of activities in the Area.

4. Any state party which has reason to believe that there has been a breach of the requirements of paragraphs 1 (b) to (d) or 3 may initiate dispute settlement procedures in conformity with paragraph 1 (f) or (g).

5. A state party may at any time bring to the attention of the Council activities which in its view are inconsistent with the requirements of paragraph 1 (b) to (d).

6. The Authority shall develop rules, regulations and procedures which ensure the implementation of the provisions of this section, including relevant rules, regulations and procedures governing the approval of plans of work.

7. The provisions of article 151, paragraphs 1 to 7 and 9, article 162, paragraph 2 (q), article 165, paragraph 2 (n), and Annex III, article 6, paragraph 5, and article 7, of the Convention shall not apply.

SECTION 7. ECONOMIC ASSISTANCE

1. The policy of the Authority of assisting developing countries which suffer serious adverse effects on their export earnings or economies resulting from a reduction in the price of an affected mineral or in the volume of exports of that mineral, to the extent that such reduction is caused by activities in the Area, shall be based on the following principles:

(a) The Authority shall establish an economic assistance fund from a portion of the funds of the Authority which exceeds those necessary to cover the administrative expenses of the Authority. The amount set aside for this purpose shall be determined by the Council from time to time, on the recommendation of the Finance Committee. Only funds from payments received from contractors, including the Enterprise, and voluntary contributions shall be used for the establishment of the economic assistance fund;

(b) Developing land-based producer States whose economies have been determined to be seriously affected by the production of minerals from the deep seabed shall be assisted from the economic assistance fund of the Authority;

(c) The Authority shall provide assistance from the fund to affected developing land-based producer States, where appropriate, in cooperation with existing global or regional development institutions which have the infrastructure and expertise to carry out such assistance programmes;

(d) The extent and period of such assistance shall be determined on a case-by-case basis. In doing so, due consideration shall be given to the nature and magnitude of the problems encountered by affected developing land-based producer States.

2. Article 151, paragraph 10, of the Convention shall be implemented by means of measures of economic assistance referred to in paragraph 1. Article 160, paragraph 2 (1), article 162, paragraph 2 (n), article 164,

paragraph 2 (d), article 171, subparagraph (f), and article 173, paragraph 2 (c), of the Convention shall be interpreted accordingly.

SECTION 8. FINANCIAL TERMS OF CONTRACTS

1. The following principles shall provide the basis for establishing rules, regulations and procedures for financial terms of contracts:

(a) The system of payments to the Authority shall be fair both to the contractor and to the Authority and shall provide adequate means of determining compliance by the contractor with such system;

(b) The rates of payments under the system shall be within the range of those prevailing in respect of land-based mining of the same or similar minerals in order to avoid giving deep seabed miners an artificial competitive advantage or imposing on them a competitive disadvantage;

(c) The system should not be complicated and should not impose major administrative costs on the Authority or on a contractor. Consideration should be given to the adoption of a royalty system or a combination of a royalty and profit-sharing system. If alternative systems are decided on, the contractor has the right to choose the system applicable to its contract. Any subsequent change in choice between alternative systems, however, shall be made by agreement between the Authority and the contractor;

(d) An annual fixed fee shall be payable from the date of commencement of commercial production. This fee may be credited against other payments due under the system adopted in accordance with subparagraph (c). The amount of the fee shall be established by the Council;

(e) The system of payments may be revised periodically in the light of changing circumstances. Any changes shall be applied in a non-discriminatory manner. Such changes may apply to existing contracts only at the election of the contractor. Any subsequent change in choice between alternative systems shall be made by agreement between the Authority and the contractor;

(f) Disputes concerning the interpretation or application of the rules and regulations based on these principles shall be subject to the dispute settlement procedures set out in the Convention.

2. The provisions of Annex III, article 13, paragraphs 3 to 10, of the Convention shall not apply.

3.   With regard to the implementation of Annex III, article 13, paragraph 2, of the Convention, the fee for processing applications for approval of a plan of work limited to one phase, either the exploration phase or the exploitation phase, shall be U.S.$ 250,000.

SECTION 9. THE FINANCE COMMITTEE

1. There is hereby established a Finance Committee. The Committee shall be composed of 15 members with appropriate qualifications relevant to financial matters.   States Parties shall nominate candidates of the highest standards of competence and integrity.

2.   No two members of the Finance Committee shall be nationals of the same state party.

3.   Members of the Finance Committee shall be elected by the Assembly and due account shall be taken of the need for equitable geographical distribution and the representation of special interests. Each group of States referred to in section 3, paragraph 15 (a), (b), (c) and (d), of this Annex shall be represented on the Committee by at least one member. Until the Authority has sufficient funds other than assessed contributions to meet its administrative expenses, the membership of the Committee shall include representatives of the five largest financial contributors to the administrative budget of the Authority.   Thereafter, the election of one member from each group shall be on the basis of nomination by the members of the respective group, without prejudice to the possibility of further members being elected from each group.

4. Members of the Finance Committee shall hold office for a term of five years. They shall be eligible for re-election for a further term.

5. In the event of the death, incapacity or resignation of a member of the Finance Committee prior to the expiration of the term of office, the Assembly shall elect for the remainder of the term a member from the same geographical region or group of States.

6. Members of the Finance Committee shall have no financial interest in any activity relating to matters on which the Committee has the

responsibility to make recommendations. They shall not disclose, even after the termination of their functions, any confidential information coming to their knowledge by reason of their duties for the Authority.

7. Decisions by the Assembly and the Council on the following issues shall take into account recommendations of the Finance Committee:

(a) Draft financial rules, regulations and procedures of the organs of the Authority and the financial management and internal financial administration of the Authority;

(b) Assessment of contributions of members to the administrative budget of the Authority in accordance with article 160, paragraph 2 (e), of the Convention;

(c) All relevant financial matters, including the proposed annual budget prepared by the Secretary-General of the Authority in accordance with article 172 of the Convention and the financial aspects of the implementation of the programmes of work of the Secretariat;

(d) The administrative budget;

(e) Financial obligations of States Parties arising from the implementation of this Agreement and Part XI as well as the administrative and budgetary implications of proposals and recommendations involving expenditure from the funds of the Authority;

(f) Rules, regulations and procedures on the equitable sharing of financial and other economic benefits derived from activities in the Area and the decisions to be made thereon.

8. Decisions in the Finance Committee on questions of procedure shall be taken by a majority of members present and voting. Decisions on questions of substance shall be taken by consensus.

9. The requirement of article 162, paragraph 2 (y), of the Convention to establish a subsidiary organ to deal with financial matters shall be deemed to have been fulfilled by the establishment of the Finance Committee in accordance with this section.

References

Agnew, Allen F., ed., *International Minerals: A National Perspective*. Published for the American Academy of Sciences. Boulder: Westview Press, Inc., 1983.

Allen, Patrick D. and Peter C. Noehrenberg. *U.S. Dependence on Strategic Materials from Southern African Nations*. Santa Monica: RAND, 1992.

Amann, Hans. "Basic Engineering and New Technologies for an Environmentally Acceptable Deep Seabed Collector" in Korea Ocean Research and Development Institute. *Proceedings of the International Advisory Conference on Deep seabed Mining Policy, Seoul, Korea (September 5-6, 1994)*.

Andreasen, C. "National Oceanic and Atmospheric Administration. "Exclusive Economic Zone Mapping Project," in M. Lockwood and G. Hill (eds.), *Proceedings: The Exclusive Economic Zone Symposium: Exploring the New Ocean Frontier*, conference sponsored by National Oceanic and Atmospheric Administration. U.S. Department of the Interior. Smithsonian Institution. and Marine Society, held at the Smithsonian Institution. Oct. 2-3, 1985, pp. 63-67.

Associated Press. "Worries About Plutonium Ship" September 21, 1992.

Barber, Ben. "Dole Bill Threatens Funding for U.N." *Washington Times* (January 18, 1996), 1.

Barraclough, Geoffrey. *An Introduction to Contemporary History*. Baltimore, 1967.

Bollow, G. E. *Economic Effects of Deep Ocean Mineral Exploitation*. Monterey, Calif.: Naval Postgraduate School, 1971.

Browne, Marjorie Ann. *The Law of the Sea Convention and U.S. Policy* Congressional Research Service. IB95010 (January 1995).

Browne, Marjorie Ann. *The Law of the Sea Conference: A U.S. Perspective.* Congressional Research Service. IB81153 (March 1983).

Burrows, James C. *Cobalt: An Industry Analysis.*, New York: D.C. Heath and Co., 1971.

Caldwell, A.B. "Deepsea Ventures Readying Its Attack on Pacific Nodules." *Mining Engineering.* (October 1971).

Cardwell, P.H. "Extractive Metallurgy of Ocean Nodules". *American Mining Congress Journal.* (November 1973)., pp. 38-43.

Clark, Maurice J. et. al, eds., *Readings in the Economics of War.* Chicago: University of Chicago Press, 1918.

Collier, Ellen C. *Senate Approval of Treaties: A Brief Description with Examples from Arms Control.* (Washington, D.C.: U.S. Congressional Research Service. Sept 11, 1991).

Edwards, Art M. "Dependence of Alloy Producers on International Strategic Minerals." in Kenneth A. Kessel. *Strategic Minerals: U.S. Alternatives* (Washington, D.C.: NDU Press, 1990), pp. 122-32.

Ely, Northcutt. "Statement Before the Senate Committee on Foreign Relations on September 30, 1982." *Congressional Digest* (January 1983), 29-31.

Farr, H. K. "Multibeam Bathymetric Sonar: Sea Beam and Hydrochart," *Marine Geodosy,* Vol. 4, No.2, pp. 88-89.

Flawn, Peter T. *Mineral Resources.* New York: John Wiley and Sons, Inc., 1966.

Gillmer. Thomas C. *Modern Ship Design.* Annapolis, MD: U.S. Naval Institute, 1970)

Glasby, G. P. *Marine Manganese Deposits,* Elsevier, Amsterdam, 1977.

Government of Japan, Deep Ocean Mining Agency. DOMA Brochure, *Manganese Nodules.*

Hayashi, Moritaka. "Prospects for a Universal Acceptance of the Part XI Agreement," Remarks to *Symposium on Implementing the United Nations Convention on the Law of the Sea.* Georgetown University Law School (27 January 1995):5-6.

Hoagland, Peter "Manganese Nodule Price Trends." *Resources Policy* (December 1993):293.

Hoyle, Brian J. *Testimony Before the U. S. House of Representatives,* Committee on Merchant Marine and Fisheries, Subcommittee on Oceanography, Gulf of Mexico and the Outer Continental Shelf, April 26, 1994.

"Hughes Glomar Explorer begins sea tests of mining systems", *Ocean Industry.* (March 1974), pp. 32-34.

Institute for Defense Analyses. IDA Document D-1264.

Institute for Defense Analyses. *Addendum to Section 8.0 Military Critical Technologies List: Marine Technology.* (March 1995):8.2-23.

Institute for Defense Analyses. *Record of Activities of Technical Review Group 6--Sensors and Sensor Systems.* IDA Document D-1404 (January 1994):182.

Institute of Geological Science, *Statistical Summary of the Mineral Industry* (London), various issues; 1969-1972.

International Nickel Co., *The Supply of Nickel*, N.Y. (May 1, 1958).

"Japanese Ship Loads Plutonium," *Washington Post*, 8 November 1992, p. A47

Justus, John R. *Ocean Mining.* Congressional Research Service. IB74024 (August 1985).

Justus, John R. *Deep Seabed Hard Mineral Resources.* Congressional Research Service. (October 1980).

Kassebaum, Nancy Landon and Lee Hamilton. "Fix the U.N.," *Washington Post* (June 25, 1995).

Kissinger, Henry. "The Law of the Sea Treaty: A Test of International Cooperation" address before the Foreign Policy Association, U.N. Association, et. al., April 8, 1976. *Department of State Bulletin* No. 1922 (April 26,1976):540-541.

Knight, Gary. "Legal Aspects of Current United States Law of the Sea Policy," Paper presented *to American Enterprise Institute Conference on United States Interests in the Law of the Sea: Review and Analysis* (October 19, 1981):1.

Landsberg, Hans H. et. al., *Resources in America's Future: Patterns of Requirements and Availabilities, 1960-2000.* Baltimore: Resources for the Future, Johns Hopkins Press, 1963.

Leipziger, Danny M. and James L. Mudge. *The Economics of Manganese Nodule Exploitation.* Ballinger Pub Co., Cambridge, Mass, 1976.

Leitner, Peter M. *Decontrolling Strategic Technology, 1990-1992: Creating the Military Threats of the 21st Century.* Lanham, Md.: University Press of America, 1995.

Lenoble, J. P. "The Future of Deep Seabed Mining: A Changing Economic and Legal Contingency" Paper Presented to the *International Advisory Committee on Deep Seabed Mining Policy*, (Seoul, Korea, September 5-6, 1994):4-15.

Lucretius. *On the Nature of the Universe.* London: Penguin Books, 1971.

Massachusettes Institute of Technology, Sea Grant Program. *A Cost Model of Deep Ocean Mining and Associated Regulatory Issues.* MIT Sea Grant Program Report MITSG-78-4 (March 1978).

Masuda, Y., M.J. Cruickshank and J.L. Mero, "Continuous Bucket Line Dredging at 12,000 feet". *Offshore Technology Conference Preprint.* (prepared for the 3rd Annual Offshore Technology Conference, Houston, Texas, 19-21 April 1971) Paper No. 1410.

Mcmanus, Doyle. "Bush's Vision of a 'New World Order' Still Unclear," *Los Angeles Times* (February 18, 1991):A9.

Mero, J. L. *Mineral Resources of the Sea.* New York: Elsiever, 1965.

Mero, J.L. "Recent Concepts in Undersea Mining.' *American Mining Congress,* 1971 Mining Show, Las Vegas, Nevada (4 August 1971).

Mero, John L.. "Will Ocean Mining Prove Commercial?" *Offshore Technology,* (April 1971).

Mielke, James E.. *Ocean Mierals/Polymetallic Sulfides: Should the United States Legislate for Future Development?* Congressional Research Service. MB82214 (August 1984).

Miller, Steven E. "Russian-American Security Cooperation on the High Seas," in Goodby (forthcoming).

"Mining System will process ore in underwater station", *Ocean Industry.* (October 1971).

National Commission on Materials Policy. *Materials and The Environment, Today and Tomorrow.*, U.S. GOP, 1973.

Negroponte, John. "Who Will Protect the Oceans?", *Department of State Bulletin,* October 1986, 41-43.

Ocean Science News. (11 January 1974), p. 1.

Offley, Ed. "U.S. To Help Japan Protect Plutonium Ship, Sources Say," *Seattle Post-Intelligencer,* 6 November 1992, p. 1.

Padleford, Norman J. and George A. Lincoln. *International Politics: Foundation of International Relations.* N.Y.: MacMillian and Co., 1954

Paul, Ron E. "Remarks Addressed to the U.S. House of Representatives on April 28, 1992" in *Congressional Digest* (January 1983), 23-25.

Radetzki, Marian "Metal Mineral Resource Exhaustion and the Threat to Material Progress: The Case of Copper". *World Development.* Vol. 3, Nos. 2 and 3 (February-March, 1975)., p. 124.

Reagan, Ronald. Statement on United States Oceans Policy, March 10, 1983, 1 *Public Papers of President Reagan* (1983):378-79.

Reid, T.R. "Japan's 'Plutonium Ship' Blows Controversial Cover," *Washington Post,* 19 August 1992, p. A15.

Revel, Jean-François. *How Democracies Perish.* Garden City, N.Y.: Doubleday & Company, 1983.

Roach, J. Ashley and Robert W. Smith. *Excessive Maritime Claims*, Newport, R.I.:Naval War College, 1994.

Sands, Jeffrey I. *Blue Hulls: Multinational Naval Cooperation and the United Nations*, CNA CRM 93-40 (July 1993).

Sanger, David E. "Japan's Plan To Ship Plutonium Has Big and Little Lands Roaring," *NY Times*, 5 October 1992, p. 1.

Singh, T.R.P. "Perspective on Deep Seabed Mining" Paper Presented to *International Advisory Committee on Deep Seabed Mining Policy* (Seoul, Korea September 5-6, 1994):19.

Slingsby Electronics, Ltd., U.K.

Smith, Robert W. and J. Ashley Roach. *Limits in the Seas*, U.S. Department of State, No. 36 (January 11, 1995).

State of Hawaii, Department of Planning and Economic Development. *The Feasiubility Impact of Manganese Nodule Processing in Hawaii*, February 1978.

Stewardson, B.R. "The Nature of Competition in the World Market for Refined Copper". *Economic Record*. (June 1970).

Taylor, D.M. "New Concepts in Offshore Production." *Ocean Industry.*, (February 1969), pp. 66-70.

Taylor, D.M. "Worthless Nodules Become Valuable", *Ocean Industry*, (June 1971):pp.27-38.

Testimony of Representative Fields, *Current Status of the Conventionon the Law of the Sea*, Hearings, Aug. 11, 1994, p. 5.

"The Future Promise of Mining in the Ocean", *Canadian Mining and Metallurgical Bulletin*. (April 1972).

"Turkey Warns Greece to Keep its Distance at Sea," *Jane's Defense Weekly* (July 15, 1995):11.

U.S. Commission on Marine Sciences, Engineering, and Resources. *Marine Resources and Legal-political Arrangements for their Uses.*

U.S. Congress, *Treaties and Other International Agreements: The Role of the United States Senate*. S. Prt. 10353, 1993, p. 84.

U.S. Congress. Office of Technology Assessment. *Marine Minerals: Exploring Our New Ocean Frontier* (Washington, D.C., 1987):40.

U.S. Department of Defense. *1992 Militarily Critical Technologies List.*

U.S. Department of State, Bureau of Public Affairs, "Navigation Rights and the Gulf of Sidra," in *CIST, a reference aid on U.S. foreign relations.*

U.S. Department of State. *Delegation Report of the Sixth Session of UNCLOS, May 23 - July 15, 1977*, pp. 5-6.

U.S. Dept. of the Interior, Bureau of Mines. *Minerals Yearbook,* Various Issues.

U.S. General Accounting Office. *The Law of the Sea Conference-- Status of the Issues, 1978.* ID-79-6 (March 9, 1979):6.

U.S. Navy.   Mine Warfare Program Executive Office. *Littoral Undersea Science and Technology Review,* (April 8, 1993).

U.S. NOAA. *Deep Seabed Mining: Workshop Report* (March 1994).

U.S. Office of Technology Assessment. *Marine Minerals: Exploring Our New Ocean Frontier.* Washington, D.C.:U.S. GPO, 1987).

U.S. Senate Foreign Relations Committee, Statement by Rear Admiral William D. Center, Deputy Director, International Negotiations, J-5 Directorate, Joint Staff, 11 August 1994.

U.S. Senate. Committee on Interior and Insular Affairs. *Current Developments in Deep Seabed Mining.,* 1975.

United Nations Document. *A/AC. 138/73.*
United Nations Document. *A/Conf.62/121.*
United Nations Document. *A/Conf.62/L.78..*
United Nations Document. *A/C/Res/482/263.*
United Nations Document. *TD/B(XIII)/Misc.3.*
United Nations Document. *TD/B/449/ADD.1.*
United Nations Document. *TD/B/483/ADD.1.*
United Nations Document. *A/Conf. 62/25.*
United Nations Document. *SEA/1398.*
United Nations Document. *SEA/1399.*
United Nations Document. *SEA/1400.*
United Nations Document. *SEA/1401.*
United Nations Document. *SEA/1402.*
United Nations Document. *SEA/1425.*
United Nations Document. *SEA/1427.*
United Nations Document. *SEA/1428.*
United Nations Document. *SEA/1429.*
United Nations Document. *SEA/1430.*
United Nations Document. *SEA/1431.*
United Nations Document. *SEA/1432.*
United Nations Document. *SEA/1433.*
United Nations Document. *SEA/1452.*
United Nations Document. *SEA/1453.*
United Nations Document. *SEA/1454.*
United Nations Document. *SEA/1455.*
United Nations Document. *SEA/1456.*
United Nations Document. *SEA/1457.*
United Nations Document. *SEA/1458.*
United Nations Document. *SEA/1461.*

United Nations Document. *SEA/1462*.
United Nations Document. *SEA/1463*.
United Nations Document. *SEA/1465*.
United Nations Document. *SEA/1466*.
United Nations Document. *SEA/1467*.
United Nations Document. *SEA/1468*.
United Nations Document. *SEA/1469*.
United Nations Document. *SEA/1470*.
United Nations Document. *SEA/1471*.
United Nations Document. *SEA/1472*.
United Nations Document. *SEA/1473*.
United Nations Document. *SEA/1474*.
United Nations Document. *SEA/1475*.
United Nations Document. *SEA/1476*.
United Nations Document. *SEA/1483*.
United Nations Document. *SEA/1484*.
United Nations Document. *SEA/1485*.
United Nations Document. *SEA/1486*.
United Nations Document. *SEA/1491*.
United Nations Document. *SEA/1494*.
United Nations Document. *SEA/1495*.
United Nations Document. *SEA/1496*.
United Nations Document. *SEA/1497*.
United Nations Document. *SEA/1498*.
United Nations Document. *SEA/1499*.
United Nations Document. *SEA/1500*.
United Nations Document. *SEA/1501*.
United Nations Document. *SEA/1502*.
United Nations Document. *SEA/1400*.
United Nations Document. *SEA/1400*.
United Nations Document. *TD/B/483*.
United Nations Document. *TD/B/483/Add.*
United Nations Document. *TD/B/484*.
United Nations Document. *TD/B/C. 1/170*.
United Nations Document. *TD/B/C.1/185*.
United Nations Document. *TD/B/C.1/120*.
United Nations Document. *TD/B/C.1/172*.
United Nations. *UNCTAD Commodity Yearbook* (Various Issues).
United Nations. *Basic Facts About the United Nations*. (New York, 1992).
Waxman, Sharon. "France Seeks To Ease Fears of Plutonium Ship," *Washington Post* 17 October 1992, p. 15.
Welling, Conrad. "Next Step in Ocean Mining Large Scale Test." Presented to *American Mining Congress Convention:*

Undersea Mineral Resources, Denver, Co. (September 26-29, 1976).

Wright, C.W.. "Germany's Capacity to Produce and Consume Metals." U.S. Bureau of Mines, *Mineral Trade Notes.*, Special Supplement, No. 4. (November 20, 1936).

Index

About the Author

Peter M. Leitner is an adjunct professor at Mount Vernon College and a senior strategic trade advisor with the Office of the Secretary of Defense in Washington, D.C. Dr. Leitner has served in advanced technology and international relations posts with several government agencies including the General Accounting Office where he was involved in diverse issues including Law of the Sea Treaty negotiations, host nation support for U.S. military forces, the Egyptian defense industry, the Sinai Field Mission, access to the Suez Canal for U.S. nuclear powered ships, accounting education in the third world, and maneuver damages caused by U.S. forces in Germany.

Over the course of the past ten years, Dr. Leitner has served as DoD's principal policy analyst and international negotiator for export controls on machine tools, controllers, robots, industrial equipment, software, and navigation and guidance equipment. He was chairman of two Paris-based eight-country study groups on advanced materials for weapons systems and defense production technology and equipment. He also served as senior licensing officer for U.S. exports to various proscribed countries including China, Libya, Iraq, former Warsaw Pact countries, Iran, and India. Dr. Leitner is currently DoD's representative to the interagency Subcommittee on Nuclear Export Controls.

Dr. Leitner has also authored the 1995 UPA book: *Decontrolling Strategic Technology, 1990-1992: Creating the Military Threats of the 21st Century*. He received his doctoral and master's degrees from the University of Southern California and holds other advanced degrees from Washington University, Northern Arizona University, and the State University of New York. He resides in Arlington, Virginia, with his wife and four children.